Modern Japan
A History in Documents

Modern Japan
A History in Documents

James L. Huffman

OXFORD
UNIVERSITY PRESS

To Grace and Simon

OXFORD
UNIVERSITY PRESS

Oxford   New York
Auckland   Bangkok   Buenos Aires   Cape Town   Chennai
Dar es Salaam   Delhi   Hong Kong   Istanbul   Karachi   Kolkata
Kuala Lumpur   Madrid   Melbourne   Mexico City   Mumbai   Nairobi
São Paulo   Shanghai   Singapore   Taipei   Tokyo   Toronto

Published by Oxford University Press, Inc.
198 Madison Avenue, New York, New York 10016
www.oup.com

Oxford is a registered trademark of Oxford University Press

Library of Congress Cataloging-in-Publication Data
Huffman, James L., 1941–
Modern Japan: a history in documents / James L. Huffman.
p. cm. — (Pages from history)
Includes index.
ISBN 0-19-514742-1 (alk. paper)
1. Japan—History—1868– 2. Japan—History—Tokugawa period,
1600-1868. I. Title. II. Series.
DS881.9.H85 2004
952.025—dc22
2004008185

Printed in the United States of America
On acid-free paper

Cover: *The main shopping street of Shinjuku,
Tokyo, Japan. Copyright © Cheryl Conlon.*

Frontispiece: *At the beginning of the twentieth
century, crowds took to the streets frequently in
Japan's cities: for festivals, to demonstrate for
lower streetcar fares, to celebrate military triumphs.
Here, residents of Yokohama celebrate with flags,
lanterns, and banners in the aftermath of Japan's
1905 victory in the Russo-Japanese War.*

Title page: *The feminist poet and essayist
Yosano Akiko sits for a formal photo in 1915
with her husband, the less-famous writer Yosano
Tekkan, and their children.*

Contents

What Is a Document?

To the historian, a document is, quite simply, any sort of historical evidence. It is a primary source, the raw material of history. A document may be more than the expected government paperwork, such as a treaty or passport. It is also a letter, diary, will, grocery list, newspaper article, recipe, memoir, oral history, school yearbook, map, chart, architectural plan, poster, musical score, play script, novel, political cartoon, painting, photograph—even an object.

Using primary sources allows us not just to read *about* history, but to read history itself. It allows us to immerse ourselves in the look and feel of an era gone by, to understand its people and their language, whether verbal or visual. And it allows us to take an active, hands-on role in (re)constructing history.

Using primary sources requires us to use our powers of detection to ferret out the relevant facts and to draw conclusions from them; just as Agatha Christie uses the scores in a bridge game to determine the identity of a murderer, the historian uses facts from a variety of sources—some, perhaps, seemingly inconsequential—to build a historical case.

The poet W. H. Auden wrote that history was the study of questions. Primary sources force us to ask questions—and then, by answering them, to construct a narrative or an argument that makes sense to us. Moreover, as we draw on the many sources from "the dust-bin of history," we can endow that narrative with character, personality, and texture—all the elements that make history so endlessly intriguing.

Cartoon
This political cartoon addresses the issue of church and state. It illustrates the Supreme Court's role in balancing the demands of the 1st Amendment of the Constitution and the desires of the religious population.

Illustration
Illustrations from children's books, such as this alphabet from the New England Primer, tell us how children were educated, and also what the religious and moral values of the time were.

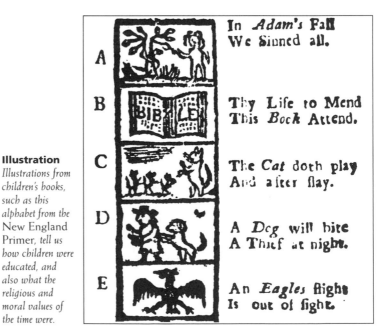

In *Adam's* Fall
We Sinned all.

Thy Life to Mend
This *Book* Attend.

The *Cat* doth play
And after slay.

A *Dog* will bite
A Thief at night.

An *Eagles* flight
Is out of sight.

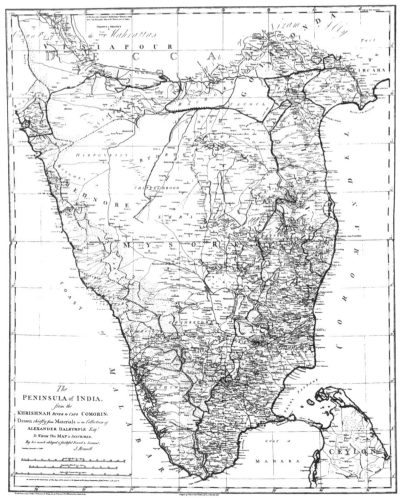

Map
A 1788 British map of India shows the region prior to British colonization, an indication of the kingdoms and provinces whose ethnic divisions would resurface later in India's history.

Treaty
A government document such as this 1805 treaty can reveal not only the details of government policy, but information about the people who signed it. Here, the Indians' names were written in English transliteration by U.S. officials; the Indians added pictographs to the right of their names.

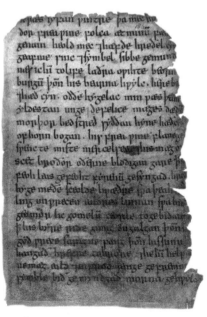

Literature
The first written version of the Old English epic Beowulf, from the late 10th century, is physical evidence of the transition from oral to written history. Charred by fire, it is also a physical record of the wear and tear of history.

How to Read a Document

This book aims to bring us close to the people who actually lived out Japan's modern era, through their letters, speeches, documents, cartoons, statistical charts, and maps. To understand those people, however, we must treat these documents as a detective would, looking for clues about what they really mean. We need to ask ourselves constant questions as we read what people in the past have written:

Is this accurate? In the first chapter of this book, a Portuguese merchant named Alvares describes Japanese "kings" of the late 1500s; history tells us, however, that Japan had no kings then. Why did Alvares make this mistake? Does his error make the document useless? If not, what does it tell us? Errors themselves often give us insights into the writer's world and worldview.

What are the writer's biases? All people are biased, but we must ask what the bias was and how it affected the source. When the nineteenth-century traveler Kume Kunitake described Christian scriptures as "delirious ravings," was he telling us more about Christianity or more about Japanese understandings of religion? Since we want to know how people saw the world, biased materials often give us as much insight as balanced materials do.

What is the context? When we hear the journalist Kiryū Yūyū decry the army's "reckless actions" in 1936 (Chapter 6), we must ask what was happening in Japan then. Does his diatribe suggest that people were free to criticize their government, or simply that a few brave men risked prison for the right to speak up?

What lies beneath a document's surface? An important trend among historians is the use of literary and visual materials, because they often tell us more than their composers intended. It is not enough to ask if the facts are accurate, however; we must ask what clues they reveal about life at the time. Omissions can tell us much about a writer's way of seeing the world.

The British historian E. H. Carr said that a fact resembles an empty sack, which the historian must fill with meaning. So too with documents. They will not yield much insight unless the reader asks the right questions. Read carelessly, documents may mislead, confuse, or hold the full picture back from us. Examined carefully, they bring the past to life.

Brackets

In translated materials, the translator often has to include words or ideas not found in the original text, so that the meaning will be clear to the English-speaking reader. Such materials normally are placed in brackets.

Tone

Tone may be as important as actual words in helping us understand a document. Kume's balanced tone here gives us immediate clues about the kind of man he was and the purpose of the writing. The fact that he sees behavioral differences as signs of variant cultures rather than as indications that Americans were just barbaric suggests to the reader that Kume was well educated and a careful observer. The tone also may be our first clue to the fact that he was on an official mission and that Japanese were quite open to cultural relativity.

Subconscious Values

Certain phrases tell the reader that the writer may have had values that even he himself (and his fellow countrymen) did not fully understand. Few people today would think of American men as having been servants of their wives in the nineteenth century. Yet that is what Kume thought when he saw American men holding chairs for women and carrying their things in public. His statement should prompt the reader to ask what Japanese values led to such an assessment. Even if Kume's evaluation of American values was wrong, it helps us understand Japan's own values then.

Unintended or Suggestive Information

Although Kume is describing American practices in this journal entry, his obvious surprise makes it clear that the gender-related behaviors he observed were not common in Japan. The careful reader would use Kume's material as a stimulus to further research, and might learn that in the 1870s Japanese women indeed did avoid going out publicly with their husbands, and that Japanese of both genders would have found it not only unusual but morally offensive for men to treat women deferentially in public.

Concrete Details

Even if an observer's interpretation of a situation is wrong, the document still may yield a rich, concrete picture of the setting. This entry makes it clear that when Kume visited the United States, men were restrained in their behavior when women were present but "lax" when by themselves. People also ate by lamplight, rode in carriages, wore shoes, and used chairs (an uncommon practice in Japan then). And Kume obviously saw (or heard about) instances of husbands being punished by their wives when they had acted offensively.

Photos

Photos may not provide the concrete facts of an era, but they help us understand the human values that undergirded those facts. The photo here, taken by a professional photographer in 1876, shows Sakai Denpatsu, Kyoto's first governor, just before a new law took effect requiring samurai to give up their swords and cut their hair. Careful readers may be impressed by Sakai's eagerness to retain a record of the traditional samurai dignity and garb, but they also will note how even he blended Japanese and Western elements: old Japanese kimono, sword, and shoes alongside a Western-style chair, the traditional hairstyle carefully combed to be recorded by a new-fangled camera.

Journal of Kume Kunitake on 1872 Visit to the United States

From the time our group boarded ship at Yokohama, [we found ourselves] in a realm of completely alien customs. What is appropriate deportment for us seems to attract their curiosity, and what is proper behavior for them is strange to us. . . . What we found most strange in their behavior was the relations between men and women.

With respect to relations between husbands and wives, it is the practice in Japan that the wife serves her husband's parents and that children serve their parents, but in America the husband follows the "Way of Serving His Wife." The [American husband] lights the lamps, prepares food at the table, presents shoes to his wife, brushes the dust off [her] clothes, helps her up and down the stairs, offers her his chair, and carries her things when she goes out. If the wife becomes a little angry, the husband is quick to offer affection and show respect, bowing and scraping to beg her forgiveness. But if she does not accept his apologies, he may find himself turned out of the house and denied meals.

When riding in the same ship or carriage, men stand up and offer their seats to the women, who accept with no hesitation at all. When women take their places sitting down, the men all crowd around them to show their respect. Men are restrained in their behavior when together [with women] at the same gathering. . . . It is only when the women retire that the men begin to become lax in their behavior. . . .

Introduction

Japan already possessed an ancient civilization when the first Western visitors, a group of shipwrecked Portuguese sailors, stumbled onto the coast of southern Tanegashima island in 1542. Though a young country in comparison with its neighbor China, this archipelago nation had been ruled at least nominally by emperors for more than a thousand years and had boasted a well-developed, community-based culture for a full two millennia. The Japanese people were as highly educated as any on the globe, and the country's literary and art worlds were sophisticated. It was little wonder that the first European arrivals called the Japanese the "best race yet discovered." Japanese culture was, after all, well in advance of that of Europe.

Until the eighth century, Japan's central regions were ruled directly by the imperial Yamato family, a clan said to have descended from the sun goddess and to have ruled these divinely created islands since 660 BCE, when the first emperor, Jimmu, came down from the heavens. The family's rule had peaked in the eighth century at Nara, a capital city of 200,000 people where taste and elegance vied with intricate law codes, adapted from China, to make Japan a model of progress. A fifty-three-foot statue of Buddha, dedicated in 752 CE and covered in 15,000 pounds of gold, showcased the new importance of Buddhism, as well as the ruling family's wealth. Although the emperors lost much of their political power to a noble family named Fujiwara after the capital moved north to Kyoto (then called Heian) to get away from Nara's meddling Buddhist influence at the end of the century, the emphasis on taste and elegance remained. During the 400 peaceful years in which Heian dominated Japanese life, a group of women produced brilliant works of literature, including what has been called the world's first novel, the *Tale of Genji*, while men vied for esteem by showing off their learning, and everyone competed to be the best dressed and the most elegant calligraphers.

The mood turned darker near the end of the 1100s, when a warrior family named Minamoto took control of the country by military

The thirty-seven-foot-high bronze statue of Buddha at Kamakura, built in the 1200s, not long after the warrior class had taken power in Japan, illustrates not only how wealthy the new samurai leaders were but how deeply they valued both art and religion. The nineteenth-century Westerners' eagerness to be photographed on the Buddha's lap showed both the statue's height and the visitors' lack of respect for Buddhism.

force and moved the administrative capital 300 miles east, to the remote region of Kamakura. For the next four centuries, the sword would dominate political life, first in the hands of powerful clans named Hōjō and Ashikaga who controlled Japan from the capital, and later under the power of regional lords, called *daimyō*, who largely ignored the central government and ruled from feudal castle towns. Even during this period, however, the emperors continued to sit on their thrones, powerless but important as high priestly symbols of Japan's link to the heavens. And while the fighting sometimes was brutal, the samurai, or warrior class, nurtured education and the arts as vigorously as the nobles of Heian had. In the 1400s and 1500s, drawing inspiration from the Zen sect of Buddhism, samurai produced some of history's most unusual and sophisticated art forms: rock gardens, flower arranging, ink paintings, and the tea ceremony. One of the most popular stories of the age was that of Atsumori, a young warrior slain by an enemy soldier who cried profusely while beheading him; when Atsumori's body was examined, he was found to be carrying a flute alongside his sword. It was thus a combination of martial vigor and cultural sophistication that set the stage for Japan's modern era.

One of the distinctive features of Japan's ancient history is its complex interactions with the rest of Asia. Living less than a hundred miles off the continent, the Japanese drew endlessly on the culture and institutions of China, adapting its religions, writing system, law codes, and cultural tastes—even while vigorously maintaining their own distinct values and styles. When one of Japan's earliest leaders, the regent Shōtoku Taishi, sent a study mission to China in 607 CE, he made it clear that his people were eager to learn from China, but he also revealed their self-confidence by giving the embassy this charge: "From the sovereign of the land of the rising sun to the sovereign of the land of the setting sun." The Chinese emperor, offended, refused to assist the mission's members.

That same tension—between a thirst to understand foreign institutions and a determination to assert and preserve native traditions—continued to shape the whole of Japan's modern era, propelling dynamic change at times, inviting calamity at others. During the early modern centuries when the Tokugawa family ruled (1600–1868), the country shut itself off from the rest of the world, fearful that trade and Christianity would undermine the Tokugawa's hold on power. Once the West reentered, in the mid-1800s, the newness of foreign technology and the military threat

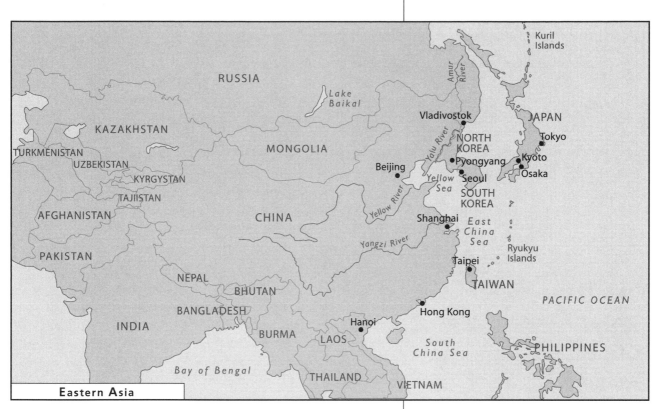

Eastern Asia

of imperialism triggered an explosion, a rush to modernize that caused urban residents to gasp: "Old things pass away between a night and a morning." The clash between national values and Westernization also triggered Japan's march down the road of imperialism. When leaders became convinced late in the nineteenth century that Japan's culture and independence could be preserved only by showing the country's strength militarily, they began wars with China and Russia, winning both, and secured their own colonies in Taiwan and Korea. The patriotism stimulated by those victories turned into aggressive nationalism in the 1930s, fueling Japan's disastrous participation in World War II.

Japan's World War II defeat in 1945 brought more than mere humiliation and devastation. It also assured the country's renewal, with even greater force, and heightened the tension between embracing foreign influences and nurturing native traditions. For at least two generations after the war, the country engaged the rest of the world almost as intensely as it had in the late 1800s, and even more successfully. It was the United States rather than China that fueled Japan's internationalism this time, with the Americans providing a government structure and constitution during the postwar

Like the British Isles on the western fringe of the Eurasian land mass, the Japanese archipelago is dwarfed geographically by continental neighbors such as China, Russia, and India. In the modern era, however, it used its location and astute policies to emerge as Asia's most powerful nation.

occupation (1945–52), then helping to build Japan's economy in the 1950s through everything from military procurements to trade and defense alliances.

By the late 1960s, Japan had become its own engine, using a combination of energy, hard work, efficient institutions, and effective education to develop the world's second-largest economy. By the 1980s, it was arguably the richest country on earth, giving out more foreign aid than any other nation and planting its businesses around the globe. The well-tailored Japanese businessman became a common sight at the best hotels of every city in the world. After the economy went into a tailspin in the 1990s, however, Japan's international profile dimmed. Japan seemed to turn inward once more, as the passage of decades made World War II an increasingly vague memory. The dynamism of its cultural life never died out; nor did its reputation as one of the world's most educated, safest, best-working societies. It continued to be one of the world's largest economies and to work quietly as an agent of change in Asia. But as several times before, the islands began to focus more heavily on domestic issues. Several generations of fierce engagement with the outside world were followed, at the turn of the twenty-first century, by an inward turn.

Finding primary sources to study Japan's last 1,500 years never has been a problem. For reasons that historians have not fully figured out, writing came late to the Japanese islands; their culture was well developed long before they began adapting China's written script to fit their own spoken language in the early fifth century. Once that process began, however, the Japanese took fervently to writing and record keeping. They compiled their first major poetry anthology, the Man'yōshū, "Collection of Ten Thousand Leaves," in the mid-700s, a few decades after they had published a monumental seventeen-volume set of legal and administrative codes. And in the 760s, the empress ordered a million copies of Buddhist incantations to be printed and distributed throughout the country. From that point on, the Japanese wrote with a passion, right down to the modern age: keeping diaries, publishing sermons and stories, composing histories, recording farming methods, and carrying on the kinds of public conversations possible only through the written word.

When a 1760 law insisted that since "books had long been published, no more are necessary," the officials were, more than anything, admitting the impossibility of stemming the flow of private writing. Indeed, one of the distinctive characteristics of Japanese writing is the fact that so much of it was private in

Kawabata Yasunari, Japan's first Nobel Prize winner in literature (1968), illustrated in his works the postwar tension between international influences and domestic traditions. He knew Western literature well and wrote about such modern topics as decay and death, yet used the literary styles of classical Japan. A traditionalist who wore the kimono, he loved the game of go, a complicated board game somewhat like chess.

nature. As early as the 1000s, much of the best writing was done by women courtiers, people without the credentials (or right) to use the Chinese script used in official documents. By the onset of the modern era in the early 1800s, when government control was particularly stringent, private scholars were issuing forth discussions of every aspect of national life, while dissidents were using cunning of every sort—including highly commercial, hard-to-suppress "newspapers" called broadsides—to get their ideas into the public arena. Once the daily newspaper press took root in the 1870s, that process gathered steam, and by the early 1900s Japan had a mass press, reflecting the views of an expanding public with as much energy and controversy as could be found anywhere in Europe or the United States. Even in the highly censored days of the 1930s and World War II, private speeches and publications continued to make a wide range of views available to those courageous enough to seek them out.

The point of all this is that historians seeking to know Japan's past, particularly in the modern era, will be hindered more by an abundance of sources than by a lack of them. No matter what the segment of society—mountain villagers, political radicals, schoolteachers, fishermen's wives, athletes, rural philosophers, prostitutes, rebel farmers, city office workers—it is well represented in the collected, preserved writings of Japan. Irokawa Daikichi, one of Japan's best-known contemporary historians, has spent a career trying to hear the voice of what he calls "grass-roots culture" and he has found it, not just in the essays of "'learned men' among the common people" but in pamphlets, records, written appeals, newspaper reports, and court documents by and about the "inarticulate masses." The Japanese are educated; they are opinionated; they are writers; they are record keepers. The historian's job—and it is not an easy one, the abundance of sources notwithstanding—is to find those records, to interpret them, and to develop as complete a picture of Japan's past as possible.

Japanese at all levels of society delight in calligraphy and are eager to show off their skills at it. One of the most popular slogans for calligraphers in the late 1940s, particularly among schoolchildren, was heiwa kokka kensetsu, *"building a nation of peace" (top). Twelve-year-old crown prince Akihito, who became emperor in 1989, reproduced the slogan on New Year's Day 1946. In a more recent example (bottom), a calligraphy student writes a modern version of an old Japanese saying.*

Chapter One

The Shogun's Realm

The viciousness of the fighting during the Tokugawa forces' attack on Toyotomi castle in Osaka in 1615 was captured by the artist Kuroda Nagamasa. Although the gun had been introduced to Japan by then, Tokugawa warriors still primarily used swords and pikes.

When the Boston journalist Edward H. House arrived in Tokyo in the summer of 1870, he proclaimed himself surprised by what he found: a people struggling with massive social changes yet gracious to the many foreigners who were pressuring Japan to make these changes, orderly and law abiding even in a time of political tumult. "The climate is lovely," he wrote to his New York editor; "the people (natives, I mean) are kind; hospitable, and courteous to a degree which more than justifies all that has been said in their praise; . . . the scenery inexhaustibly attractive, and the cost of living is light." It was not the first time Westerners had been impressed by Japan. The initial European visitors, nearly three centuries earlier, had found the Japanese people handsome, intelligent, orderly, and gracious. Some even commented on how quickly they adapted, then surpassed, the Westerners in skills as varied as making bread and turning a profit at trade.

One reason the visitors were impressed lay in the ages-old ability of the Japanese to structure their surroundings and institutions so that a large segment of the populace enjoyed the "good" life. Though plagued as much by strife as other peoples, the Japanese elites had focused for a millennium on education and harmony as keys to civilization. Another reason, by House's time, lay in the specific political and social structures of the Tokugawa era (1600–1868), which had given the country two and a half centuries of peace by emphasizing loyalty and learning, while providing enough money and freedom to spawn vibrant cities, alive with commerce and trade, up and down the islands. It was this time that laid the foundations for Japan's modern era.

One of the remarkable features of life under Tokugawa rule was its peaceful nature. For four centuries prior to consolidation of control by

This depiction of Tokugawa Ieyasu, who took power in 1600, was sketched in the formal style typical of portraits of powerful men of the seventeenth century, with the subject dressed in heavy court robes and sitting, unsmiling, on a dais. He had himself named shogun in 1603.

family head Tokugawa Ieyasu in 1600, the country had been at war, held together loosely in the better times by national overlords who called themselves "shoguns," and ruled during less stable periods by as many as 250 regional lords known as *daimyō*, "great names." By the late fifteenth century, fighting had laid waste to the capital city of Kyoto, turning both the shogun and the emperor into figureheads and plunging Japan into a feudal era in which competing members of the military class ruled relatively small domains from massive defensive castles. After Ieyasu had consolidated his victory by leveling the castle of chief rival Toyotomi in 1615, the country remained at peace for 250 years. There were peasant uprisings—during the famine-plagued period of 1833–37, for example, when the annual frosts came as early as August. But these uprisings were local and isolated, no threat to Japan as a whole.

At the base of the stability was a sophisticated, well-run administration, grounded in a unique system called *bakuhan* in Japanese and "centralized feudalism" in English. In this system, the Tokugawa rulers adopted a Neo-Confucian philosophy from China that demanded loyalty to parents and rulers and allowed the *daimyō* to retain control of their own domains (to the extent of collecting taxes and maintaining local armies). But the Tokugawa held onto absolute allegiance through a set of regulations that kept the lords in the capital city of Edo (today's Tokyo) half the time. They also adopted an elaborate legal system that kept people satisfied yet controlled. And they barred most foreigners from coming to the country and Japanese from leaving, thus making sure their opponents got neither money nor ideas from abroad. The ruling samurai class, focused on maintaining status and privilege, eventually grew stagnant.

Although this system was tightly controlled, it provided enough flexibility and opportunity to make the Tokugawa years energetic. Merchant firms flourished, as sake, or rice wine, brewers and soy sauce manufacturers with names like Mitsui and Kikkoman moved into ever wider fields of operations, founding silk spinning and cotton weaving factories, establishing rice exchanges, and even managing the shogun's finances. By the early nineteenth century, many of them had become financial giants, making loans to cash-strapped rulers and accumulating wealth

that made Japan's towns and cities prosper. One result of the economic vitality was the appearance of schools in every region: public academies in the capital of each domain (now called a *han*), private institutions run by leading scholars, and more than 10,000
popular schools—many of them taught and operated by
women—run out of homes, shops, or even temples. As the
Tokugawa era moved into its last half-century, literacy rates had
risen as high as those in England, and a healthy intellectual life
supported a large array of thought systems: national learning that
focused on the uniqueness of Japan's past, study of the West called
"Dutch learning" (so-called because the only Westerners allowed
in Japan were from the Netherlands), and Neo-Confucianism,
which emphasized character development, public service, and
loyalty to a benevolent state, as well as a more practical approach
to Japan's contemporary problems.

The most dramatic evidence of Tokugawa vitality came in the
urban areas, where merchant wealth undergirded entertainment
centers that were as lively as they were lowbrow. Every city had a
geisha quarter, presided over by female entertainers who danced,
sang, and made conversation with male visitors. These centers
produced some of the most interesting arts of Japanese history.
The *kabuki* theater, for example, provided plays that were known
for both intricate plots and dramatic staging, such as temple
bells falling on worshipers and samurai disguised as women.
Novelists spun tales of love and moneymaking that sold into
the hundreds of thousands. Poets wrote three-line, seventeen-
syllable poems called *haiku* and composed sets of spontaneous but
elaborately linked verses, while they drank
wine and engaged in witty repartee. Tattoo-
ists worked wonders on the arms and chests
of the fashion conscious. And artists produced multicolored woodblock illustrations
of women in the pleasure quarters and commoners in the fields, provoking scorn from
the samurai but creating art forms that would
influence Western artists from Vincent van
Gogh to Paul Cézanne. When the American naval officer Matthew Perry pressured
Japan to reopen its ports to Western ships in
1853, the country was as well integrated
politically and as sophisticated culturally as
any on Earth.

*Japan's first prominent woodblock artist
was Moronobu Hishikawa, a native of
Chiba, on Edo Bay, who illustrated
nearly 150 books on everything from
kimono patterns and puppet plays to life
in the cities' entertainment quarters. He
was well known for his portrayals of
women dressed in the latest fashions,
along with men who came to visit them.*

Closing the Country

The first Westerners arrived in Japan from Portugal in the mid-1500s, and across the next half-century traders and missionaries created a European boomlet, serving as intermediaries for an expansive trade within Asia, introducing such popular European objects as eyeglasses and clocks, demonstrating the art of shipbuilding, and converting as many as 200,000 Japanese to the Christian faith. A number of the coastal *daimyō* grew richer as a result of the trade that the Portuguese, Dutch, and Spanish encouraged. And European guns helped to shift the military balance, leading to the country's reunification and the Tokugawa family's triumph in 1600 as national overlords.

Although the Western presence would not last long beyond the Tokugawa victory, most of the visitors themselves were impressed by this "new" Asian people. They

Prints of the "exotic" Westerners, called Namban art, became extremely popular in Japan in the late 1500s and early 1600s. Portuguese sailors, in baggy pants, arrived in the port city of Nagasaki late in the sixteenth century, bringing with them Catholic missionaries, as well as items for trade. The size and sophisticated structures of the Portuguese ships impressed the Japanese greatly.

found them different from the Chinese, Indians, and Filippinos, more curious and more accepting of outsiders. The Jesuit priest and commercial agent João Rodrigues, who spent more than thirty years in Japan, wrote two volumes about the Japanese, *Arte da Lingoa de Iapan* in 1608 and *Lingoa de Iapan* in 1620. He reveals a typical Westerner's ambivalence toward the sixteenth-century Japanese, whom he saw as intelligent and principled, yet unduly self-impressed. His observations also reveal the ethnocentrism that characterized most European travelers at that time.

The Japanese tend to be of medium build and on the short side rather than tall, although they admire well-built men. They have many natural talents and an alert understanding, and experience shows that they are competent in all our moral and speculative sciences and the Chinese language. This can be seen in those who profess their sciences and letters, and in the discerning and subtle questions put by even pagans when they listen to sermons about the mysteries of the faith preached to the pagans. . . . In general the Japanese are very much ruled by natural reason and submit to it. . . .

As the Japanese have been brought up here at the end of the world without knowing or being in contact with anybody save the Chinese and Koreans, they naturally have a high opinion of themselves and of their nation. They accordingly have a haughty and proud spirit, and however much they see or hear about other nations, they always think that their own country is the best, especially as regards weapons and their use in war. They have an intrepid and bold spirit, and they believe that nobody in the whole world equals them in this respect and that all are far inferior to them. . . . They are so punctilious and meticulous that they do not hesitate to lay down their life on a single point of honour. . . .

They welcome foreigners with much kindness and they are very trusting in allowing them to enter their country. In this respect they are very different from the Chinese and Koreans, who despise foreigners and are very apprehensive as regards their kingdoms, because they are weak and timid, while the Japanese are courageous and intrepid. They wonder at the civil practice of killing tame and domestic animals and things of that sort, for they show great pity and compassion in this respect.

Jorge Alvares, a Portuguese merchant who visited Japan briefly in the mid-1500s, reported to Jesuit mission leaders

European women use artificial means to make their teeth white; Japanese women use iron and vinegar to make their mouth and teeth black.

—Portuguese priest Luis Frois's accounts of travel in Japan, *Kulturgegensätze Europa-Japan* (Cultural Differences: Europe and Japan), 1585

Fish is with them an ordinary article of diet and is so plentiful as to cost very little. They usually eat this in a practically raw state, after having dipped it in boiling vinegar.

—Report from Japan by Italian traveler Francesco Carletti, 1597–98, published in *Ragionamenti* (1701)

The food is placed in little bowls or platters of wood, covered with a red lacquer, in the most cleanly fashion. And then the whole is eaten without touching anything with their fingers. For this purpose they make use of two little round sticks, with blunt ends, about the size of a quill pen, which are made of either wood or gold. These are called *hashi*.

—Report from Japan by Italian traveler Francesco Carletti, 1597–98, in *Ragionamenti* (1701)

One of the early Tokugawa period's most influential samurai was the swordsman Miyamoto Musashi, whose exploits and writings became the source of many later legends. The nineteenth-century woodblock artist Utagawa Kuniyoshi captured Miyamoto's aura by showing a wandering priest holding a magnifying glass to his head, trying to see if some minute, hard-to-see feature of his face might explain the swordsman's great skill and wisdom.

on social interactions between people of different classes. He mistakes the domain lord, or *daimyō*, for a "king," but shows a keen understanding of Japanese etiquette.

The people greatly venerate their king and it is reckoned a high honour for the sons of the greatest nobles of the kingdom to serve him. They kneel down, placing both hands on the ground, when they receive or hand anything over in his presence. They like speaking softly and look down on us for speaking roughly. Etiquette demands that a man receives guests of equal rank by kneeling with his hands on the floor until they are seated. When the king goes abroad, he is attended by his guards. When the people meet him in the streets, they all bow low with their shoes in their hands until he passes. Inferiors do the same for superiors, and if they meet noble and honourable people they take off their shoes and bow very low with their hands between their thighs.

No matter how astute Western visitors were in describing Japanese practices, they had a harder time grasping the value system that lay behind daily behavior. Nor were they quick to see how perceptive and erudite Japan's own writers had been for centuries in assessing the country's complicated social norms. Perhaps the clearest view of Tokugawa-era customs and values was presented by fiction writers like Ihara Saikaku, who in 1688 published *Tales of Samurai Honor*, a series of short stories illustrating the nature of warrior life. In "His Own Money Put Him Naked into the River," Saikaku describes how the samurai Aoto Zaemon treated two workers who tried, but failed, to find some coins he had dropped into a river. The first worker lies, substituting his own coins for the lost ones in order to curry Aoto's favor, while the second acts honorably, chiding his greedy fellow yet refusing to reveal that man's dishonesty to others. Saikaku's tale depicts both the era's norms and the tendency of many people to stray from the accepted path.

Although the man said nothing, Aoto heard the whole story by chance and had the dishonest laborer seized. Aoto ordered him to atone for his misdeeds by hunting for the lost money every day until he found it. This time, Aoto assigned him a strict supervisor and had him stripped naked so that there would be no further opportunity for trickery.

The man suffered greatly as fall turned into winter on the river. The river began to dry up and finally nothing was left but bare sand. On the ninety-seventh day of his search, he found every last one of the coins and so narrowly escaped with his life. . . .

Aoto later made secret inquiries about the laborer who had spoken out for the cause of righteousness. He turned out to be a descendant of the distinguished samurai family of Chiba no Suke, and his real name was Chiba Magokurō. Circumstances had forced Magokurō's father to conceal his identity and that of his son, and they had lived as commoners among the people. Deeply moved by Magokurō's demonstration of true samurai spirit, Aoto Zaemon spoke about the matter to Lord Tokiyori with successful results. Magokurō was summoned and was restored to samurai status.

Japanese officials found the Europeans increasingly worrisome as a potential threat to power as the decades passed. They puzzled over the unfamiliar Christian doctrines and practices, such as consuming Christ's "body and blood" in the sacrament of communion. And they debated about whether the visitors' true motives were commercial or religious, particularly when they learned that priests often were employed by the ship captains as linguists and commercial agents. Many stories and songs such as those compiled in the 1639 book *Kirishitan monogatari*, "Christian Tales," caricature everything from the Christians' self righteousness to their consumption of meat, which offended the Buddhists, who were vegetarians.

How different are the habits of Japanese monks from the customs of South Barbary! . . . It is not by a miracle that the Kirishitans [Christians] are not covetous and refrain from fawning on their parishioners. For the King of South Barbary each year dispatches a Black Ship or a *galliot*, to eliminate any want in all their temples; and everyone gets his share—including simple parishioners, if their faith be deep. So it is no wonder that they appear to be uncovetous and prudent. And, moreover, day and night they eat the flesh of cows, horses, swine, chickens, and meaner yet! Anxious thus to adopt the manner of wild beasts, many became members of their religion mainly for the taste of such foods.

By 1612, the Tokugawa government—worried over the potential political and economic power of the Europeans—had banned Christianity in Japan, and by 1616 it had limited European trade to Nagasaki and the small southern island of Hirado. During the next two decades, the officials carried out

Lord Tokiyori

The Chiba family became prominent in the 1100s; Lord Tokiyori ruled Japan as a regent of the Hōjō family in the 1200s.

South Barbary

"South Barbary" or *nanban* was the Japanese name for Spain, Portugal, and Italy in the 1500s and 1600s. Like the Chinese, the Japanese regarded all foreigners as barbarians, and since the missionaries and traders most often arrived in Japan from Macao, the island off south China, or the Philippines to the south, they were labeled "southern barbarians."

Early seventeenth-century paintings exaggerated the features of European priests that distinguished them most from the Japanese: heavy eyebrows, overpowering, fleshy faces, and flowing black clerical robes.

a bitter persecution of Japanese Christians, forcing them to renounce their faith under threat of torture, imprisonment, or even death. As a result, all missionaries were banished, and some 3,000 Japanese Christians were executed, many of them by crucifixion. After a bloody 1636 uprising against the lord of the Shimabara region of Kyushu by 40,000 peasants, most of them Christians, the government issued edicts that effectively banned Europeans from Japan. The only exception was the Dutch, who had avoided proselytizing and thus were allowed to remain under severe restrictions on a small, man-made island called Dejima in Nagasaki harbor. A 1640 government edict, which ordered the lord of Chikugo in northern Kyushu to be vigilant against Christians, illustrates the vigor of the officials who pursued the "closed country" policy across the next century.

No Japanese ships may leave for foreign countries.

Any Japanese now living abroad who tries to return to Japan will be put to death.

No offspring of Southern Barbarians will be allowed to remain. Anyone violating this order will be killed, and all relatives punished according to the gravity of the offence.

—From Closed Country Edict, June 1636

In recent years there have been instances of those who used the cover of the Macao trade to venture by ship to Nagasaki with the secret intent to spread the pernicious creed of the Lord of Heaven and thus to delude the populace. This was immediately detected by the perspicacious and valiant government, which instituted stringent proscriptions. If worshippers of this pernicious creed were discovered, punishment was extended unto their relations.

Nevertheless, *Bateren* continued being hidden in the Macao vessels and brought over to delude our populace. For that reason, last year an even more stringent prohibition was issued and traffic from Macao was stopped altogether, with the injunction that any ship coming again would be completely demolished and its passengers killed. And yet the barbarians transgressed our country's prohibition and under the false pretence of presenting their side of the matter came again. Once again they dispatched ambassadors to the port of Nagasaki. Seventy of the gang were arrested and their heads put on exhibition; the ship and its various implements were broken up and sunk to the bottom of the sea. This is something you have seen before your very eyes. From now and ever after you must observe our proscriptions. . . .

Now that those who came from Macao have met their punishment the prohibition of the Jesuits is ever more stringent: that they should come is not permissible. And yet the possibility cannot be excluded that the barbarians in their surfeit of zeal to disseminate their accursed doctrine will hide within your ships, the ministers of monstrosity and preachers of perdition venturing secretly across to work deceit upon the populace. They may arrive with shaved heads or unshaven, dressed in Chinese robes or affecting our country's costume—but where will they hide their cat's eyes and protruding noses, their red hair and shrike's tongues! . . . Anything of the sort will mean that all on board that ship, the old and the young, will be executed and the ship burnt and sunk. . . . Take care to observe the official proscriptions of our country; do not be taken in by the barbarians!

During the years when Japan was closed to the world, an average of two Dutch vessels and a few Chinese ships were allowed to visit Nagasaki yearly to ensure that Japan had access to certain desirable items from abroad and to enable its rulers to keep up with foreign developments. While the Chinese traders—Japanese viewed them as representatives of Earth's most advanced land—were allowed to live in Nagasaki proper, the Dutch were confined to prison-like conditions at Dejima island, which could be traversed in 236 steps. They sold the luxury items that had been brought from Europe, collected Japanese goods for sale back home, and spent their hours chatting, playing games, and smoking drowsily. A few traders took advantage of the idle hours to study Japan. One of the most astute observers was Engelbert Kaempfer, a German doctor who gave his interpreters

Bateren

Bateren or "bugbear Padres" was the derogatory label applied to Christian priests, particularly those of the Jesuit order, in sixteenth-century Japan. These men often were depicted as having long noses, strange complexions, and uncouth, aggressive habits.

shrike

Shrikes are shrill-sounding birds with long tails and hooked beaks; their plumage is gray, white, and black.

liquor and medical treatments in ex-change for knowledge and books during his two years at Dejima (1690–92). His two-volume *History of Japan*, published in 1727–28, tells much about the Japanese attitude toward foreigners then.

This jail goes by the name Dejima, that is, the *island* which lies *in front* of the city. It is also called Dejima *machi*, because it is counted as one street: the street of the in-front-lying island. The island is situated next to the city and has been built up with boulders one and a half by two fathoms from the ocean floor, which at this point is rocky and sandy and at low tide emerges from the water; the island rises half a fathom above the highest water level. It has the shape of a fan without a handle, or rounded square following the curve of the city, to which it is linked by a bridge of hewn stones a few steps long. . . . The area of the island is estimated to be one stadium, or 600 steps in length and 240 in width. According to my measurements it is 82 ordinary steps in width and 236 in length through the middle, following the curve, being shorter on the side of the city and longer on that facing the sea on account of its shape. Two roads crossing each other run through the whole island, and in addition there is a circular road within the barricades, which can be closed off when necessary. The rain gutters run into the sea in a deep curve, so that they cannot be used for passing anything in or out of the island. . . . Three guard houses are also situated within the limits of the island, one at each end and in the middle. At the entrance there is moreover a place with the necessary equipment to extinguish fires.

Kaempfer's *History of Japan* also describes the way the shogun treated the Dutch during one of their annual trips to

Dutchmen stroll in the garden-like area outside their living quarters in Dejima, the two-block-long island that served as their home and headquarters during the seventeenth and eighteenth centuries. The artist captured the quietness and boredom that marked the months they had to spend in Dejima between ship arrivals from Holland.

the capital in Edo, which were required so that the government could stay informed about European affairs.

The shogun had first been seated next to the women at some distance in front of us, but now he moved to the side, as close to us as he could behind the blind. He had us take off our *kappa*, or ceremonial robes, and sit upright so that he could inspect us; had us now stand up and walk, now pay compliments to each other, then again dance, jump, pretend to be drunk, speak Japanese, read Dutch, draw, sing, put on our coats, and take them off again. During this process I broke into the following song:

Wretched me! Impudently I thought
That the ordeal of wild escape to distant lands
Would permit me to forget you,
My angel.
Yet neither Taurus nor Caucus,
Turks nor heathens,
Indus nor Ganges River,
Can part us,
Can quell the fire. . . .

Away with you, court of empty pleasures!
Away with you, land of immense treasures!
Nothing can give me earthly pleasure,
But the chaste loveliness,
Of my precious Florimene.
Deeply longing for each other,
She for me, and I for her.

At the demand of the shogun we had to put up with providing such amusements and perform innumerable other monkey tricks. The captain, however, was excused so that the light of authority of our superiors, whom he represented, would not be blemished. Moreover, his poised demeanor made him an unlikely candidate for such impositions. After we had drilled for two hours—albeit always after courteous requests— . . . servants served each of us with small Japanese dishes on separate little tables; instead of knives we were given two small sticks. We ate just a little. The remains had to be taken away by the old interpreter, carried with both hands in front of him, by him who hardly had the strength to drag his feet. Thereupon we were told to put on our coats and take our leave; we complied immediately.

It is prohibited

—that women enter, except prostitutes.

—that monks and mountain priests enter, except the priests from Mount Kōya.

—that people enter who ask for alms or bet for a living.

—to enter inside the posts placed around Dejima or to pass below the bridge.

—that, unless it be unavoidable, the Dutch leave Dejima.

The above order is to be strictly obeyed.

—Sign posted outside Dejima during Engelbert Kaempfer's stay there, 1690–92

Taurus nor Caucus

The Taurus are mountains in southern Turkey, and the Caucus is a mountain range north of Turkey.

A Feudal Regime

In the spring of 1615, Tokugawa Ieyasu destroyed the last vestiges of opposition in a vicious attack on the rival Toyotomi family castle in Osaka. Using nearly 200,000 men, he laid waste to the castle defenses and forced the suicide of the defending lord. Ieyasu's victory established the Tokugawa as Japan's rulers and created the groundwork for a peace that would last for 250 years. The bloody battle inspired what generally is considered Japan's first example of journalism: a broadside illustrating the battle and showing the consternation inside the Toyotomi castle. Published by Ieyasu on June 4,

This artist's depiction of Tokugawa troops attacking the Osaka Castle in 1615 marked a major journalistic milestone as the first broadside, or single-page newspaper, ever published in Japan. The written characters at the bottom describe the battle.

the day the battle ended, the sheet was intended to inspire lords across the country to give the new rulers their loyalty.

The Tokugawa system for controlling the country was unusually effective, a family-based structure that gave autonomy to each domain even while ensuring loyalty to the central regime in Edo. Scholars have criticized the mature Tokugawa government for being inflexible and insulated. The truth is, however, that this government—called *bakuhan* because of the way it balanced the *bakufu,* "central government," and the *han,* "regional domains"—was both flexible and resilient enough to keep Japan peaceful and vibrant for the better part of 300 years.

At the base of the Tokugawa system was a commitment to the Neo-Confucianism that had undergirded Chinese dynasties for half a millennium. Under that doctrine, emphasis was placed on the four-class status system, in which samurai officials lorded it over farmers, craftsmen, and merchants (in that order). It was the ruler's responsibility to see that people lived in comfort and fairness. Of special importance was loyalty. All people—villagers, townspeople, workers, priests, even samurai—were to faithfully follow those above them in rank. At the same time, balance was equally important; even loyalty or the rank system would become destructive if used by the upper class to oppress the lower class. Lords and followers alike were to seek the good of the country. The shogun's advisor Ogyū Sōrai explains this system of balance in a series of letters to warrior friends in the 1720s.

The division of everything in the world into four classes—warriors, peasants, artisans, and merchants—is something that the sages devised long ago; the four classes of people did not exist naturally in heaven and on earth. Farmers cultivate the fields and feed the people of the world. Artisans make household goods for the people of the world to use. Merchants keep produce and goods circulating and thus benefit the people of the world. And the warriors oversee all of this and prevent disorder. Although each class performs its own duties, each assists the others, and so if any one class were lacking, the country would be the worse for it. And so because people live together, they all are officials helping the ruler become the "father and mother of the people. . . ."

One's first concern should be Humane Government—for without the unity of rulers and their subjects, military victory is impossible. Thus the lord of a province should regard his warriors

"Filial piety" entails serving one's parents. "Brotherly Respect" entails serving one's elder brother. "Loyalty" entails taking on and doing for others—whether a lord or anyone else—what one would do for oneself. "Trust" requires speaking carefully and not lying or making mistakes in one's dealings with friends and others as well.

—Shogun's advisor Ogyū Sōrai in a letter of 1727

Buddhist sects such as Shingon, which was founded by the priest Kōbō Daishi, provided a popular, more devotional alternative to the philosophical approach of Neo-Confucianism. This devotional scroll shows Kōbō Daishi during his student years in China, at a banquet celebrating his ordination. Though the scroll does not identify the celebrants, Kōbō is probably seated in the center at the top table.

* Man's life is like going on a long journey under a heavy burden: one must not hurry.
* If you regard discomfort as a normal condition you are not likely to be troubled by want.
* When ambition arises in your mind consider the days of your adversity.
* Patience is the foundation of security and long life: consider anger as an enemy.
* He who only knows victory and doesn't know defeat will fare badly.
* Blame yourself: don't blame others.
* The insufficient is better than the superfluous.

—Maxims of Tokugawa Ieyasu

and the general population as a family that has been given him by Heaven, a family that he cannot abandon. He should make their hardship his hardship and do what he can to make them enjoy their lives in the province. . . .

The general population is dumb and does only what they are used to doing. This being so, one must plan even everyday matters, grow grasses and trees locally, carry out the annual tree cutting at New Year's, assemble the hundred craftsmen, and encourage commerce. If the root (read agriculture) is slighted and the branch (read commerce) is favored, the province will decline, and the resulting mob of merchants will become the bane of the province. But there are cases in which a poor province became rich through its merchants. In any event, one should pay attention to the ebb and flow of commerce. Because extravagance and gambling signal the deterioration of the population at large, one should prohibit gambling, using harsh punishments to enforce the prohibition, and set up a system regulating dress and house wares. If you are cautious, your province should become as wealthy as you want. . . .

The idea that our bodies belong to our lords and are no longer ours is popular nowadays. Yet this does not appear in the Way of Sages and should be seen as the stuff of flattery and sycophancy. . . . "Loyalty" is seeing another person's affairs as one's own and nothing more. . . . Retainers are a lord's assistants, not his personal toys. The practice of treating retainers as toys originates in the mistake mentioned earlier—namely, the idea that a retainer's body is not his own property—and this violates the Way of Sages.

At the center of the Tokugawa system was the *bakufu's* control of every aspect of the feudal lords' lives under military "house laws." These laws, issued in 1615, provided instructions on everything from *daimyō's* etiquette to their ways of spending money. The most important of the regulations was Number Nine, which required that lords spend regular periods in Edo serving the shogun. It laid the basis for the

innovative governmental system that made *daimyō* simultaneously lords of their own domains and submissive servants of the Tokugawa rulers.

1. The study of literature and the practice of the military arts, including archery and horsemanship, must be cultivated diligently. "On the left hand literature, on the right hand use of arms" was the rule of the ancients. Both must be pursued concurrently. Archery and horsemanship are essential skills for military men. . . .

2. Avoid group drinking and wild parties. The existing codes forbid these matters. Especially, when one indulges in licentious sex, or becomes addicted to gambling, it creates a cause for the destruction of one's own domain.

7. If innovations are being made or factions are being formed in a neighboring domain, it must be reported immediately. Men have a proclivity toward forming factions, but seldom do they attain their goals. There are some who [on account of their factions] disobey their masters and fathers, and feud with their neighboring villages. Why must one engage in [meaningless] innovations, instead of obeying old examples?

8. Marriage must not be contracted in private. . . . The thirty-eighth hexagram *k'uei* [from the *Book of Changes*], says "marriage is not to be contracted to create disturbance. Let the longing of male and female for each other be satisfied. If disturbance is to take hold, then the proper time will slip by." . . . To form a factional alliance through marriage is the root of treason.

9. The *daimyō*'s visits (*sankin*) to Edo must follow the following regulations: . . . It is not permissible to be accompanied by a large

the *Book of Changes*

The *Book of Changes*, one of Confucianism's five ancient classics, explained various combinations of short and long lines, to enable readers to divine the future.

Nijō Castle was constructed by the Tokugawa government in the 1600s as a residence for the shogun when he visited Kyoto. It was noted for its "nightingale floors," which warned of approaching enemies by making a chirping sound when people walked on them. All Japanese castles were surrounded by moats to protect them from enemy armies.

koku

A *koku* was the standard unit of pay and taxation during the Tokugawa era. It equaled about five bushels of unpolished rice. Despite the prohibition on taking "a large force of soldiers" along, powerful daimyō often took hundreds—or even thousands—of men with them to Edo.

force of soldiers. For the *daimyō* whose revenues range from 1,000,000 *koku* down to 200,000 *koku* of rice, not more than twenty horsemen may accompany them. For those whose revenues are 100,000 *koku* or less, the number is to be proportionate to their incomes. On official business, however, the number of persons accompanying him can be proportionate to the rank of each *daimyō*.

12. The samurai of all domains must practice frugality. When the rich proudly display their wealth, the poor are ashamed of not being on a par with them. There is nothing which will corrupt public morality more than this, and therefore it must be severely restricted.

A 1635 amendment to House Law Number Nine stipulated that *daimyō* service in Edo would occur in alternating years. This created the *sankin kōtai*, "alternate attendance," system that required lords to spend every other year in the capital while their wives and children remained there permanently, as hostages. This system did more than anything else to integrate the Tokugawa realm.

It is now settled that the *daimyō* . . . are to serve in turns (*kōtai*) at Edo. They shall proceed hither (*sankin*) every year in the summer during the course of the fourth month. Lately the numbers of retainers and servants accompanying them have become excessive. This is not only wasteful to the domains and districts, but also imposes considerable hardship on the people.

An important feature of the Tokugawa system was the respectful but condescending way in which officials treated the emperor. Japan has the oldest unbroken imperial line in the world, with successive generations of the same family having held the throne for more than 1,700 years. Since the ninth century, however, the emperors had had little more than spiritual power, with people outside the imperial family running the country. During the 200 years prior to the Tokugawa victory, the emperors had been not only powerless but impoverished, as rival lords were too busy fighting each other to pay much attention to the throne. In an effort to shore up its own legitimacy, the Tokugawa family restored the emperors' palaces, built grand gardens for them, and provided them with money to live well. The Tokugawa did not, however, restore power to the throne. By keeping the

This illustration accompanied an 1872 Harper's Weekly *article on the godlike status of Japan's ruler. This image shows an imagined audience before the emperor by samurai officials, who dare not look upon his divine face. The emperor appears partly veiled at the top, in the middle of the room, sitting behind a screen.*

emperors in Kyoto while setting up the *bakufu* three hundred miles to the east, in Edo, the shogun made it clear: emperors would be high priests, shoguns would rule.

Three pieces of literature illustrate the changing role of the emperors across time. The first, this poem from the ancient anthology *Man'yōshū* (A Collection of Ten Thousand Leaves), written in 759 CE, indicates the power and prestige of the sovereigns in the 700s, a century when both males and females ruled.

Our great Sovereign, a goddess,
Of her sacred will
Has reared a towering place
On Yoshinu's shore,
Encircled by its rapids;
And, climbing, she surveys the land.

The overlapping mountains,
Rising like green walls,
Offer the blossoms in spring,
And with autumn, show their tinted leaves,
As godly tributes to the Throne.
The god of the Yu River, to provide the royal table,
Holds the cormorant-fishing
In its upper shallows,
And sinks the fishing-nets
In the lower stream.

Thus the mountains and the river
Serve our Sovereign, one in will;
It is truly the reign of a divinity.

In the early eleventh century, the female courtier Murasaki Shikibu wrote the *Tale of Genji*, a 1,000-page masterpiece depicting the lavish lives of the aristocrats that is often called the world's first novel. By this time, most emperors had grown politically weak, symbolic figureheads who enjoyed luxurious living and romance while regents and nobles exercised power.

In a certain reign there was a lady not of the first rank whom the emperor loved more than any of the others. The grand ladies with high ambitions thought her a presumptuous upstart, and lesser ladies were still more resentful. Everything she did offended someone. Probably aware of what was happening, she fell seriously ill and came to spend more time at home than at court. The emperor's pity and affection quite passed bounds. No longer caring what his ladies and courtiers might say, he behaved as if intent upon stirring gossip. . . .

It may have been because of a bond in a former life that she bore the emperor a beautiful son, a jewel beyond compare. The emperor was in a fever of impatience to see the child, still with the mother's family; and when, on the earliest day possible, he was brought to court, he did indeed prove to be a most marvelous babe. The emperor's eldest son was the grandson of the Minister of the Right. The world assumed that with this powerful support

Episodes from the Tale of Genji *inspired countless artists across Japanese history. Here the seventeenth-century artist Iwasa Matabei depicts a spring storm at the isolated beach at Suma in western Japan, where Prince Genji was exiled after a scandalous love affair. Blooming cherry trees, which symbolize sadness because of the blossoms' short lives, suggest the prince's anguish and loneliness.*

he would one day be named crown prince; but the new child was far more beautiful. On public occasions the emperor continued to favor his eldest son. The new child was a private treasure, so to speak, on which to lavish uninhibited affection.

The mother was not of such a low rank as to attend upon the emperor's personal needs. In the general view she belonged to the upper classes. He insisted on having her always beside him, however, and on nights when there was music or other entertainment he would require that she be present. Sometimes the two of them would sleep late, and even after they had risen he would not let her go. Because of his unreasonable demands she was widely held to have fallen into immoderate habits out of keeping with her rank.

With the birth of the son, it became yet clearer that she was the emperor's favorite.

By the early 1600s, Tokugawa Ieyasu saw the emperor's role as largely ritualistic and spiritual, in contrast to his own more powerful role. His attitude is revealed in this story from the *Historical Records of Great Japan*.

Once, Lord Tosho [Tokugawa Ieyasu] conversed with Honda, Governor Sado, on the subject of the emperor, the shogun, and the farmer. "Whether there is order or chaos in the nation depends on the virtues and vices of these three. The emperor, with compassion in his heart for the needs of the people, must not be remiss in the performance of his duties—from the early morning worship of the New Year to the monthly functions of the court. Secondly, the shogun must not forget the possibility of war in the peacetime, and must maintain his discipline. He should be able to maintain order in the country; he should bear in mind the security of the sovereign; and he must strive to dispel the anxieties of the people. One who cultivates the way of the warrior only in the times of crisis is like a rat who bites his captor in the throes of being captured. The man may die from the effects of poisonous bite, but to generate courage at the spur of the moment is not the way of a warrior. To assume the way of the warrior upon the outbreak of war is like a rat biting its captor. Although this is better than fleeing from the scene, the true master of the way of the warrior is one who maintains his martial discipline even in time of peace.

The Tokugawa legal system was well developed, with laws for each institution and status group, as well as detailed administrative and criminal codes for the nation. Constant

The best-known judicial decision of the
Tokugawa era inspired the *Tale of the Forty-
Seven Masterless Warriors* (*Chūshingura*), which
narrated the experience of servants whose
lord, Asano Naganori, was sentenced to commit suicide after he lost his temper in 1701
and drew his sword in the shogun's court
against an arrogant superior named Kira. His
forty-seven retainers spent much of the next
two years throwing Kira off guard by pretend-
ing to have become dissolute, then regrouped,
charged Kira's estate, found him hiding in a
storeroom, and killed him. They took his head
to Sengakukji temple, where Asano's remains
had been interred, and presented it to their
lord. The case created a sensation for the
nation and a problem for the government,
because while contemporary laws demanded
execution for murder, the public was impressed
by the retainers' faithfulness to the old feudal
code of vengeance. In the end, the men were
ordered to commit suicide, thus upholding
both the law and their own honor. The event
has inspired endless stories and dramas over
the last 300 years.

**discussions by scholars and writers of how to apply legal
principles to daily life supplemented the formal laws. This
account by the scholar-statesman Arai Hakuseki about a
young warrior who was jailed in 1716 for running away from
his lord typically reflects the widespread concern with applying laws justly to life's complex situations.**

In the region of the Sagami River . . . a young samurai who had
killed a robber had been detained by the men of Nakajima in that
neighborhood and had been brought to the Daikansho [steward's
office]. When the incident was looked into, it was ascertained that
the samurai was called Sakai. . . . On his way to Suruga Providence,
between Totsuka and Fujisawa, a big man began following him,
and when he got near the river, the fellow had put his hand into
the samurai's bosom and stolen his purse, so the samurai drew his
sword and cut him down with one stroke. When the local people
were interrogated about the man who had been killed, they
replied that they did not know anything about him but that he
might be a robber plying up and down the highway. It was also
said that this young samurai was a retainer in the house of Honda
Totomi-no-Kami Masatake and that he had recently run away
from his lord's house. Although his slaying of the robber was a fine
deed, since he had run away from his lord's house, he had, for the
time being, been put into prison on the grounds that his offense
could not be overlooked.

I told Akifusa that if this man were punished, the rest of the
robber-band would spread a false report, and that if the story got
about that he had been punished for killing a robber, in the future
people traveling along the highway would suffer beyond
endurance at the hands of robbers. However, I said there was a
way to deal with the matter and he should delay his decision for
a while. I sent a message to Asakura Yoichi Kagetake telling him
there was something I wanted to see him about. He came at once,
and I asked him if someone had recently run away from his master's house. He replied: "That is so. A man named Sakai has run
away and killed a robber near the Sagami River." I told him that it
was because of that man that I had asked him to see me and said:
"It will be very cruel if, despite the fact that the young fellow has
killed a robber, he is punished because he has run away from his
lord's house. What should we do?" "I see," he said, and came the
next day and told me he had spoken to his lord who had agreed
not to inflict any punishment on the man. I told him that was wise
and reported what had happened to Akifusa.

Life Under the Tokugawa

The samurai class dominated the Tokugawa world. They rested atop the status system, held all offices, operated most of the schools, and received government stipends for their service to society. However, with the honors came restrictions that prevented samurai from going into business or participating—except in disguise—in the popular culture of the cities. As a result, although many of them lived well, an even greater number lived at the edge of poverty. Many samurai were unemployed because there were too few government (i.e., respectable) jobs, which forced them to idleness and decadence because they had no other work options. By the early 1800s, many *daimyō* were deeply in debt, in hock to the merchants who lived free of the restrictions. Regardless of their personal condition, all samurai strove for the ideal. One of its foremost spokesmen was Yamamoto Tsunetomo, who became well known in the eighteenth century for a 1716 book of sayings called *Hagakure* (In the Shadow of Leaves), on the way samurai should live.

The way of the Samurai is found in death. When it comes to either/or, there is only the quick choice of death. It is not particularly difficult. Be determined and advance. To say that dying without reaching one's aim is to die a dog's death is the frivolous way of sophisticates.

It is bad taste to yawn in front of people. When one unexpectedly has to yawn, if he rubs his forehead in an upward direction, the sensation will stop. If that does not work, he can lick his lips while keeping his mouth closed, or simply hide it with his hand or his sleeve in such a way that no one will know what he is doing. It is the same with sneezing.

These are from the recorded sayings of Yamamoto Jin'emon:

If you can understand one affair, you will understand eight.

An affected laugh shows lack of self-respect in a man and lewdness in a woman. . . .

A samurai with no group and no horse is not a samurai at all. . . .

It is said that one should rise at four in the morning, bathe and arrange his hair daily, eat when the sun comes up, and retire when it becomes dark.

A samurai will use a toothpick even though he has not eaten.

There are two kinds of dispositions, inward and outward, and a person who is lacking in one or the other is worthless. It is, for example, like the blade of a sword. . . . If a person has his sword out all the time, he is habitually swinging a naked blade; people will not approach him. . . . If a sword is always sheathed, it will become rusty, the blade will dull, and people will think as much of its owner.

—Yamamoto Tsunetomo,
Hagakure: The Book of the
Samurai, 1716

The samurai's most important talent was the ability to use his sword skillfully and justly. Each samurai wore two swords, a long one for battle and a short one with which to kill himself if the occasion demanded it. These swords, made in the fifteenth century, were approximately 25 and 20 inches long, respectively.

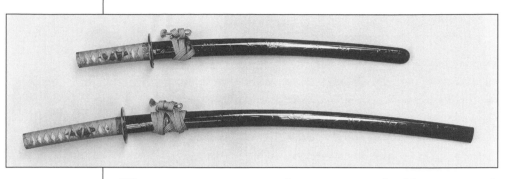

When someone is giving you his opinion, you should receive it with deep gratitude even though it is worthless. If you don't, he will not tell you the things that he has seen and heard about you again. It is best to both give and receive opinions in a friendly way.

Lord Naoshige said, "An ancestor's good or evil can be determined by the conduct of his descendants." A descendant should act in a way that will manifest the good in his ancestor and not the bad. This is filial piety.

At the other end of the samurai spectrum was Katsu Kokichi, a ne'er-do-well of the early 1800s who wrote an autobiography under the pseudonym *Musui's Story*, revealing just about every trait—dishonesty, womanizing, brawling, idleness—a samurai should avoid. His summation at the end of his memoir pretends shame, but exudes self-satisfaction.

At my brother's office in Edo there was a man by the name of Kuboshima Karoku. One day he tricked me into going with him to the pleasure quarters in the Yoshiwara. I enjoyed myself immensely and after that went every night. I used up all my money. Just as I was wondering what to do, the annual tax money—about seven thousand *ryō*—arrived from the shogunate land under my brother's jurisdiction in Shinano. My brother ordered me to guard the money until it was delivered to the shogunate treasury. I kept an eye on the funds, but then my friend Karoku suggested, "Without money it isn't much fun in the Yoshiwara, is it? Go ahead and steal one hundred *ryō*." "Not a bad idea," I said, and prying open the strongbox, I removed two hundred *ryō*.

The box rattled rather suspiciously afterward, but Karoku fixed that by putting in some stones wrapped in paper. The two of us went about our business looking very innocent. Several days later my brother Hikoshirō discovered the theft, and when he angrily cross-examined everyone, the damned errand boy blurted out that

I had stolen the money. . . . It was plain as day that I had stolen the money. All the same, everyone looked the other way, and the incident passed over. As for the two hundred *ryō*, I spent it all in the Yoshiwara in less than a month and a half. After that I had to scrounge from the rice agents at the shogunate warehouse and other moneylenders. . . .

Reflections on My Life

Although I indulged in every manner of folly and nonsense in my lifetime, Heaven seems not to have punished me as yet. Here I am, forty-two, sound of health and without a scratch on my body. Some of my friends were beaten to death; others vanished without a trace or suffered one fate or another. I must have been born under a lucky star, the way I did whatever I pleased. No other samurai with such a low stipend spent money as I did. And how I blustered and swaggered about with a trail of followers at my beck and call!

I wore kimonos of imported silk and fine fabrics that were beyond the reach of most people. I ate my fill of good food, and all my life I bought as many prostitutes as I liked. I lived life fully. Only recently have I come to my senses and begun to act more like a human being. When I think of my past, my hair stands on end.

He who would call himself a man would do well to not imitate my ways.

Any grandchildren or great-grandchildren that I may have—let them read carefully what I have set down and take it as a warning. Even putting these words on paper fills me with shame. . . .

I am most fortunate in having a filial and obedient son. My daughters, too, are very devoted. My wife has never gone against my wishes. I am altogether satisfied to have lived until now without any serious mishap. At forty-two I have understood for the first time what it means to follow the path of righteousness, to serve one's lord and one's father, to live with one's kinsmen in harmony, and to have compassion and love for one's wife, children, and servants.

My past conduct truly fills me with horror. Let my children, their children, and their children's children read this record carefully and savor its meaning. So be it.

Early in Japan's history, women had held prominent roles, reigned as empresses, written much of the best literature, and on occasion even served as warriors. By the feudal era, however, their status had declined to that of subservient

wives responsible for rearing families and serving their husbands. But the reality was more complex, and many Tokugawa women exerted power in fields as varied as literature, business, and the entertainment world. The official values of an ideal woman were encapsulated in a widely circulated 1716 manual *Onna daigaku* (Great Learning for Women). It calls for wo-men to be obedient, quiet, hard-working, and self-controlled.

More precious in a woman is a virtuous heart than a face of beauty. The vicious woman's heart is ever excited; she glares wildly around her, she vents her anger on others, her words are harsh and her accent vulgar. When she speaks it is to set herself above others, to upbraid others, to envy others, to be puffed up with individual pride, to jeer at others, to outdo others—all things at variance with the way in which a woman should walk. The only qualities that benefit a woman are gentle obedience, chastity, mercy and quietness.

From her earliest youth a girl should observe the line of demarcation separating women from men, and never, even for an instant, should she be allowed to see or hear the least impropriety. The customs of antiquity did not allow men and women to sit in the same apartment, to keep their wearing apparel in the same place, to bathe in the same place, or to transmit to each other anything directly from hand to hand. . . .

The great lifelong duty of a woman is obedience. In her dealings with her husband, both the expression of her countenance and style of her address should be courteous, humble, and conciliatory, never peevish and intractable, never rude and arrogant—that should be a woman's first and chiefest care. When the husband issues his instructions, the wife must never disobey him. . . . Should her husband be roused at any time to anger, she must obey him with fear and trembling, and not set herself up against him in anger and forwardness. A woman should look on her husband as if he were Heaven itself. . . .

Let her never even dream of jealousy. If her husband be dissolute, she must expostulate with him, but never either nurse or vent her anger. If her jealousy be extreme, it will render her countenance frightful and her accent repulsive, and can only result in completely alienating her husband from her.

The most lively sector of Tokugawa life probably was the entertainment quarter in each of the large towns and cities,

One of the tasks demanded of women in Tokugawa society was to hang out both clothes and books each year in order to prevent mildew and kill insects. One woman stops to peruse the book she has opened.

The five worst infirmities that afflict the female are indocility, discontent, slander, jealousy, and silliness. Without any doubt, these five infirmities are found in seven or eight out of every ten women.

—Great Learning for Women, 1716

an area known for its free-wheeling style as the "floating world" of *geisha*, theater, dance, music, woodblock art, and popular literature. Condemned by the ruling elites as bastions of moral decay, these centers fostered new artistic forms that in later generations would be hailed as creative, avant-garde—and distinctly Japanese. One product of this world was the *ukiyo-e*, or woodblock print of the floating world: from the early illustrated guides to courtesan life by the artist Moronobu Hishikawa to the depictions of natural wonders and commoner life by the era's most celebrated printmaker, Andō Hiroshige. No one captured the spirit of this world more fully than the novelist Ihara Saikaku, who wrote about samurai justice, vendettas, love affairs, and moneymaking. His 1688 accounts of merchant greed in *The Eternal Storehouse of Japan* ridicule men willing to bend any rule in search of riches.

Fuji-ichi was a clever man, and his substantial fortune was amassed in his own lifetime. But first and foremost he was a man who knew his own mind, and this was the basis of his success. In addition to carrying out his own business, he kept a separate ledger, bound from old scraps of paper, in which, as he sat all day in his shop, pen in hand, he entered a variety of information. As the clerks from the money exchanges passed by he noted down the market ratio of copper and gold; he inquired about the current quotations of the stock brokers; he sought information from druggists' and haberdashers' assistants on the state of the market at Nagasaki; for the latest news on ginned cotton, salt, and saké, he noted the various days on which the Kyoto dealers received dispatches from

The most popular poetic form of the Tokugawa era was the three-line, seventeen-syllable *haiku*, and the greatest master of the form was Matsuo Bashō, who spent years wandering on foot across Japan, writing travel accounts interlaced with poetry.

Men have grieved to hear monkeys—
What of a child forsaken
In the autumn wind?

My summer clothing—
I still have not quite finished
Picking out the lice.

Octopus in a trap—
Its dreams are fleeting under
The summer moon.

I can see how she looked—
The old woman, weeping alone,
The moon her companion.

The passing of spring—
The birds weep and in the eyes
Of fish there are tears.

One of the earliest eighteenth-century ukiyo-e artists, Miyagawa Chosun, was known for his attention to the elegant attire of the geisha and their visitors. Here, in the scroll "Festivals of the Twelve Months," he shows a group of geisha dancing, while several musicians play the flute, drums, and three-stringed shamisen (lute) during an autumn festival.

Andō Hiroshige was the first prominent artist to add landscapes and daily scenes to the woodblock genre, of which this depiction of a flash rainstorm at Ohashi is typical. Andō is known to have designed more than 10,000 prints.

the Edo branch shops. Every day a thousand things were entered in his book, and people came to Fuji-ichi if they were ever in doubt. . . .

Once, on the evening of the seventh day of the New Year, some neighbors asked leave to send their sons to Fuji-ichi's house to seek advice on how to become millionaires. Lighting the lamp in the sitting room, Fuji-ichi sent his daughter to wait, bidding her let him know when she heard a noise at the private door from the street. The young girl, doing as she was told with charming grace, first carefully lowered the wick in the lamp. Then, when she heard the voices of visitors, she raised the wick again and retired to the scullery. By the time the three guests had seated themselves the grinding of an earthenware mortar could be heard from the kitchen, and the sound fell with pleasant promise on their ears. They speculated on what was in store for them.

"Pickled whale skin soup?" hazarded the first.

"No. As this is our first visit of the year, it ought to be rice-cake gruel," said the second.

The third listened carefully for some time, and then confidently announced that it was noodle soup. Visitors always go through this amusing performance. Fuji-ichi then entered and talked to the three of them on the requisites for success. . . .

"As a general rule," concluded Fuji-ichi, "give the closest attention to even the smallest details. Well now, you have kindly talked with me from early evening, and it is high time that refreshments were served. But not to provide refreshments is one way of becoming a millionaire. The noise of the mortar you heard when you first arrived was the pounding of starch for the covers of the Account Book."

The Shogunate Under Challenge

In 1771 the physician Sugita Genpaku discovered a Dutch anatomy book that illustrated the body's internal organs in ways wholly at variance with Chinese medical texts. When

an autopsy supported the Dutch version, he decided to study the West more earnestly. It was a sign that a new world was arriving. Japan had always looked to China as the font of wisdom and culture, dominating the world like the shogun dominated his domains. But in the next decades, the old order began to crumble. Western ships breached the coast, scholars began to question both Chinese scholarship and Japan's defenses, and some officials began raising doubts about Tokugawa legitimacy. All the while, the *bakufu* was growing old and less capable of handling change.

The Tokugawa rulers issued a decree after British ships showed up in Nagasaki harbor in 1825, ordering the immediate expulsion of all foreign visitors and revealing both the rulers' fears and their inflexible mindset.

One sign of the changing times in the late Tokugawa years was the appearance of paintings depicting the functions of the human body. This print by the nineteenth-century woodblock artist Utagawa Kunisada shows a man digesting a carp, one of Japan's favorite seafoods.

Because there has been an increase in the number of ships [coming to our shores], a new decree is needed. . . . A British ship carried out violent acts in Nagasaki several years ago; more recently they have been using rowboats to approach shore at several places, asking for firewood, water, and provisions. Last year, they landed without permission and attacked cargo vessels, then stole rice, grain, and livestock. They also have engaged in the unacceptable behavior of encouraging their evil religion. Nor are the English alone responsible. The Southern Barbarians and other Westerners all come, despite our prohibitions on their evil religion, landing at whatever port village they desire. We will send men to those areas and expel them. . . . If they insist on landing and trying to push us aside, we have no choice but to destroy them. . . . Chinese, Korean, and Okinawan vessels are easy to recognize. Dutch ships, which are harder to recognize, must be inspected and checked carefully. Boats from anywhere else should be sent away without a second thought.

While some scholars called for Japan to open up to the West—to begin trading and develop a modern army—others focused on the need to strengthen Japan by renewing ancient values. Japanese culture, said the nationalist scholar Aizawa Seishisai, was inherently superior to that of the West, but the regime needed to be strengthened by placing the emperor at the center, just as Europe had made Christianity the core of Western institutions. Aizawa's *Shinron* (New Theses), published in 1825, argues that even though Christianity is evil, it unifies the Westerners and makes them strong. Japan, it says, must return to "the way," to the emperor-centered values that had enabled it to triumph over foreign challenges such as that of the Mongols in the thirteenth century.

For close to three hundred years now the Western barbarians have rampaged on the high seas. Why are they able to enlarge their territories and fulfill their every desire? Does their wisdom and courage exceed that of an ordinary man? Is their government so benevolent that they win popular support? Are their rites, music, laws, and political institutions superb in all respects? Do they possess some superhuman, divine powers? Hardly. Christianity is the sole key of their success. It is a truly evil and base religion, barely worth discussing. But its main doctrines are simple to grasp and well-contrived; they can easily deceive stupid commoners with it. . . .

They win a reputation for benevolence by performing small acts of kindness temporarily to peoples they seek to conquer. After they capture a people's hearts and minds, they propagate their doctrines. Their gross falsehoods and misrepresentations deceive many, particularly those who yearn for things foreign. Such dupes, with their smattering of secondhand Western knowledge, write books with an air of scholarly authority; so even *daimyō* or high-ranking officials at times cannot escape infection from barbarian ways. Once beguiled by Christianity, they cannot be brought back to their senses. Herein lies the secret of barbarians' success.

Whenever they seek to take over a country, they employ the same method. By trading with that nation, they learn about its geography and defenses. If these be weak, they dispatch troops to invade the nation; if strong, they propagate Christianity to subvert it from within. Once our people's hearts and minds are captivated by Christianity, they will greet the barbarian host with open arms, and we will be powerless to stop them. . . .

To defend the nation and improve military preparedness, we first must determine our fundamental [foreign] policy—war or peace. Otherwise we will drift aimlessly, morale and discipline will slacken, high and low will indulge in the ways of ease and comfort, intelligent men will be unable to devise stratagems, and courageous men will be unable to work up their anger. . . . When the Mongols sullied our honor, Hojo Tokimune resolutely beheaded their envoy and ordered that an army be raised to smite them. His Imperial Majesty, Emperor Kameyama, prayed that a disaster befall himself rather than the nation. In that hour of crisis, we willingly courted oblivion and the people ceased fearing death. Indeed, did anyone *not* aspire to die ardently in the realm's defense! Hence, we once again attained spiritual unity, and the purity and intensity of our sincerity unleashed a raging typhoon that destroyed the barbarian fleet. Ah, the ancients expressed it well when they said, "Place a man between the jaws of death, and he will emerge unscathed." Or again, "If officials and commoners are led to believe that savage hordes are closing in, fortune will be with us." Therefore I say that we must once and for all establish our basic foreign policy and place the realm between the jaws of death. Only then can we implement defense measures.

The Tokugawa government's opposition to Christianity is symbolized by this carved stone on the island of Amakusa, marking the place where thousands of Christians were buried after being killed in an uprising against the government in 1636. The stone, dedicated to the "martyrs" of a region known for its resistance against the Tokugawa government, was photographed by a Christian missionary early in the 1900s.

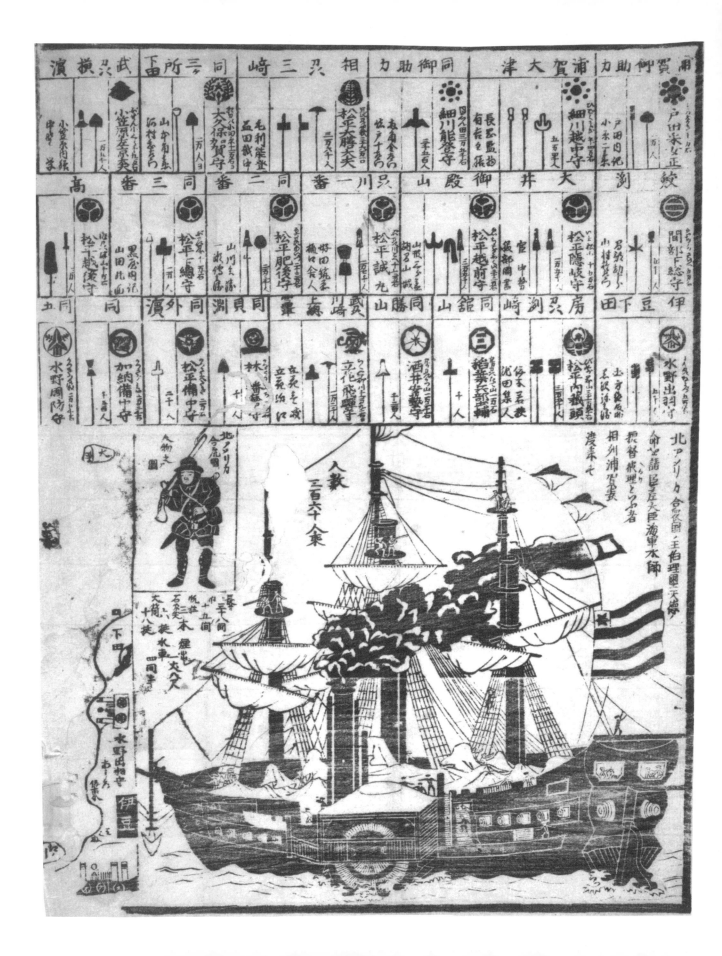

The Old Order Topples: 1853–68

Japanese leadership circles were filled with talk about *naiyū gaikan* at the beginning of the 1850s. The phrase, which means "troubles at home and dangers from abroad," came from the ancient Chinese idea that when serious foreign and domestic troubles occur simultaneously, the dynasty is about to fall. And troubles of every sort were plaguing the ruling Tokugawa family. The *bakufu* administrative structures were old and creaky, leading one young upstart to say that hidebound officials acted like "wooden monkeys." The ruling elites were laden with debts so heavy that, for some, loan interest alone consumed 90 percent of their annual income. Discontented urbanites in Osaka, angry over high taxes, famine, and poor services, had destroyed a quarter of the city during the late 1830s. And though the rebellion was put down fairly easily, the regime had not been able to quell a deluge of ensuing criticism from the political and intellectual elites. Scholars decried official inability to meet the needs of the poor. Dutch-learning scholars complained that Japan had not kept up with the West. Traditionalists lamented the movement of job-seeking peasants into the cities. Domain lords were frustrated over the costs of the alternate attendance system.

As if to underline the instability, foreign ships were showing up with increasing frequency in Japanese waters. When U.S. Commodore Matthew Perry arrived in Edo Bay in 1853 with black ships laden with nearly a hundred cannons, the Japanese concluded that the "dangers from abroad" were imminent. The Tokugawa's hold on power seemed tenuous.

A nineteenth-century print entitled "United States of North America: Perry Arrives in Uraga, Soshu Province" shows the steamship on which Commodore Matthew Perry entered Edo Bay in July 1853 to open relations between Japan and the United States. His ship flies the American flag and belches black smoke.

It should have surprised no one, then, that the decade and a half after Perry's arrival plunged Japan into tumult, leading finally to a change in regimes. The first obvious result of the government's 1854 decision to let the Americans in was the arrival of Westerners, at first by scores, then hundreds, then thousands. By 1858, a Japan-U.S. commercial treaty was in place, bringing Japan into the arena of world trade. By the early 1860s, the ports of Nagasaki, Kōbe, Hakodate, and Yokohama bustled with merchants, newspapers, theaters, brothels, churches—and Japanese eager to make money off the foreigners. The Westerners also brought guns, and on several occasions used them to pressure the Japanese into opening more ports and following the new treaties.

The second major result of the opening was the emergence of an active domestic opposition movement. Almost as soon as the traders began coming, low-level samurai called *shishi*, "men of zeal," took to the streets and alleyways, signing oaths in blood to drive out the "barbarians" and punish the officials who had let them in. Sometimes called the world's first urban guerillas, they named their cause *sonnō jōi*, "revere the emperor, expel the barbarians," and assassinated the American consul general's secretary, Henry Heusken, one of their first victims. In 1860, a group of them killed Ii Naosuke, the regent they held responsible for signing the commercial treaty. Even more important to the regime, several of the powerful regional lords, as well as an increasing number of highly placed officials and court nobles, began maneuvering actively against the regime. By the early 1860s, they had destroyed the Tokugawa's power to act unilaterally, and by the mid-1860s the large Chōshū domain on the western tip of Japan's main island was in open rebellion against the regime. The culmination of these domestic problems came in January 3, 1868, when the emperor claimed ownership of the Tokugawa lands and took power into his own hands through a coup d'etat. The Tokugawa army resisted briefly, but by February the shogun had surrendered. The new era was given the emperor's rule name, Meiji, which means "bright or enlightened rule."

Abe Yasuyuki's 1853 map of the world reflects the imprecision of the Japanese understanding of the world beyond their shores. The legend at the bottom says the world has four great seas (which it does not identify) and six continents: Asia, North America, South America, Europe, Rimiya (Africa), and Mecalanica, the huge land mass at the southern extreme. It identifies seas by names such as Great Western Ocean (eastern Atlantic), Large Eastern Ocean (western Atlantic), South Sea (southern Pacific), and North Sea (northern Pacific).

Japan's Sense of the World

Mapmaking in Japan goes back at least to the eighth century and became popular in the 1600s, stimulated by improved survey techniques, European influence, and the growth of woodblock printing, which made multiple copies easy to produce. The Japanese understanding of the globe remained crude during the Tokugawa years, but maps of the Japanese islands became increasingly accurate, and by the early 1800s the Japanese were making large and detailed maps, some of them based on a 1:200,000 scale. Since the Japanese typically read maps while sitting on the floor, characters were printed in four different directions. Thus it was impossible to tell which was the top or bottom unless one knew which locations were in the north, which usually was regarded as the top.

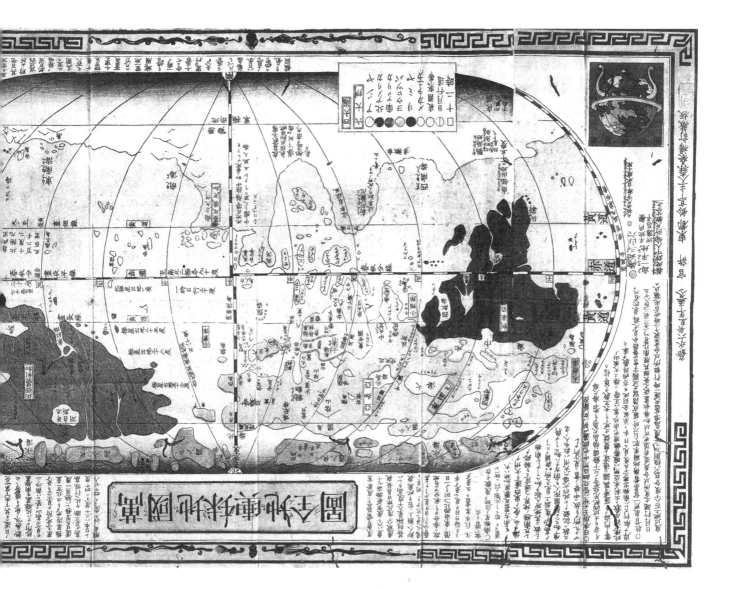

Perry's Arrival

Commodore Perry came to Japan twice, first in July 1853 with four ships to demand that Japan open its ports to American sailors, then again in February 1854, when he returned with a quarter of the U.S. Navy—nine vessels—to receive the shogun's response. His first visit triggered a vigorous debate, when the Tokugawa rulers departed from their traditional practice of acting unilaterally and asked more than sixty opinion leaders what they should do. The opinions were as varied as the leaders; so the officials had to make up their own minds,

and by the time Perry came back, they had concluded that there was no choice but to negotiate with Perry. The resultant Treaty of Kanagawa in 1854 opened two ports—Kanagawa near present-day Yokohama and Hakodate on the northern island of Hokkaidō—to U.S. ships for refueling and storage, and provided for the exchange of consuls general after 1856. Commercial relations and full diplomatic relations between the two nations had to wait until 1858.

J. G. Sproston, one of Matthew Perry's assistants when he returned to Japan to sign a treaty in 1854, drew a sketch of a negotiating session between Japanese officials (right) and Perry's group. Henry A. Adams, captain of Perry's flagship, and Sproston are third and fourth from the left, respectively. The man seated on the floor is a Japanese interpreter.

Photographs and drawings often tell us a great deal about an artist's viewpoint. An official American photograph of Commodore Perry (left) conveys a solemn, dignified man of confident but thoughtful manner, with the symbols of authority and military might off to the side and beneath him. Many Japanese saw Perry differently, as a watercolor by an unknown artist illustrates (right). The artist emphasized the commodore's heavy eyebrows, lengthened his nose, highlighted the creases in his jowls, added facial hair, and placed the sword in a threatening position.

A Land in Transition

Coming after two and a half centuries of isolation, the Kanagawa Treaty opened the door to what seemed to many like a whole new world. Though the most important changes related to domestic politics, as rival lords and groups vied for a say in national decisions, the most dramatic transformation was found in the presence of the Europeans and Americans who brought more variety to Japan's port cities than the country had ever known. Stories about their strange hairy-bodied looks and even stranger behavior—ballroom dancing, weekly church attendance, street brawling after weekend drinking bouts—began to circulate across the land. And their technologies, beliefs, and merchandise gave rise to political discussions of the sort never heard in Japan before. They also stimulated the growth of trade in Yokohama, where nearly a hundred Japanese businesses opened soon after Westerners were allowed there in 1859.

One of the major new factors in Japanese life after the coming of the Westerners was the advent of foreign trade; foreigners and Japanese sold each other tea, Mexican silver, woolens, and art objects. A woodblock artist rendered his vision of American merchants transporting goods into Yokohama harbor in 1861; elegant Western travelers stood on deck, while an American flag graced the small boat used for transporting goods in the harbor.

One of the most popular ways to make money from foreigners was to sell them woodblock prints that depicted their lives. Below, the era's most popular printmaker, Utagawa Hiroshige III, shows the foreign business district in Yokohama in the 1870s, with its Western-style buildings, European women in formal dresses, European men leading dogs, Japanese women in kimono, and well-off foreigners riding in a carriage. Ships laden with trading goods fill the harbor in the background.

Symbols of Change

In Yokohama, the first Japanese-language newspaper, *Shimbunshi*, was produced by Joseph Heco, a Japanese fisherman who had been rescued by an American ship when his boat was wrecked at sea in 1850. Returning to Japan early in the 1860s, he took up a number of business projects and taught his compatriots about the West by translating articles from British papers.

Quite a number of Japanese also began going abroad after the late 1850s, in a dramatic break from the centuries of isolation. The most heralded late-Tokugawa mission was the first: an embassy of seventy-seven diplomats and officials sent to the United States in 1860 to exchange ratifications of the 1858 commercial treaty. American reporters covered their travels with great curiosity and in meticulous detail, describing the endless gifts they handed out, the solemnity of their visit with President James Buchanan, the flirtations of a teenage member of the entourage nicknamed Tommy, the swords and straw sandals that the ambassadors wore, and the 10,000 rambunctious New Yorkers who attended a ball in their honor.

Both the formality of the visit and the contrast in cultures shine out from a photograph that was taken on the arrival of the Japanese ambassadors at the Washington Naval Yard in 1860. The Japanese wore swords and formal kimono called hakama, whereas the Americans wore suits or military uniforms and hats—and sported considerable facial hair.

The Nagasaki Shipping List
AND
Advertiser.

Vol. I. No. 4.]   NAGASAKI, JAPAN, WEDNESDAY, 10TH JULY, 1861.   [$20 PER ANNUM, PAYABLE IN ADVANCE.

OFFICIAL NOTIFICATION.—It is hereby notified that from and after this date, and until further orders, the "*Nagasaki Shipping List and Advertiser,*" is to be considered the Official Organ of all Notifications proceeding from HER BRITANNIC MAJESTI'S LEGATION, CONSULATE GENERAL, and CONSULATES IN JAPAN.

By Order,

(Signed)   ADOLPHUS A. ANNESLEY.

H. B. M.'s Consulate, Nagasaki, 22nd June, 1861.

OFFICIAL NOTIFICATION.—Is is hereby notified that from this date until further orders, the "*Nagasaki Shipping List and Advertiser,*" is to be considered the Official Organ of all Notifications proceeding from this Consulate.

Consulate of Portugal, Nagasaki, 22nd June, 1861.

J. LOUREIRO,
Consul for Portugal.

THE NAGASAKI SHIPPING LIST AND ADVERTISER, WILL be published every Saturday and Wednesday Morning Subscription.—$20 per Annum, payable in advance. For less time than one year (or if not paid in advance) $6 per quarter. The quarters will date on the last day of publication in September, December, March and June, at which date only can Subscriptions be discontinued, but new Subscribers entering at intermediate dates will only be charged from the commencement of the then current month. Captains of vessels in the harbour will be supplied with single copies at the

JAMES MITCHELL,
SHIP BUILDER,
ABERDEEN YARD, SAGAROMATCH, NAGASAKI.
Vessels of every description built to order with despatch, &c., at very moderate rates.

KEPPEL & Co.,
SHIP BUILDERS AND CHANDLERS, AND BLACKSMITHS.
NAGASAKI.
A heaving-down Hulk ready for immediate use. All repairs promptly executed.

FOR SALE BY FRAZAR & Co.
IRON SAFES, warranted Fire and Burglar Proof.
Dr. S. P. TOWNSEND'S Compound Extract of SARSAPARILLA for Purifying the Blood.
Also,
A small stock of Liquors very cheap.
Nagasaki, 22nd June, 1861.

FOR SALE.
At WACHTEL & Co.'s (next door to Messrs. TEXTOR & Co.,
Desima.
GENTLEMEN'S Clothing in suits of 1 Pantaloon, 1 Waistcoat and 1 Coat.

COMMERCIAL HOTEL.
THE undersigned begs to invite the attention of residents and visitors to his house, and to assure them that they will at all times find there supplies of Liquors of every description and of the best quality, which he will be happy to supply wholesale as well as retail.
The House is a commodious building conveniently situated and fitted to accommodate visitors. There is a bowling alley attached, for which the undersigned has just received a new set of ligum vitæ balls.
WM. WARREN.
Nagasaki, 10th July, 1861.

NOTICE.
I beg to give notice that I have established myself as Agent here to carry on business generally with the Chinese in Imports and Exports, having had twenty one years' experience in business in China, and being acquainted with the language sufficiently to transact business without the assistance of Compradors. I am also about to open a Branch of my business at Newchwang during the Summer season under the superintendence of a European gentleman who is well versed in the Chinese anguage, which will also be conducted without the assistance of Compradors.
P. F. RICHARDS.

One of the most influential Western imports was the newspaper, which appeared first in the treaty ports for Westerners' consumption and then spread to the Japanese. The first paper published in Japan was the Nagasaki Shipping List and Advertiser, *a semiweekly published by an English grocer, Albert Hansard, who wanted to introduce Japanese culture to the foreign community. After twenty-eight issues, Hansard moved the paper to Yokohama, where a larger foreign population promised higher profits.*

The basic Japanese coin in the late Tokugawa years was the koban or ryō, which was made of gold and weighed a little more than a third of an ounce. This 1861 manen oban, also gold, was worth ten koban, and weighed three and a half ounces. In 1871, one ryō became one yen, the currency still used in Japan today.

Tumultuous Times

By the early 1860s, foreign pressures and internal dissent were creating troubles for the Tokugawa in every region of the country, as people of all classes clamored for change. Antiforeign activists forced the *bakufu*, or central government, late in 1862 to issue an unenforceable order that all foreigners leave Japan within six months—triggering, in the process, attacks by antiforeign forces on Western ships and heavy retaliation by the foreigners. Radical samurai overthrew the pro-Tokugawa domain administration in Chōshū, and began scheming with subversives in other fiefs to topple the Tokugawa house. More moderate regional leaders maneuvered, though never with much effect, to bring the opposing sides together.

The culmination of the national tumult came on January 3, 1868, when a coup called the Meiji Restoration toppled the 268-year-old Tokugawa government and opened the door to one of the most remarkable periods of change in the history of humankind. The major rebel figures were young, relatively low-ranking samurai from western domains, who acted in name of the fifteen-year-old Emperor Meiji, shown here in military dress, just five years into his reign.

Opposition to the Tokugawa regime was not limited to the official classes. Indeed, one of the more worrisome features of the 1860s was the increase in peasant and commoner protests and uprisings, such as the one depicted in this ink painting by Hosoya Syomo, in which workers in Edo ransack the home of a despised member of the wealthy class. Nearly 3,000 documented rebellions occurred during the Tokugawa period, and a rash of them broke out after the Western incursion began to increase the commoners' economic difficulties. Though most of these uprisings were put down quickly, their spread made it clear that ordinary people would not always be docile in the face of power. There also were seventy urban riots in the 1850s and 1860s. And by 1867, tens of thousands of peasants across the country had begun taking part in wild *ee ja nai ka*, "Why not, it's okay!" movements, dancing wildly in streets and town squares, breaking into the homes of the wealthy, and demanding a new, more just world.

Demise of a Domain Lord

No one symbolized all of this controversy better than Ii Naosuke, a crusty domain lord from Hikone on Lake Biwa north of Kyoto, who had become active in national affairs after Perry's arrival. By 1857, Ii had been named *tairō*, "Great Elder," and was a virtual dictator of Japan, running the shogun's administration and working to smooth relations with the Western nations. He triggered widespread anger in 1858 when he pushed through the commercial treaty with the United States, named an unpopular man as heir to the shogun, and jailed or executed almost 100 of his opponents. In a foreshadowing of the coming decade, eighteen anti-Tokugawa zealots waylaid Ii's palanquin outside Edo castle during an angry snowstorm on the morning of March 3, 1860. They pulled him out of the palanquin, shot him, then cut his head off, plunging the government into crisis.

The woodblock artist Ōso Hōnen captured the chaotic scene when antiforeign, anti-Tokugawa zealots waylaid, then beheaded, Regent Ii Naosuke on March 3, 1860, outside Edo Castle, shaking the government to its core.

Chapter Three

Confronting the Modern World: 1868–89

The ricksha, the train, the trolley, the bicycle: in the late nineteenth century Japan saw its city streets erupt with a variety of transportation methods never seen before. The artist captures the things in urban life that use wheels, including the pulley on an ancient well and a set of "wind wheels," known to Westerners as pinwheels, carried by the mother with a baby on her back, at the bottom left of the drawing.

W hen eight-year-old Inagaki Etsubo arrived home from school one day early in the 1880s, her grandmother and a maid were covering the family altar with sheets of white paper. Puzzled and slightly frightened, she asked if someone were about to die. No, her grandmother replied resignedly; no one was ill. Much worse, the father had commanded that the household begin eating meat that night, and the family gods must be protected from having to see it happen. Eating meat might make children healthy, Grandma said, but it was wrong; it violated Buddhist doctrine.

Before long, Etsubo would learn to enjoy meat, along with a hundred other innovations of the new Meiji era. She would become the wife of a businessman, sail off to America, become a Christian, and rear two daughters who would marry educated, elite fellow Japanese. Born in a stronghold of tradition and reared early in isolation from foreign influences, she would know enough change as an adult to overwhelm someone of less strength. Her life mirrored Japan's rapidly changing Meiji era. And like Japan, she would embrace the changes and adapt, even as she clung almost effortlessly to such traditional values as loyalty, hard work, and filial piety.

A British professor who came to Japan in 1873, a year before Etsubo's birth, wrote at the end of the century that he felt as if he were 400 years old, so rapidly had the changes occurred. Indeed, while most other nations suffered paralysis or decline when challenged by

One of the most important symbols of the new political order ushered in by the Meiji Restoration was the decision to have the Emperor Meiji move from his palace in Kyoto to a new home in Tokyo. Here, he and his entourage enter Tokyo Castle for the first time on November 26, 1868.

the imperialist powers, after the installation of the Meiji government in 1868 Japan transformed itself with a skill that amazed even its critics, moving from feudal isolation to world-power status in half a century.

Two elements lay at the core of Japan's successes: the solid Tokugawa-era institutions—education, national markets, political integration—and the intelligent pragmatism of the young Meiji leaders. Aware that their regime was shaky at home and frightened by the imperialist threat abroad, the new officials discarded their antiforeign views and adopted two slogans: *kuni no tame*, "for the good of the country," and *fukoku kyōhei*, "rich country, strong army." They brought the emperor to Edo, where he could be consulted and controlled, ensconced him in the old Tokugawa castle, and renamed the city Tokyo, "eastern capital." They committed themselves to seeking knowledge from around the world and to leveling the classes. They also addressed the massive debts and regionalism that continuously threatened to undermine the new government. And they set out to bring distant rural regions, where thousands of peasants were in revolt, under central control.

The outcome was that modernity reached the entire country, though not always with positive results. The government structure was reorganized under an emperor who was turned into both a divine oracle and a secular sovereign, though in actuality he remained more a figurehead than a power holder. The samurai class was disbanded; the military draft was made compulsory, as was education (for both boys and girls); a standard currency replaced the complex and disunified old domain-by-domain monetary system; a national land tax was enacted. And politics became the preoccupation of all men who had enough money and leisure to be politically active. All of this culminated in 1889 in Asia's first national constitution, which created an independent judiciary as well as a relatively strong legislature.

Heightening the impact of these changes was the reach of modernization into the private realm. Freed from the bonds of isolation and the Confucian-oriented restrictions of class and status rules, many people in every sphere pursued new practices and modern ideas, while others launched rear-guard actions in defense of old values and ways. Following the modernizer Fukuzawa Yukichi's dictum that "the independence of a nation springs from the independent spirit of its citizens," thinkers demanded freedom and democracy, journalists criticized the government, businessmen pursued long-despised profits, and novelists, known for stopping "at nothing to squeeze in a moral," devised complex plots and realistic characters. Even villagers in deep mountain valleys took to discussing the new order. One popular ditty warned: "Don't despise the lodger; tomorrow he may be the Minister's secretary." By the 1870s concepts such as progress and modernity had become the goals of most leading citizens.

Envisioning a New World

The tone of the new regime was set by officials such as Kido Kōin and Iwakura Tomomi, who issued an "imperial oath of five articles" on April 6, 1868, outlining the Meiji government's central goals. The document, which is known by Western historians as the Charter Oath, was not considered particularly important at the time. Indeed, few of the top officials showed up for the ceremony in which it was presented, and Kido said he had forgotten all about the docu-

Emperor Meiji (in a white robe, on the right) listens to his minister Sanjō Sanetomi (in a black robe, center) read the Charter Oath, which outlined the central goals of the Meiji government, on April 6, 1868. The emperor sat inside an enclosure, in keeping with the tradition that set him apart from—and above—his subjects.

At a bound Japan leapt out of the darkness of the Middle Ages into the fiercest light of the nineteenth century. . . . Perhaps no revolution of equal magnitude has ever been carried into effect with less shedding of blood, or accepted in the end with less bitterness of spirit.

— Memoir of Algernon Bertram Mitford, British diplomat in Japan, 1866–70

ment when a friend asked him about it four years later. But it set out the philosophical principles that were to guide the Meiji government for decades to come, and by the 1900s it was seen as one of the era's foundational documents.

By this oath we set up as our aim the broad-based establishment of national well-being and the framing of a constitution and laws.

1. Assemblies shall be widely convoked, and all measures shall be decided by open discussion.

2. High and low shall be of one mind, and the national economy and finances shall be greatly strengthened.

3. Civil and military officials together, and the common people as well, shall all achieve their aspirations, and thus the people's minds shall not be made weary.

4. Evil practices of the past shall be abandoned, and actions shall be based on international usage.

5. Knowledge shall be sought all over the world, and the foundations of Imperial rule shall be strengthened.

If the new rulers' first goal was to make Japan strong, their second aim was to win the world's respect. A set of "Imperial Precepts," distributed by the government in 1869, illustrates how far officials had come from the earlier determination to "expel the barbarians." It also shows their resolve to make people everywhere see the superiority of the Japanese spirit. In a foretaste of the approach the officials would take through much of the Meiji era, they used traditional rhetoric in the document to justify radical innovations.

Now, the spirit of the present differs from the spirit of the past. The countries of the world have joined themselves in a relationship of peace and friendship. Steamers are sent round the world heedless of stormy waves or of foul winds. The communication between lands distant ten thousand miles from one another is as that between neighbors. Country competes with country in producing rifles and guns and machinery, and each revolves plans for its own advantage and profit. Each vies with the other in devising schemes to obtain the mastery; each exerts itself to keep up the strength of its armies; each and every one strives to invent warlike contrivances. But in spite of all this there is a great principle existing all over the world, which prevents civilized countries from being lightly and lawlessly attacked. This principle is called International Law.

How much the more, then, would our divine country, the institutions of which excel those of all other countries, be turning her back upon the sacred precepts established by the heavenly ancestors of the Emperor, should she be guilty of violent and lawless acts! Such a thing would be the greatest shame and disgrace to the country of the gods. Hence it is that the Emperor has extended a faithful alliance to those foreigners who come here lawfully and rightly, and they are allowed free and uninterrupted access to this country. Following this example set by the Emperor, his subjects, when they receive no insult from the foreigner, should . . . refrain from blows and fighting. If by any chance we should be put to shame before the foreigner, it is hard to say what consequences may ensue.

No episode better illustrated the Meiji officials' determination to follow "civilized" rules than the Iwakura Mission of 1871–73. Convinced that they must understand the institutions of the imperialist powers more fully in order to compete effectively, the government sent an expedition of fifty of its most competent leaders to the United States and

The famed Civil War photographer Matthew Brady took this 1872 photograph of Prince Iwakura Tomomi, leader of the mission to the United States and Europe and nominal head of the Japanese government. His progressive nature is apparent in the fact that he is wearing a Western suit, sports a modern haircut and watch chain, and holds a cane rather than a sword.

I cannot express my feelings, but I could not help recalling what my mother said to me just before I started for America: "I have heard, my daughter, that it is the custom of foreign people to lick each other as dogs do."

—Sugimoto Inagaki Etsu in her memoir *A Daughter of the Samurai* (1926), on seeing Americans kiss for the first time, in the 1880s

Europe. Headed by chief of state Iwakura Tomomi, along with such powerful men as finance minister Ōkubo Toshimichi and junior councilor Kido, the men spent eighteen months abroad. They studied constitutions and military institutions, visited schools, negotiated (unsuccessfully) for fairer treaties, examined factories and industrial systems, and explained to their Western counterparts how far Japan had come along the road to modernity. The fact that the very highest officials would give a full year and a half to such a mission illustrated both how stable the government had become in less than four years and how important they thought it was to acquire firsthand knowledge of the West. In an 1871 letter to Ulysses S. Grant, President of the United States, the emperor explains the Embassy's mission.

Mr. President: . . . We have thought fit to select our trusted and honored minister, Iwakura Tomomi, the Junior Prime Minister (*udaijin*), as Ambassador Extraordinary, . . . and invested [him] with full powers to proceed to the Government of the United States, as well as to other Governments, in order to declare our cordial friendship, and to place the peaceful relations between our respective nations on a firmer and broader basis. The period for revising the treaties now existing between ourselves and the United States is less than one year distant. We expect and intend to reform and improve the same so as to stand upon a similar footing with the most enlightened nations, and to attain the full development of public rights and interest. The civilization and institutions of Japan are so different from those of other countries that we cannot expect to reach the declared end at once. It is our purpose to select from the various institutions prevailing among enlightened nations such as are best suited to our present conditions, and adapt them in gradual reforms and improvements of our policy and customs so as to be upon an equality with them. With this object we desire to fully disclose to the United States Government the condition of affairs in our Empire, and to consult upon the means of giving greater efficiency to our institutions at present and in the future, and as soon as the said Embassy returns home we will consider the revision of the treaties and accomplish what we have expected and intended. The Ministers who compose this Embassy have our confidence and esteem. We request you to favor them with full credence and due regard, and we earnestly pray for your continued health and happiness, and for the peace and prosperity of your great Republic.

The mindset of early Meiji officials showed up in the detailed observations members of the Iwakura Mission made about American and European life during their travels. They were far more sophisticated than their predecessors, who on an 1862 diplomatic mission had packed a thousand pairs of straw sandals, expecting to walk their way through Europe. But Western practices were so far removed from their own customs and experiences that they often shook their heads in wonderment. Ideas and practices like Christianity, male-female relationships, democratic government, and the apparent lack of respect for family members and rulers left mission members befuddled. They recorded both their observations and how they felt about what they saw in voluminous diaries that show both keen powers of observation and refreshing candor. In the minds of the Japanese, the Western lands had much to teach, but they also had much to be avoided, as the journal, published in 1877, of Iwakura's private secretary Kume Kunitake illustrates.

From the time our group boarded ship at Yokohama, [we found ourselves] in a realm of completely alien customs. What is appropriate deportment for us seems to attract their curiosity, and what is proper behavior for them is strange to us. . . . What we found most strange in their behavior was the relations between men and women.

With respect to relations between husbands and wives, it is the practice in Japan that the wife serves her husband's parents and that children serve their parents, but in America the husband follows the "Way of Serving His Wife." The [American husband] lights the lamps, prepares food at the table, presents shoes to his wife, brushes the dust off [her] clothes, helps her up and down the stairs, offers her his chair, and carries her things when she goes out. If the wife becomes a little angry, the husband is quick to offer affection and show respect, bowing and scraping to beg her forgiveness. But if she does not accept his apologies, he may find himself turned out of the house and denied meals.

When riding in the same ship or carriage, men stand up and offer their seats to the women, who accept with no hesitation at all. When women take their places sitting down, the men all crowd around them to show their respect. Men are restrained in their behavior when together [with women] at the same gathering. . . . It is only when the women retire that the men begin to become lax in their behavior. . . .

Wealth is the sole object of ambition of the people at large. I . . . observe a strange inconsistency of the Americans. Though they thus neglect their moral training at home, they send missionaries to teach the wretched heathen to be good, and at the same time send a company of practical men who show their practicability by extracting the riches in every way, and when they could, by cheating those men whom their fellow-countrymen undertake to teach—to be what?—to be good!

—E. R. Enouye, Japanese student in America, 1872, reflecting on the Iwakura mission, in Charles Lanman's The Japanese in America

To explain the conditions of the people in the countries of the West, one must by all means understand their religion. . . .

People in the West vie with one another in the pursuit of civilization, but we find only absurd tales if we peruse the Old and New Testaments they respect so much. It would not be wrong to regard [tales about] voices from Heaven and criminals raised from the dead as similar to the delirious ravings of madness. . . . They hold that someone crucified was the son of the Heavenly Lord and they kneel, reverently wailing in lamentation. Where do these tears come from? we wonder to ourselves. In all European and American cities, pictures of crucified criminals, profuse with ruby-red blood, are hung everywhere on building walls and rooms, making one feel as though one is living in a cemetery or staying in an execution ground. If this is not bizarre, then what is? . . .

In the teachings of Christ, there is much that is bizarre. . . . However, when it comes to earnestness of practice, we must blush with shame. Everyone from kings and princes to servants and small children understands what is said in this one book, the Bible. High and low alike carry it to the temple on the weekly day, returning home after hearing sermons and carrying out their worship. Parents teach their children to worship at the temple and study the scriptures, masters preach the same to their servants, and innkeepers urge it on travelers as well. From the moment they leave the womb as infants, they absorb [Christianity] into their blood along with their mother's milk, and they are enveloped in its teachings until they depart from this world. They contribute money for the translation of the scriptures so that it will be easy to read. . . . Wherever there is a village, there is a temple, and wherever people gather, there is a congregation. Even though the level of discourse is not elevated, they are fervent. . . . What we should respect in a religion is not its argument but its practice.

Not all Japanese were as progressive, or as eager to adopt Western ways, as the Meiji leaders. For the first decade of the new era, many people challenged the new regime. They criticized the departure from time-honored customs, called for a restoration of samurai dominance, and often made life uncomfortable for foreigners. A number of peasant rebellions kept things unsettled in the countryside, while malcontents stirred up trouble in the cities. In 1873 Saigō Takamori, probably the most popular of the new leaders, stormed out of the government over its unwillingness to force Korea to open trade with Japan. And in 1877, some 40,000 former

In the most dramatic campaign of the 1877 rebellion by Satsuma troops against the Meiji government, rebels besieged the government's old castle in the southern city of Kumamoto, shelling the fortress from a nearby hillside. The government forces finally put down the rebellion in October, after more than eight months of fighting.

samurai in Saigō's home domain of Satsuma carried out a devastating, though unsuccessful, rebellion in which more than 6,000 government troops lost their lives. Although the majority of Japanese supported the new Meiji policies, or at least kept their reservations about the policies to themselves, the nostalgic minority continued to challenge the new regime and for years kept the Meiji officials worried.

A dramatic example of this nostalgia for the old system came in the first year of Meiji, when the French demanded that the Japanese execute twenty commoner-soldiers from Tosa domain who had killed several Frenchmen during a military confrontation at the town of Sakai. The soldiers asked that they be given samurai status and be allowed to commit *seppuku*, ritual suicide, so that their deaths would be honorable, and the officials agreed. An execution date was set, with both French and Japanese officials scheduled to attend. On the scheduled date, however, things did not go as planned. The Meiji novelist Mori Ōgai retold the event in "Incident at Sakai" (1914), a story that follows the basic facts carefully. When the soldiers began taking their own lives, the French consul became increasingly queasy. In the end, the French diplomat left and the sentence was reversed for the nine men who had not already committed suicide.

hakama, haori

Hakama are the kimono-like robes with pleated skirts that Japanese men wear on formal occasions; the *haori* is a short coat worn over the *hakama*.

Alas, your face looks serene. For your sake I have not been at ease for half a year. Now I am at peace; but you were one of the greatest heroes of our land. . . . It is a pity that this should be your fate.

—Yamagata Aritomo, commander of government forces, when the head of rebel leader Saigō Takamori was brought to him at the end of the Satsuma Rebellion, 1877, quoted in Tokutomi Sohō, *Kōshaku Yamagata Aritomo den* (Biography of Prince Yamagata Aritomo), II (1933), 753

The official finally called out the first name: "Shinoura Inokichi." The areas inside and outside the temple became hushed. Shinoura walked to the place of *seppuku* wearing a white *hakama* and a black felt *haori*. . . . After bowing to Prince Yamashina and the other officials, Shinoura took a short sword in his right hand from a box of unpainted wood held by another official. Then he cried out in a voice like thunder:

"Frenchmen! I am not dying for your sake. I am dying for my Imperial nation. Observe the *seppuku* of a Japanese soldier."

Shinoura relaxed his garment, pointed the sword downward, made a deep thrust into the right side of his stomach and upwards three inches on the left. Because of the depth of the initial thrust, the wound gaped widely. Releasing his sword, Shinoura then placed both hands within the cut and, pulling out his own guts, glared at the French consul. . . .

The French consul, his eyes riveted on Shinoura from the start, was increasingly overcome by a mixture of shock and fear. Unable to stay in his seat after hearing Shinoura's overwhelming cry during what was for him a totally new experience, he finally stood up, looking as if he were going to faint. . . .

Nishimura, . . . Sugimoto, Katsugase, Yamamoto, Morimoto, Kitashiro, Inada, and Yanase committed *seppuku* in sequence. Yanase drew his sword across from left to right, then back again from right to left, and so his entrails came gushing out of the opening.

The twelfth man to commit *seppuku* was Hashizume. As he appeared and advanced toward the mat, it was already growing dark and lanterns were lit in the main hall.

To this point, the French consul had been continually standing up and sitting down again, and seemed to be almost beside himself. His nervousness spread increasingly to the French soldiers who provided his escort. Their military stance completely collapsed; they began to move their hands and whisper among each other. Just as Hashizume reached the *seppuku* mat, the consul gave some kind of order, and the whole contingent left their places and surrounded the consul who, without making any apology or explanation to Prince Yamashina or to the other dignitaries, hurriedly left the tent. Taking the shortest line across the temple garden, the soldiers who enveloped the consul broke into a run for the harbor as soon as they were outside the temple gate.

At the place of *seppuku* Hashizume had already loosened his garments and was about to thrust in his sword. At that instant an official came running in and broke Hashizume's concentration with a cry of "Wait!" The official informed him of the French consul's departure and declared that the *seppuku* ceremony was being temporarily delayed. Hashizume returned to the other eight men and communicated this information to them.

Creating a New System

The early Meiji government developed new laws and structures with a speed that made some journalists question their wisdom. As a *New York Times* correspondent wrote on April 5, 1872: "The question is not unfrequently asked . . . , is not Japan going ahead too fast? In some respects we fear she is." Taking a lesson from the troubles that apathy had created for their Tokugawa forebears, the officials were determined that Japan should become as modern as possible, as quickly as possible. They replaced the old feudal domains with modern prefectures, or states, and devised a series of central governing bodies; they reorganized national finances, created model industries to encourage commerce, and began reworking the law codes; they nurtured the spread of information by subsidizing newspapers, and hired thousands of foreigners to provide technological and administrative expertise. In any year during the 1870s, one could find some 800 engineers, language teachers, political advisers, surveyors, and writers from Great Britain, Germany, the Netherlands, the United States, and elsewhere—all of them hired by the Meiji government, often at stunningly high salaries.

The three fields that consumed the officials' greatest energy were finances, education, and the military. The government devised a standard land tax, which put the burden of paying for the massive changes primarily on the farmers. They created the world's first system of compulsory education for all the nation's children in 1872. And they instituted a draft under which all young men, commoner and samurai alike, were required to give three years of military service to the nation.

The announcement of the draft, issued November 28, 1872, explains the rationale for compulsory conscription by drawing on both Japan's past and the new demands of the modern age. It reflected the views of Yamagata Aritomo, who would guide Japanese military policy into the next century.

Sakai Denpatsu, an early governor of Kyoto, had his photograph taken in traditional garb in 1876, shortly before complying with a government decree to stop wearing swords in public and to have his hair cut. The government order symbolized the end of the samurai class.

In this print of a hot air balloon test at the Navy Department in Tokyo in 1877, the prominent woodblock artist Utagawa Hiroshige III caught the frenzied, innovative approach of modernizing Meiji-era officials. While the military envisioned balloons for transporting goods, late-nineteenth-century city dwellers turned out by the thousands to watch performers do stunts and acrobatics with balloons. Balloon candy and balloon prints became popular in the 1890s.

In the system in effect in our country in the ancient past everyone was a soldier. In an emergency the emperor became the Marshal, mobilizing the able-bodied youth for military service and thereby suppressing rebellion. When the campaign was over the men returned to their homes and their occupations, whether that of farmer, artisan, or merchant. They differed from the soldiers of a later period who carried two swords and called themselves warriors, living presumptuously without working, and in extreme instances cutting down people in cold blood while officials turned their faces. . . .

Feudal conditions spread throughout the country, and there appeared among the people a distinction between the farmer and the soldier. Still later, the distinction between the ruler and the ruled collapsed, giving rise to indescribable evils. Then came the great Restoration of the government. All feudatories returned their fiefs to the Throne, and in 1871 the old prefectural system was restored. On the one hand, warriors who lived without labor for generations have had their stipends reduced and have been stripped of their swords; on the other hand, the four classes of the people are about to receive their right to freedom. This is the way to restore the balance between the high and the low and to grant equal rights to all. It is, in short, the basis of uniting the farmer and the soldier into one. Thus, the soldier is not the soldier of former days. The people are not the people of former days. They are now equally the people of the empire, and there is no distinction between them in their obligations to the State. . . .

Everyone should endeavor to repay one's country. The Occidentals call military obligation "blood tax," for it is one's repayment in life-blood to one's country. When the State suffers disaster, the people cannot escape being affected. Thus, the people can ward off disaster to themselves by striving to ward off disaster to the State. And where there is a state, there is military defense; and if there is military defense there must be military service.

Occidentals

Yamagata refers to Westerners as Occidentals, "residents of the West," in contrast to Orientals, "residents of the East."

One of the daring decisions of the early Meiji years came when the government announced in 1872 that both boys and girls would be required to attend school for at least three years. Although decades would pass before many localities could afford to send all of their children to school, the decree resulted for a time in a great increase in education for girls. The first government-sponsored girls' school, named Takebashi, opened in Tokyo in 1872 with about forty girls. A classroom essay by Takebashi student Aoki Koto reveals a less-than-perfect grasp of English. But it also reflects her enthusiasm about learning the ways and words of the new world. Her English eventually would become impeccable, and she would become a teacher, translator, and interpreter for the government.

Although Japanese students spent most of their time in the classroom, at their desks, they also found time for pleasure. Accompanied by teachers, these Tokyo schoolgirls take part in one of Japan's most beloved annual events: heading for a city park to view the spring cherry blossoms.

Aoki Koto, June 20, 1874. I was born at Owari which is my province. . . . The customs of this country are very good temper, because the people are honest and gentle and the women never go out without their girdle, but the women of Tokio [Tokyo] are very bad for sometimes I see them who has no girdle or dress on the summer. . . . My parents loved me very much, but my mother died when I was three years old; consequently I do not know what face she had, and my father told me that she had a great trouble for me and she thought that I was a cripple, because I could not stand nor walk before she died. . . . When I arrived to Tokio, I thought the cities of here are much dirtier, more than my province's and I was very glad that I met my father and he told me "you must begin to learn and study . . . ," and I answered him "Yes, I want to do so and I wish to learn English language; therefore let me learn it please, if you find some good teacher;" yet we could not find her and I was waiting, waiting all days. One day my father's friend came to my house and he told me that the ladies' school will open to let the ladies and girls to learn; then I was very joy.

Japan's political life became volatile after 1874, when Itagaki Taisuke, an official who had left the government in protest with Saigō Takamori the year before, sent the emperor a petition that called for the creation of a national legislative assembly. Although Itagaki desired a fairly limited electorate, the very fact that he wanted a legislature was precedent-shattering. His petition sparked the Japanese press's first major political debate, with editorialists arguing over how soon Japan should have representative government and what kind of legislature it needed.

When we humbly reflect upon the quarter in which the governing power lies, we find that it lies not with the Crown (the Imperial House) on the one hand, nor the people on the other, but with the officials alone. We do not deny that the officials respect the Crown, and yet the Crown is gradually losing its prestige, nor do we deny that they protect the people, and yet the manifold decrees of the government appear in the morning and are changed in the evening, the administration is conducted in an arbitrary manner, rewards and punishments are prompted by partiality, the channel by which the people should communicate with the government is blocked up and they cannot state their grievances. . . . We fear, therefore, that if a reform is not effected the state will be ruined. Unable to resist the promptings of our patriotic feelings,

Ah, democracy, democracy! Absolute monarchy is stupid. It is unaware of its faults. Constitutionalism is aware of its faults but has corrected only half of them. Democracy, though, is open and frank, without a speck of impurity in its heart. . . .

All enterprises of human society are like alcohol, and liberty is the yeast. If you try to brew wine or beer without yeast, all the other ingredients, no matter how good they are, will sink to the bottom of the barrel, and your efforts will be in vain. Life in a despotic country is like a brew without ferment: sediments at the bottom of a barrel. Consider, for example, the literature of a despotic country. Occasionally some work appears to be noteworthy, but closer scrutiny reveals that nothing new is produced in a thousand years, nothing unique among ten thousand works. The kinds of phenomenon that would ordinarily appeal to an author's sight and hearing are, in these societies, merely sediments at the bottom of a barrel, and the author copies these phenomena with a spirit which is also a sediment. Isn't it only natural then, that there should be no change in the arts? . . .

—Political theorist Nakai Chōmin, *Discourse by Three Drunkards*, 1887

we have sought to devise a means of rescuing it from this danger, and we find it to consist in developing public discussion in the empire. The means of developing public discussion is the establishment of a council-chamber chosen by the people. Then a limit will be placed on the power of the officials, and both governors and governed will obtain peace and prosperity. We ask leave then to make some remarks on this subject.

The people whose duty it is to pay taxes to the government possess the right of sharing in their government's affairs and of approving or condemning. This being a principle universally acknowledged it is not necessary to waste words in discussing it. . . .

By establishing such a council-chamber, public discussion in the empire may be established, the spirit of the empire be roused to activity, the affection between governors and governed be made greater, sovereign and subject be brought to love each other, our imperial country be maintained and its destinies be developed, and prosperity and peace be assured to all. We shall esteem ourselves fortunate if you will adopt our suggestions.

A movement for "freedom and popular rights" also sprang to life in the wake of the Itagaki petition, and for a decade people across the country discussed governmental policies through debating societies, speeches, political parties, and newspaper editorials. Even farmers in remote regions gathered in village squares to discuss politics under the moonlight, sometimes producing their own thoughtful essays on the kind of constitution Japan should have. A schoolteacher, Chiba Takasaburō, wrote an essay in 1882 in Istukaichi, a mountain village west of Tokyo. It draws on a traditional Confucian concept of the "Way of the King" in which virtuous rulers set an example for their subjects of compassionate, just rule. Chiba demanded both a constitution and a legislature; he also wrote a draft of a constitution.

All governments, whether they be dictatorships, aristocracies, or republics, must be in accordance with the Way of the King if they are faithful to the nation. It is the very foundation of a government's or monarch's qualification to rule. . . .

Those who manifest the following signs believe in the Way of the King. They want to establish constitutional government—and that constitution is a national contract. They want to open a parliament. They want to maintain the esteem for the crown and secure the welfare of all the people. They want to see the hopes

A clear indication of the growth of popular rights ideas in the 1870s was the convening of public assemblies in areas far from Tokyo. These proceedings of an assembly in the southern nineteenth district of Nagano Prefecture in February 1878 record the daily work of assemblymen elected from a small pool of high-ranking officials.

of all the classes for constitutional government realized, and they observe the spirit [of the Charter Oath]—"unite in carrying out vigorously the administration of affairs of state." Finally, they will be untiring in the performance of government. You men in our country who are loyal subjects of His Majesty and truly cherish the people as brothers should accept this theory and accomplish in your own lives the Way of the King. . . .

Without exception those who bring about the decline of the Way of the King disdain the people and destroy the people's liberties. Such instances are not confined to China and Japan, but have occurred in a number of European countries as well. The reason is that when the monarch destroys the people's liberties, he first abandons and disregards the imperial prerogatives. He exercises unlimited sovereignty, ignoring virtue and proper rule. He makes the nation his household and the people his slaves. Consequently, when the people rise up against oppression, they do not care for virtue and rule, and it often happens that they start a rebellion and scheme a violent and odious disturbance to overthrow the government. . . .

Those who do not know what constitutional government, a constitution, or a parliament really mean, should read this essay carefully and then they will be able to speak of the Way of the

King and understand the times we live in. I hope that this essay will serve as a ship to carry them to the shores of understanding.

Most officials worried about the rise in popular activism. Their goal was to make Japan strong, not democratic. In the 1880s, they issued several regulations that limited the groups of people who could take part in politics. The harsh Peace Preservation Regulation of December 25, 1887, outlawed secret assemblies, allowed the Cabinet to prohibit public meetings in regions "imperiled by popular excitement," and forbade political enemies from even residing near the capital. Immediately after this order, more than 500 men were banished from Tokyo.

Any person residing or sojourning within a distance of three *ri* [7-1/2 miles] radius around the Imperial Palace or around the Imperial place of resort, who plots or incites disturbance, or who is judged to be scheming something detrimental to public tranquillity, may be ordered by the police, or local authorities, with the sanction of the Minister of State for Home Affairs, to leave the said district within a fixed number of days or hours. And anyone who, being thus ordered to depart, fails to comply within the appointed time, or who, after departure, is again guilty of any of the aforesaid offences, shall be liable to a penalty of from one to three years' minor confinement, and further, to police surveillance for a period not exceeding five years, such surveillance to be exercised within the district of the offender's original registration.

The Meiji officials who devised the harsh measures to stamp out dissent were also determined that Japan should have a "modern" government based on laws. They spent much of the 1880s preparing Japan's first constitution. They visited Europe to study constitutional systems, invited German scholars to Japan to help in the drafting of their fundamental law, set up a modern cabinet system, and created a body of peers with noble titles to lay the foundation for a two-house legislature. The result was the promulgation of the first national constitution in the Asian hemisphere on February 11, 1889. This event gave Japan a constitutional monarchy, and the country celebrated, with fireworks, banquets, and proud celebrations in communities across the nation. The Meiji Constitution places sovereignty in the emperor and gives the bulk of power to the cabinet members

Reports in the newspaper *Jiji Shinpō* (1887) illustrate the confusion caused by the deportation of opposition leaders under the Peace Preservation Law:

December 29. At one point, sixty-six deportees from the Kōchi region all were staying at the Matsui Inn on 5 Honchō Street. With a ratio of one policeman per deportee, the inn was virtually surrounded by police.

December 30. With the recent increase in criminals, the Metropolitan Police Department has experienced a shortage of horse-drawn wagons for transporting criminals; new wagons are being built to meet the growing demand.

December 30. The sudden increase in the construction of telephone lines has accompanied the . . . issuance of the Peace Preservation Law. Technicians have been working night and day to set up lines between the homes of the Police Superintendent, the Minister of Internal Affairs, and the Minister of Agriculture and Commerce, among others.

In the 1880s, the following ancient poem was set to music. Since then it has been used as an unofficial national anthem and sung at most state ceremonies and sports events. It never has been officially adopted.

Thousands of years of happy reign be thine;
Rule on, my lord, till what are pebbles now
By age united to mighty rocks shall grow
Whose venerable sides the moss doth line.

14th year

Years were (and still are) numbered from the date of the ascension of the reigning emperor, though the Western system was also used fairly widely. Meiji 14 was 1881.

Diet

The *kokka*, or Japanese national legislature, is typically translated "Diet" in English, because the constitutional system was based on German legal concepts. Meiji 23 was 1890.

who surround him. Yet it also provides for an elected assembly and an independent judiciary. At the time, it was regarded as conservative but fully in line with Europe's national constitutions.

Having by virtue of the glories of Our Ancestors, ascended the throne of a lineal succession unbroken for ages eternal; desiring to promote the welfare of, and to give development to the moral and intellectual faculties of Our beloved subjects, the very same that have been favoured with the benevolent care and affectionate vigilance of Our Ancestors; and hoping to maintain the prosperity of the State, in concert with Our people and with their support, We hereby promulgate, in pursuance of Our Imperial Rescript of the 12th day of the 10th month of the 14th year of Meiji, a fundamental law of State, to exhibit the principles, by which We are to be guided in Our conduct, and to point out to what Our descendants and Our subjects and their descendants are forever to conform.

The rights of sovereignty of the State, We have inherited from Our Ancestors, and We shall bequeath them to Our descendants. Neither We nor they shall in future fail to wield them in accordance with the provisions of the Constitution hereby granted.

We now declare to respect and protect the security of the rights and of the property of Our people, and to secure to them the complete enjoyment of the same within the extent of the provisions of the present Constitution and of the law.

The Imperial Diet shall first be convoked for the 23rd year of Meiji, and the time of its opening shall be the date when the present Constitution comes into force.

When in the future it may become necessary to amend any of the provisions of the present Constitution, We or Our successors shall assume the initiative right, and submit a project for the same to the Imperial Diet. The Imperial Diet shall pass its vote upon it, according to the conditions imposed by the present Constitution. . . .

Our Ministers of State, on Our behalf, shall be held responsible for the carrying out of the present Constitution, and Our present and future subjects shall forever assume the duty of allegiance to the present Constitution.

A New Society

In Japan in the 1870s and 1880s, change was as unpredictable, as ferocious, and as all-consuming as the coming of

typhoons. Westerners who had left for a year or two invariably pronounced Japan changed beyond recognition when
they returned. They saw cities filled with new skyscrapers,
fresh translations of Shakespeare, new crops under cultiva-
tion, unprecedented debates about the ideas of philosophers Herbert Spencer, John Stuart Mill, and Jean-Jacques
Rousseau. The 1926 memoir of a young samurai girl from
Echigo in northeastern Japan, *Daughter of the Samurai*,
details the full story of what happened when her father
declared in the 1880s that the family's diet would be modernized. It also shows just how pervasive change had become.

How well I remember one day when I came home from school
and found the entire household wrapped in gloom. I felt a sense
of depression as soon as I stepped into the "shoe-off" entrance, and
heard my mother, in low, solemn tones, giving directions to a
maid. . . .

"Honorable Grandmother, I have returned," I murmured, as I
sank to the floor with my usual salutation. She returned my bow
with a gentle smile, but she was graver than usual. She and a maid
were sitting before the black-and-gold cabinet of the family shrine.
They had a large lacquer tray with rolls of white paper on it and
the maid was pasting paper over the gilded doors of the shrine. . . .

I remember that my voice trembled a little as I asked,
"Honourable Grandmother, is—is anybody going to die?"

I can see now how she looked—half
amused and half shocked.

"Little Etsu-ko," she said, "you talk too
freely, like a boy. A girl should never
speak with abrupt unceremony." . . .

Presently she straightened up and
turned toward me.

"Your honourable father has ordered
his household to eat flesh," she said very
slowly. "The wise physician who follows
the path of the Western barbarians has
told him that the flesh of animals will
bring strength to his weak body, and also
will make the children robust and clever
like the people of the Western sea. The
ox flesh is to be brought into the house in
another hour and our duty is to protect
the holy shrine from pollution."

Notifications have been posted in the
native town during the week, warning all
who still persist in shaving their heads, that
they will be severely punished if they do not
discontinue the practice after this date. . . . It
is estimated that about 300 non-conformists to
the new regulations are now living in the
native town, setting authorities at defiance
with their shaven crowns.

Girls are also forbidden to sing or play on
the Samseng and other musical instruments,
when riding in the Jinrickishas.

—*Nagasaki Express*, February 15, 1873

*Scenes of modern city life provided
material for hundreds of popular picture
postcards in the Meiji era. In this one,
urbanites try their hands—and ears—
at the newfangled phonograph, which
arrived in Japan in 1888. The presence
of women along with men shows the
increasing involvement of women in life
outside the home.*

There she learned that hearts are the same on both sides of the world; but this is a secret that is hidden from the people of the East, and hidden from the people of the West. . . . The red barbarians and the children of the gods have not yet learned each other's hearts; to them the secret is still unknown, but the ships are sailing—sailing—

—Sugimoto Etsu, *A Daughter of the Samurai* (1926), describing what her American experience taught her

Inoue

Inoue Kaoru, then minister of finance, was a fiscal conservative, like Shibusawa, who fought, often unsuccessfully, against big government deficits.

That evening we ate a solemn dinner with meat in our soup; but no friendly spirits were with us, for both shrines were sealed. Grandmother did not join us. . . . That night I asked her why she had not come.

"I would rather not grow as strong as a Westerner—nor as clever," she answered sadly. "It is more becoming for me to follow the path of our ancestors."

No sector of society was transformed more dramatically than business. Tokugawa mores had ranked merchants as the lowest class, but the Meiji era encouraged them to develop their own—and their nation's—wealth. The era's most famous entrepreneur, Shibusawa Eiichi, explained in an 1894 autobiography why he left a prestigious post in a disorganized government bureau, where he saw little chance of advancement, to make money in the private sphere.

Thoroughly discouraged, I went to see Inoue at his home in Kaiunbashi (he was then living in a house owned by Mitsui) and told him I had decided to quit. . . . "If we continue to function in this fashion, I doubt we'll ever be able to put finances in order. I've mentioned this before, but I would rather be in the business world, where I have better hopes for the future. Today, people with any education, ambition, brains, or skills all enter government service and no one goes into private business. That imbalance will prevent us from building a strong country. Anyway, I'll be handing in my resignation soon, and since I consider you my friend, I wanted you to know first.

Not long before his death in 1931, Shibusawa dictated another autobiography to a friend, reiterating his conviction that Japan needed talented men with management skills and a commitment to ethical behavior to create private companies.

The business world around 1873, when I resigned from my post in the Ministry of Finance, was filled with inertia. . . . There was a tradition of respecting officials and despising commoners. All talented men looked to government service as the ultimate goal in their lives, and ordinary students followed their examples. Practically no one was interested in business. When people met, they discussed only the affairs of the nation and world. There was no such thing as practical business education. . . .

三菱造船株式會社　長崎造船所

Among the Meiji period's most successful businessmen was Iwasaki Yatarō, who founded the Mitsubishi Commercial Company in 1873, with a gift from the government of eleven ships at its core. The hub of the company's success, shown on this postcard, was its Nagasaki shipyards, the largest shipping facility in Japan and a center of both trading and military empires until the end of World War II.

In organizing a company, the most important factor one ought to consider is to obtain the right person to oversee its operation. In the early Meiji years, the government also encouraged the incorporation of companies and organized exchange companies and development companies. . . . However, most of these companies failed because their management was poor. To state it simply, the government failed to have the right men as managers. I had no experience in commerce and industry, but I also prided myself on the fact that I had greater potential for success in these fields than most of the non-governmental people at that time.

I also felt it necessary to raise the social standing of those engaged in commerce and industry, and to set an example, I began studying and practicing the teachings of the *Analects of Confucius*. . . . It supplies the ultimate in practical ethics for all of us to follow in our daily living.

Not all Meiji changes improved people's lives. Young girls were forced to work by the thousands in the growing silk and cotton factories. They had to endure confinement, long hours, poor wages, inadequate food, and sexual harassment—all in the name of "serving the nation." The great majority of farmers found life as difficult as it had been centuries earlier. The novel *Tsuchi* (The Soil), by the Meiji-era

Analects of Confucius

The *Analects*, one of Confucius's most famous works, contained hundreds of axioms on how to live and how to govern.

1. Factory work is prison work,
All it lacks are iron chains.
More than a caged bird, more than a prison,
Dormitory life is hateful. . . .
How I wish the dormitory would be washed
   away,
The factory burn down,
And the gatekeeper die of cholera!

2. In this troubled world
I am just a silk-reeling lass,
But this lass wants to see
The parents who gave her birth.
Their letter says they are waiting for the
   year's end.
Are they waiting more for the money than
   for me?

—Songs by girls working in the silk and
cotton factories, quoted in Patricia Tsurumi,
*Factory Girls: Women in the Thread Mills of
Meiji Japan*

*Farmers, wearing broad straw hats and
head kerchiefs to protect themselves from
the heat, pick mulberry leaves to be fed
to silkworms. Their backbreaking labor
produced the raw materials for the silk
factories in which hundreds of thousands of Meiji girls worked to bring
trade and cash to Japan.*

**schoolteacher Nagatsuka Takashi describes the conditions
under which a farmer named Kanji, and millions like him,
had to live.**

Kanji's fields yielded a pitifully small harvest that fall. It was not
that the weather had been bad or that the soil itself was poor. He
had got his crops in late and had not applied much fertilizer. No
matter how much energy he expended the results were bound to
be disappointing. It was the same for all poor farmers. They spent
long hours in their fields doing all they could to raise enough food.
Then after the harvest they had to part with most of what they had
produced. Their crops were theirs only for as long as they stood
rooted in the soil. Once the farmers had paid the rents they owed
they were lucky to have enough left over to sustain them through
the winter. During the growing season itself they had to abandon
their own fields to do day labor for others to earn money for that
day's food. . . . Nor could they do much about fertilizer. It was no
longer possible to obtain free compost from the forests as they
had always done in the past. Now the forests were privately
owned, and one had to pay to collect leaves or cut green grass. . . .

   At the end of the harvest season poor farmers withered up like
the vegetation around them. There was little for them to do during the fifty or sixty days until the next growing season began but
hoe the furrows in their barley fields and hunt for fallen leaves and
firewood in the forests. Virtually no paying work was to be had at
this time of year. While the frogs and insects hibernated peace-
fully, farmers had to consume their meager
stores of grain just to keep themselves alive from
day to day. Inevitably a time would come when
they had nothing left to eat. . . .

   Kanji worked every day, except when it
rained. One day he got the blade of his mattock
stuck solidly in a tree stump. When he tried to
wrench it free he suddenly found the handle
swinging loosely in his hands. There was a large
crack in the metal ring that secured the handle
to the blade.

   "Dammit," he grumbled, "there's a day's
money gone to the blacksmith."

   He set off the next morning at dawn. . . .

   Kanji crossed the Kinu River and walked
along the embankment on the other side, the
blade in one hand. The smith was busy when he

arrived, but he finished up quickly. No one in his profession would make a man wait to have such a vital tool repaired.

The world of literature and the arts also felt the waves of change in the 1870s and 1880s. During previous eras, writers had been expected to tailor their works to uphold Confucian moral teachings. Although they produced titillating and amusing works, most fiction, forced to be didactic, contained flat characters and weak story lines. So too with the visual arts; the elites deemed the most interesting prints and plays of the pleasure quarters coarse or immoral. The 1885 book-length essay *Essence of the Novel* by the novelist Tsubouchi Shōyō shows the path-breaking determination of early Meiji writers to escape those Confucian restrictions. Tsubouchi's followers would produce some of the world's most varied and deeply human novels over the next several decades.

The writers of popular fiction seem to have taken as their guiding principle the dictum that the essence of the novel lies in the expression of approved moral sentiments. They accordingly erect a framework of morality into which they attempt to force their plots. . . . It has long been the custom in Japan to consider the novel as an instrument of education, and it has frequently been proclaimed that the novel's chief function is the castigation of vice and the encouragement of virtue. In actual practice, however, only stories of bloodthirsty cruelty or else of pornography are welcomed, and very few readers indeed even cast so much as a glance on works of a more serious nature. Moreover, since popular writers have no choice but to be devoid of self-respect and in all things slaves to public fancy and the lackeys of fashion, each one attempts to go to greater lengths than the last in pandering to the tastes of the time. They weave their brutal historical tales, string together their obscene romances, and yield to every passing vogue. Nevertheless they find it so difficult to abandon the pretext of "encouraging virtue" that they stop at nothing to squeeze in a moral, thereby distorting the emotion portrayed, falsifying the situations, and making the whole plot nonsensical. . . .

I hope that this book will help clear up the problems of readers and, at the same time, that it will be of service to authors, so that by dint of steady planning from now on for the improvement of our novels we may finally be able to surpass in quality the European novels, and permit our novels to take a glorious place along with painting, music, and poetry on the altar of the arts.

To avoid freezing during the long winter months, most farmers had to gather their own firewood from the forests on the edge of their fields and then carry it home in heavy bundles at the end of the workday. This man was photographed around 1902.

Forgetting how old
my body has become
I spend my life praying
for the day when the emperor's reign
is not buffeted by change.

—Female peasant-poet Matsuo
Taseko, 1870s

Chapter Four

Turning Outward: 1890–1912

The modernizing policies of the early Meiji years bore fruit in the two decades that sandwiched 1900, often in unpredictable ways. If leaders during the 1870s and 1880s threw their energy into making Japan up-to-date and holding off the imperialists, after 1890, they began to ponder Japan's world role and debated how to control and channel the social and intellectual forces that modernity had set off. Before the Meiji emperor breathed his last in 1912, Japan had become a fully modern society, less a victim than an imperialist colonizer.

One sign of just how much Japan had changed appeared in the celebrations and tumults that hailed the promulgation of the new constitution on February 11, 1889. Many scholars have called nationalism the most important force of the 1890s, and that day showed how right they are. Not only did farmers and city-dwellers alike celebrate Asia's first constitution, a nationalist zealot assassinated the education minister the same day for not respecting the emperor enough. And the young journalist Kuga Katsunan launched the newspaper *Nihon* to proclaim support for a new philosophy called *Nihonshugi*, "Japanism." Sometimes the patriotic spirit took the form of resentment, particularly of the unequal treatment Japan had so long received in its treaties with the Westerners. Sometimes it showed up in pride over the Meiji era's accomplishments. But for the great majority of leaders, the time had come, as the journal *Taiyō*, "Sun," argued in July 1900, for "proclamation of the unique spirit of the Japanese people, handed down across the generations."

At the policy level, this resurgence of nationalism turned people's eyes outward. One intellectual wrote that the British were great

Japanese workers load coal by the armload onto the Pacific Mail ship SS Siberia *at a naval station in Nagasaki in 1904. Though Japan had become an international power by then, having defeated China in war in 1895, and having signed an equal alliance with Great Britain in 1902, it still relied heavily on human labor for many industrial processes.*

Japan took a major step toward democratic government when the first session of the national legislature, called the Imperial Diet, was convened by the Meiji Emperor (standing, center) on November 29, 1890. He is surrounded by leading cabinet and court officials, all in formal attire, while the speaker of the House of Representatives stands on the floor beneath the dais.

because they thought of themselves as great; Japan needed to assert itself in ways that would make its people think of themselves as great too. The result was Japan's first period of territorial expansion: first, a war with China in the mid-1890s that dramatically changed the balance of power in Asia, then a war with Russia ten years later, which proved that Asians were capable of defeating Europeans. The forces unleashed by this outward turn were complex, involving mixtures of modernity, international cooperation, and aggressive chauvinism. But the national sentiment at the end of the Meiji era came as near to consensus about Japan's world role as any nation ever experiences. The drive to modernity had moved Japan from feudal isolation to worldwide leadership in just two generations; it had been mightily successful.

There was less consensus on what modernity had done to popular society. On one level, new jobs and opportunities brought 40,000 new residents a year into each of Japan's biggest cities during this period, giving them endless new possibilities: electric lights, streetcars, purified city water, department stores, mass-circulation newspapers, and entertainment quarters with baseball, beer halls, and, after 1897, moving pictures. On another level, many observers—not least the urban immigrants themselves—found the world worrisome, sometimes downright unbearable. Many a commentator noted changes in value systems, as the anonymity of the cities undermined the social fabric and mores of the old villages. One journalist observed couples making out at night in a downtown park and called them "depraved."

Even more writers worried about the poverty spawned by industrialization and urbanization. In the countryside north of Tokyo, at a copper mine in Ashio, Japan experienced its first major environmental pollution scandal in the 1890s. In the poor sections of Osaka and Tokyo, workers were crowded into teeming slums where food was scarce and filth abundant. Writers described the *shakai mondai*, "social problems," in vivid terms—prostitution, inhuman working conditions, ricksha pullers driven out of work by the new streetcars, low wages, epidemics caused by river pollution and inadequate sanitation, and cheap housing. On the surface at least, Japan seemed a far more complex place in 1912 than it had been when Meiji had seized the throne forty-five years earlier. It abounded now in the signs of modern civilization. It had become an empire, respected (and sometimes feared) by the entire world. But it seemed to the doomsayers to be losing its moorings, to be as full of social problems as it was driven by hope.

Rising Nationalism

The nationalism that swept Japan in the 1890s had many sources. One lay in officials' concerted efforts, so intense since the very beginning of the era, to make people more patriotic and, thus, more determined to face the Western challenges. Another was found in the angry reaction against Japan's submissive approach to the imperialist powers during the early Meiji years. "It was always 'America this and America that,'" fumed one young intellectual who had studied under Christian missionaries; "this I detested." Still a third source was anger over the humiliating treatment Japan continued to receive at the hands of Americans and Europeans: both the unequal treaties that prevented Japan from setting its own tariffs and trying Westerners in its own courts and the high-handedness of Western diplomats.

Japanese intellectuals saw from the first encounter with Westerners the inequities that lay behind the imperialist system, and concluded that they must master that system or be destroyed. An 1877 editorial on international relations, from

the daily newspaper *Tokyo Nichi Nichi Shimbun*, justifies the use of force to ward off western governments that have "neither reason nor morality."

The friendship between western powers is not governed by reason nor by morality. One nation will take advantage of the troubles of another and desire to benefit itself by seeking a quarrel with the one that is in trouble. Equitable principles have been discarded on the European continent, and each nation has to preserve its peace by being well prepared for war. . . . Such is the political condition of Europe. How can we hope to preserve friendly relations with foreigners by relying on their integrity if we are not prepared to use force. . . .

In Europe neither reason nor morality is needed to preserve the independence of nations. If a person desires to cover his bad actions he can do so on various pretexts. An ancient sage says that, when a weak man happens to tread on the toes of a strong man, the latter becomes angry and inflicts punishment upon him. But when the strong man happens to tread on the toes of the weak man, he also becomes angry and punishes him for putting his feet in the way. Such will be the diplomatic action of Europe. This is not the golden age in which morality controls force; but it is an age when every man in the world strives for his own advantage, regardless of the injuries inflicted upon others or the trouble they may be in. . . . How can we hope that foreigners who regard eastern nations as half civilized will behave with reason and morality towards us! Consider the behavior of foreigners towards us! It is not right at all! The face of our independent country was stained, as our countrymen know, by the convention which was signed by the Tokugawa government. It is now useless to talk of it; but foreigners have taken advantage of various disturbances which occurred at the decline of the Siogun's [sic] power. They forced their way into the heart of our country for the promotion of their own benefit and convenience. . . .

Our government treats foreigners with respect, wishing to hasten the time of the alteration of the convention, by which we shall hold the taxation and judicial powers in our hands. But we fear that the western governments, where no morality nor reason is preserved, will not accede to our desire in this respect.

One of the first people to advocate a more aggressive international stance was Fukuzawa Yukichi, the era's leading journalist-educator. In this much-discussed 1885 essay, "*Datsua*

the convention

The writer refers to the unequal treaties signed in the 1850s, which limited the tariffs Japan could levy on imported goods and provided that foreigners charged with crimes in Japan would be tried by their fellow countrymen, not by Japanese.

Alphabet woodblock prints were distributed to schoolchildren in the late Meiji years, giving them vocabulary words in pictures, in English, in Chinese characters, and, at the top of each box, in phonetic symbols (known as kana) representing the English sounds.

ron" (Cast-Off Asia), he argues that Japan, if it were to make genuine progress and gain the respect of the West, must stop thinking of itself as one of Asia's "backward" nations, that it even must forgo talk about helping neighbor states become modern. The times demand, he declares, that Japan proudly march forward along Western lines.

At a time when the spread of civilization and enlightenment has a force akin to that of measles, China and Korea violate the natural law of its spread. They forcibly try to avoid it by shutting off air from their rooms. Without air, they suffocate to death. It is said that neighbors must extend helping hands to one another because their relations are inseparable. Today's China and Korea have not done a thing for Japan. . . . Civilized Westerners . . . may see what is happening in China and Korea and judge Japan accordingly, because of the three countries' geographical proximity. The governments of China and Korea still retain their autocratic manners and do not abide by the rule of law. Westerners may consider Japan likewise a lawless society. Natives of China and Korea are deep in their hocus pocus of nonscientific behavior. Western scholars may think that Japan still remains a country dedicated to the yin and yang and five elements. . . . There are many more examples I can cite. It is not different from the case of a righteous man living in a neighborhood of a town known for foolishness, lawlessness, atrocity, and heartlessness. His action is so rare that it is always buried under the ugliness of his neighbors' activities. When these incidents are multiplied, they can affect our normal conduct of diplomatic affairs. How unfortunate it is for Japan.

What must we do today? We do not have time to wait for the enlightenment of our neighbors so that we can work together toward the development of Asia. It is better for us to leave the ranks of Asian nations and cast our lot with civilized nations of the West. . . . Any person who cherishes a bad friend cannot escape his bad notoriety. We simply erase from our minds our bad friends in Asia.

No single document did more to stimulate Japan's rising nationalism than the Imperial Rescript on Education, issued by the emperor on October 30, 1890. Conceived as an antidote to Western individualism and as a way to make all Japanese aware of their responsibility to serve the emperor and the state, it functioned much like the Pledge of Allegiance in the United States. For generations to come, students would repeat it at the start of the school day. Along with the national song, the observance of holidays such as National Foundations Day, and the rising emphasis on the emperor's role as high priest of the nation, the rescript went far in turning schoolgirls and schoolboys into loyal subjects, willing to work and die for their country.

Know ye, Our Subjects:

Our Imperial Ancestors have founded Our Empire on a basis broad and everlasting, and have deeply and firmly implanted virtue; Our subjects ever united in loyalty and filial piety have

yin and yang

Traditional Chinese philosophy held that the functioning of the world depends on a balance between passive (*yin*) and active (*yang*) forces. Yin is feminine, dark, and wet; yang is male, light, and dry.

from generation to generation illustrated the beauty thereof. This is the glory of the fundamental character of Our Empire, and herein also lies the source of Our education. Ye, Our subjects, be filial to your parents, affectionate to your brothers and sisters; as husbands and wives be harmonious, as friends true; bear yourselves in modesty and moderation; extend your benevolence to all; pursue learning and cultivate arts, and thereby develop your intellectual faculties and perfect your moral powers; furthermore, advance public good and promote common interests; always respect the Constitution and observe the laws; should emergency arise, offer yourselves courageously to the State; and thus guard and maintain the prosperity of Our Imperial Throne coeval with heaven and earth. So shall ye not only be Our good and faithful subjects, but render illustrious the best traditions of your forefathers.

The way here set forth is indeed the teaching bequeathed by Our Imperial Ancestors, to be observed alike by Their Descendants and the subjects, infallible for all ages and true in all places. It is Our wish to lay it to heart in all reverence, in common with you, Our subjects, that we may all attain to the same virtue.

There are two indispensable elements in the field of foreign policy: the armed forces first and education second. If the Japanese people are not imbued with patriotic spirit, the nation cannot be strong. . . . Patriotism can be instilled only through education.
—Prime Minister Yamagata Aritomo, speaking to the first Diet, 1890

An Expansionist Turn

The Meiji leaders left little to chance, including the attitudes of the young men drafted into the military. In the early 1880s, under the guidance of Yamagata Aritomo, architect of Japan's modern military structure, officials drafted an Imperial Rescript to Soldiers and Sailors designed to make the troops loyal to the emperor. Like the educational rescript, it was read to soldiers and sailors on a regular basis and served as the cornerstone of military values. It also was the first imperial rescript to be presented directly, by the emperor in person, to the army minister, and the first to be written in classical Japanese rather than in the classical Chinese used for earlier documents. After outlining Japan's military history, the emperor (using the imperial "we") called on the troops to be faithful to the throne and to lead exemplary lives, guided by traditional Confucian principles such as loyalty, uprightness, simplicity, and integrity.

Whether We are able to guard the Empire, and so prove Ourself worthy of Heaven's blessings and repay the benevolence of Our Ancestors, depends upon the faithful discharge of your duties as

Every year on the anniversary of Emperor Jimmu's accession, February 11, and on the anniversary of his passing, April 3, . . . we should ceremonially increase the territory of the Japanese Empire, even if it be only in small measure. Our naval vessels should . . . sail to a still unclaimed island, occupy it, and hoist the Rising Sun. . . . Not only would such a program have direct value as a practical experience for our navy, but it would excite an expeditionary spirit in the demoralized Japanese race.

—Geographer Shiga Shigetaka, *Conditions in the South Seas*, 1887

soldiers and sailors. If the majesty and power of Our Empire be impaired, do you share with Us the sorrow; if the glory of Our arms shine resplendent, We will share with you the honour. If you all do your duty, and being one with Us in spirit do your utmost for the protection of the state, Our people will long enjoy the blessings of peace, and the might and dignity of our Empire will shine in the world. As We thus expect much of you, Soldiers and Sailors, We give you the following precepts:

(1) The soldier and sailor should consider loyalty their essential duty. Who that is born in this land can be wanting in the spirit of grateful service to it? No soldier or sailor, especially, can be considered efficient unless this spirit be strong within him. A soldier or a sailor in whom the spirit is not strong, however skilled in art or proficient in science, is a mere puppet; and a body of soldiers or sailors wanting in loyalty, however well ordered and disciplined it may be, is in an emergency no better than a rabble. . . . Bear in mind that duty is weightier than a mountain, while death is lighter than a feather. Never by failing in moral principle fall into disgrace and bring dishonor upon your name.

(2) The soldier and the sailor should be strict in observing propriety. . . . Always pay due respect not only to your superiors but also to your seniors, even though not serving under them. On the other hand, superiors should never treat their inferiors with contempt or arrogance. Except when official duty requires them to be strict and severe, superiors should treat their inferiors with consideration, making kindness their chief aim. . . .

(3) The soldier and the sailor should esteem valour. Ever since the ancient times valour has in our country been held in high esteem, and without it Our subjects would be unworthy of their name. . . . But there is true valour and false. To be incited by mere impetuosity to violent action cannot be called true valour. The soldier and the sailor should have sound discrimination of right and wrong, cultivate self-possession, and form their plans with deliberation. . . .

(4) The soldier and the sailor should highly value faithfulness and righteousness. Faithfulness and righteousness are the ordinary duties of man, but the soldier and the sailor, in particular, cannot be without them and remain in the ranks even for a day. Faithfulness implies the keeping of one's word and righteousness the fulfilment of one's duty. . . .

(5) The soldier and the sailor should make simplicity their aim. If you do not make simplicity your aim, you will become effeminate and frivolous and acquire fondness for luxurious and extrava-

gant ways; you will finally grow selfish and sordid and sink to the last degree of baseness, so that neither loyalty nor valour will avail to save you from the contempt of the world. It is not too much to say that you will thus fall into a life-long misfortune. . . .

When domestic disturbances broke out in Korea early in 1894, the Korean government asked China for military assistance; and when the Chinese sent troops, the Japanese press exploded with jingoism, arguing that China was using the episode to undermine Korean independence. Fukuzawa's newspaper *Jiji Shinpō* demanded that Japan confront China, go to war, and lead Korea to "civilization." His colleagues in the papers and opinion journals followed suit, and by August 1894, Japan was engaged in the Sino-Japanese War of 1894-95, its first modern war. As it turned out, the struggle was a mismatch. Fukuzawa was right: China had not modernized, and despite its rich history and massive size, it was no rival for Japan's well-trained, well-equipped troops. The Japanese won every battle, and by fall, the Chinese were seeking a negotiated settlement.

Nothing about this war was more striking than the popular nationalistic fervor it engendered. The journalist-novelist Ubukata Toshirō, a teenager in mountainous Gifu prefecture at the time, recaptures in a 1931 memoir both the people's thirst for battlefront news and the complexities of their feelings about China, the source of so much Japanese culture.

The popular feeling about Japan's victory in China is clear in this 1895 New Year's cartoon in the newspaper Jiji Shinpō, where a small, sprightly Japanese officer rejoices over the fallen body of a large, flabby Chinese. The headline reads "Cheers to Great Imperial Japan."

Until the day this war began, we never had felt any kind of antipathy toward the Chinese people; we had never harbored hatred toward that country. . . . I learned classical Chinese from my father. From the spring of my ninth year until the winter when I was eleven, I studied the *Great Learning,* the *Golden Mean,* and the *Confucian Analects,* and then father died. . . . And we learned Chinese every day at school. Ninety-nine percent of Japanese civilization thirty years ago, prior to the modern westernization of Japan, was derived from China. . . . As far as we children were concerned before the Sino-Japanese War, the Chinese were all graceful, romantic, or heroic. Nothing we saw or heard about China was menacing or trifling; China was simply the greatest of the Asian empires. . . .

In the spring of 1894, I had just advanced to the second year of upper school, what we now call sixth grade. A long-faced teacher with a mole beside his nose told us that a gang of rebels

Great Learning, the Golden Mean, and the Confucian Analects

These three works are among the most important texts of ancient China, filled with quotations from Confucius himself.

A Japanese artist depicted Chinese officials surrendering to Japanese naval officers in 1895, near the end of the Sino-Japanese War. He captured the predominant Japanese view of things then: erect, modern, powerful Japanese in Western attire standing before bowing, humble Chinese wearing old-fashioned robes.

Toshima

The Toshima sea battle occurred off the coast of central Korea, southwest of Seoul. Pyongyang was the major city of northern Korea and the site of a major Chinese base. It fell to Japan on September 16. Though most Japanese thought of Great Britain as pro-Chinese, because of its heavy presence in that nation, it generally was neutral in the war.

called the Tonghaks was very active in Korea. Before long, he told us that the Japanese ambassador, Ōtori Keisuke, was in Seoul, negotiating with the Chinese ambassador to Korea. . . . Just before summer vacation, the situation suddenly began to get worse. I saw a neighbor from the other side of the street one evening, fanning air into the sleeves of his robe and holding a Tokyo newspaper. "Looks like we are going to have a war on our hands," he murmured. Two days later a Japanese war ship sank two Chinese war vessels in the open sea off Toshima. . . .

Everybody agreed that it would be very difficult to capture Pyongyang, since the city held huge British cannons. However, in August, the Japanese army overpowered Pyongyang with so little effort that it almost was disappointing—and the Japanese people were enraptured. My hometown had no telephone system back then. News of victories came to the police before the newspaper received it, thanks to a telegraph line between the post office and police station. All news was put up on the message board in front of the police station, and we children ran to check it several times a day. The excitement of the Japanese people was beyond imagination. After all, China was thirty times as big as Japan, and its population was over 200 million, compared to our 30 million. It had such a competent leader in Li Hongzhang too. And this was our first war with a foreign country, a country supported, moreover, by the British. Everyone—adults, children, the aged, the women—talked about war and nothing else, day and night. Even illiterate bumpkins put on their serious faces to discuss the war. My mother would order me to go to the message board at the police station several times a day. Each time, I read news of some Japanese victory and felt overjoyed. No one ever had been as happy, however, as when we learned of the fall of Pyongyang. A worker stopped his labor and rejoiced; a cleaning woman threw her broom into the air and jumped for joy; children yelled jubilantly; women and old people shed tears of joy. One of our household servants, a twenty-seven- or twenty-eight-year-old clerk who called himself Doctor Hōgō, ran out of the house like a mad man on hearing the news, and did not come back for quite some time.

The national frenzy reached even greater, but more complicated, heights in the weeks right after the Sino-Japanese War. First came the April 17, 1895, peace treaty, which gave Japan Taiwan and Manchuria's southern peninsula, called Liaodong, as well as an indemnity of 300 million yen, enough to more than pay for the entire war effort. (Wars in the nineteenth and early twentieth centuries typically ended with the loser required to pay a sum, called an "indemnity," that underwrote the victor's war costs.) Then, two weeks later, Russia, France, and Germany intervened, urging Japan to give Liaodong back to China to preserve long-term peace in the region. The motives behind the intervention were cynical and transparent; with its own designs on eastern Asia, Russia did not want a Japanese presence on the Asian continent. After bitter internal wrangling, however, the Japanese cabinet decided that it had no choice. Fearing that the Western powers might attack if Japan refused, it returned Liaodong and increased the indemnity by 15 percent to save face.

The psychological impact of this episode, known as the Triple Intervention, was huge. The Japanese public felt betrayed and humiliated by the Western powers. Newspapers decried their own officials' "cowardice." Ubukata said his classmates "cried in mortification." Observers and officials alike concluded that Japan must increase military spending so that it could not be put in such a situation again. In a memoir written late in 1895, immediately after the war, Foreign Minister Mutsu Munemitsu explains both the popular pressures that caused the Japanese negotiators to demand the acquisition of Liaodong in the initial peace treaty and the difficulties officials faced after the European intervention.

In the struggle for prestige and interests which goes on today among the world's powers, each power must always be willing to placate the others. While the word "placate" itself may be

JAPAN IS IN REVOLT.

People are Determined to Throw the Present Ministry Out of Power.

THINK THEIR INTERESTS BETRAYED.

Weighty Responsibilities of War Were Too Much for Ito and His Associates.

RULERS TAUNTED WITH TIMIDITY.

New York World *headlines captured the anger of the Japanese public on May 22, 1895, after their government agreed, under pressure from Russia, Germany, and France, to return the Liaodong Peninsula to China. That peninsula had been secured by Japan weeks earlier in the negotiations that ended the Sino-Japanese War, but the Western powers (with their own designs on Liaodong) contended that Japan had taken too much. The strong press reaction prompted the Japanese government to temporarily suspend more than 200 newspapers for stirring up public tumult.*

misunderstood as implying servility, the simple fact is that each power must be extremely sensitive to the disposition of the others and avoid areas likely to provoke jealousies in negotiating with them. This mode of interaction lays the foundation for averting future conflict, and is highly expedient from the viewpoint of diplomacy. But the state of public opinion in Japan at the time would not permit us to utilize this expedient without the most severe apprehensions as to the domestic consequences. . . . The only thing that the public and, indeed, even many officials wanted was ever larger concessions from China and ever greater glory for Japan. Indeed, when I first presented my peace treaty draft at the imperial conference in Hiroshima, some protested that the better part of Shantung Province should be demanded in addition to the Liaotung peninsula. . . . It was a time when the entire nation seemed delirious with victory, when ambitions and vain hopes ran at a fever pitch. Imagine how chagrined the public would have felt if the peace treaty had omitted that one clause relating to the cession of the Liaotung peninsula, an area taken at cost of so much Japanese blood! The nation's feelings might well have run beyond chagrin; quite possibly, the prevailing spirit of the moment would have prohibited the implementation of such a treaty.

It was extremely difficult to harmonize the requirements of our foreign policy with these popular sentiments, for the two were essentially incompatible. If we had tried too hard to reconcile them at the time, we would inevitably have faced a domestic reaction of such scope and intensity that it would have been far more menacing than any conceivable international incident. No one can say, therefore, that we left any stones unturned in the conduct of our foreign policy.

Shantung

Shantung, spelled Shandong in the pinyin romanization system commonly used today, is the large peninsula to the south and east of Beijing; Liaotung is an older spelling for Liaodong.

The government of His Majesty the Emperor of All the Russians, in examining the conditions of peace which Japan has imposed on China, finds that the possession of the peninsula of Liaotung, claimed by Japan, would be a constant menace to the capital of China, would at the same time render illusory the independence of Korea, and would henceforth be a perpetual obstacle to the peace of the Far East. Consequently, the government of His Majesty the Tsar would give a new proof of its sincere friendship for the government of His Majesty the Emperor of Japan by advising it to renounce the definitive possession of the peninsula.

—Russian statement delivered to Japan's foreign ministry, April 23, 1895

One of Japan's objections to the imperialist treaties was erased in 1899, when Japan was allowed to assume legal jurisdiction over foreigners living within its borders. By the beginning of the 1900s, Japan also had begun moving more aggressively on the international scene, enlarging its navy, expanding its influence in Korea, and settling in as colonial master of Taiwan. Over the next half-century, Japan created an empire of its own. It was a costly move that would drain resources and pull Japan into conflict with other nations. But it was a popular move, defended by officials and public alike as essential to gaining world respect. General Katsura Tarō's 1896 memorandum makes clear why Japan should use Taiwan as a base for expanding national strength.

Taiwan looks over the Pescadores to the China coast and is linked, through Amoy, to all of southern China. It leads onto the South Sea islands and offers potential for controlling the distant South Seas. . . . In China, whenever a pretext arises, the powers compete for spheres of influence. If we stand idly by, we will not survive. We must prepare if we are to use these troubled times to raise our national strength. We must make the south China–Fujian zone ours. To do this, we must open close contacts with Amoy and protect our opportunities in Fujian. . . . When considering national strength, we should take account of the real world and differences in real power. Even if our borders come into contact with strong nations, they only expand their dominions and establish colonies. They keep their main force in the far-off West. The hatreds of the powers mean they look for ways to stab each other in the back; none can relax for a moment and they clearly cannot send their main force to distant lands.

Japan's most immediate international concern in the early twentieth century was Russia, which had kept several thousand troops in Manchuria after the Boxer Rebellion of 1900, in which soldiers from several nations put down antiforeign violence by Chinese citizens. The British were worried too, fearing that Russia would threaten England's heavy investments in northern and central China. As a result, England and Japan concluded the Anglo-Japanese Alliance in 1902, recognizing each other's respective interests in China and Korea. The agreement had an important strategic impact, which allowed both nations to curtail military spending a bit, but its most important effect was psychological. For the first time in history, a European power had signed an equal alliance with an Asian nation—one more sign that Japan had become one of the world powers.

Article I. The High Contracting Parties, having mutually recognized the independence of China and Korea, declare themselves to be entirely uninfluenced by any aggressive tendencies in either country. Having in view, however, their special interests, of which those of Great Britain relate principally to China, while Japan, in addition to the interests which she possesses in China, is interested in a peculiar degree politically as well as commercially and industrially in Korea, the High Contracting Parties recognize that it will be admissible for either of them to take such measures as may be indispensable in order to safeguard those interests if

Amoy

Amoy was the capital of Fujian province, located opposite Taiwan on the south-central coast of China.

Ministers of the foreign powers—including Japan, Great Britain, Russia, France, the United States, Germany, Italy, and Spain—met in Beijing late in the summer of 1900 to negotiate a settlement with China, whose armies had just been defeated in the Boxer Rebellion battles. For the first time in history, the Western leaders included Japan as one of the powers.

threatened either by the aggressive action of any other Power, or by disturbances arising in China or Korea, and necessitating the intervention of either of the High Contracting Parties for the protection of the lives or property of its subjects.

Article II. If either Great Britain or Japan, in the defence of their respective interests as above described, should become involved in war with another Power, the other High Contracting Party will maintain a strict neutrality, and use its efforts to prevent other Powers from joining in hostilities against its Ally.

Article III. If in the above event any other Power or Powers should join in hostilities against the Ally, the other High Contracting Party will come to its assistance and will conduct the war in common, and make peace in mutual agreement with it.

Article IV. The High Contracting Parties agree that neither of them will, without consulting the other, enter into separate arrangements with another Power to the prejudice of the interests above described.

When Russia retained a military presence in Manchuria early in the 1900s despite repeated promises to withdraw its troops, the Japanese public began to react as it had when Chinese troops had entered Korea a decade earlier. Academics, columnists, and many officials began demanding that their leaders take action to get the Russians out. Some called attention to former Prime Minister Yamagata's doctrine that

Japan needed to maintain two strategic lines: a "line of sovereignty," referring to the four main islands that constituted Japan's formal borders, and a "line of advantage," or buffer zone, for protection against foreign aggressors. Others saw the Russian challenge as an opportunity to gain still more respect on the international stage.

The Russo-Japanese War (1904–5) was a less decisive victory for Japan than the earlier war against China. It lasted a year and a half, resulted in more than 125,000 Japanese casualties, and exhausted Japan's resources. At the same time, the Japanese public was as feverishly committed to this war as it had been to the war with China. A 1903 elementary textbook story shows the patriotic passion that had become ingrained in Japanese citizens by the time of the Russo-Japanese War. It describes a sailor reading a letter from his mother during the Sino-Japanese War.

It was the time of the War of 1894–95. One day on our ship the *Takachiho*, a sailor was weeping as he read a letter written in a woman's handwriting. A passing lieutenant saw him and, thinking his behavior unmanly, said, "Hey, what have we here? Has life become so valuable? Are you afraid to die? Are you lonely for your wife and children? Don't you think it's an honor to become a soldier and go to war—What kind of attitude is that?"

"Sir, don't think that of me. . . ."

[The officer reads the letter:]

"You said you did not fight in the battle of Feng-tao, and you did not accomplish much in the August 10th attack at Weihaiwei either. I am very disappointed in you. Why did you go into battle?

The Emperor of Korea wholly and forever yields all governing power over the Korean nation to the Emperor of Japan.

—August 22, 1910, treaty annexing Korea to Japan, in one of the long-term results of the Russo-Japanese War

Several of the 591 Japanese soldiers taken prisoner during the Russo-Japanese War pose for a picture postcard in front of a war camp near St. Petersburg, Russia. On the reverse side (far left), five of them write in February 1905 to an officer named Otani, thanking him for gifts and saying that though they have been ill, they are "doing fine now" and hope to leave the prison hospital soon.

Wasn't it to sacrifice your life to repay the emperor? The people in the village are good to me and offer help all the time, saying kindly: 'It must be hard on you having your only son off fighting for the country. Please don't hesitate to tell us if there is anything we can do.' Whenever I see their faces, I am reminded of your cowardice and I feel as if my heart will break. I wish you would try to understand a little of what I feel."

As he heard this, the Lieutenant's eyes welled with tears in spite of himself.

"Oh, pardon, I'm sorry. You have a good mother. You must come from a good family."

The sailor left, smiling.

Length and battlefield difficulties were not the only things that set this war apart from the Sino-Japanese War. The Russo-Japanese War also produced more domestic disputes, a sign that Japanese society was becoming more complicated. Violent controversy erupted at the end of the war, when Japan's negotiators failed to secure an indemnity or signifi-

The bombproof dugout headquarters of General Nogi Maresuke lay within the range of Russian guns, just outside the walls of Port Arthur. Japan's victory in that battle, which took nearly a year and resulted in more than 100,000 deaths (16,000 of them Japanese), proved pivotal in the Russo-Japanese War.

cant territory from the Russians. The citizens of Tokyo and other cities, kept in the dark by the press about how fragile the victory had been, reacted with bitter demonstrations in early September 1905. Thousands took to the streets, burning buildings, killing seventeen people—and demanding that the treaties be renegotiated.

Another kind of dissent also emerged during the fighting, when leftists produced Japan's first antiwar movement. The activists numbered no more than a few hundred, but their very presence suggested that Japan's intellectual life was getting more complex. "Little Brother, Do Not Die," a poem written for a literary magazine in 1904 by the young feminist essayist Yosano Akiko, was addressed to her brother, who was fighting the Russians in Manchuria. Patriotic columnists denounced the poem as "traitorous."

Oh my little brother, I weep for you
And beg you: do not die—
You, last-born and most beloved.
Did our parents
Put a blade into your hand
And teach you to kill men?
"Kill men and die in battle," did they say
And raise you so 'til twenty-four?

I beg you: do not die.
His Imperial Majesty—he himself—
Enters not the field of battle.
So vast and deep his sacred heart:
He cannot wish for you to spill
Your own blood and another's,
To die the death of beasts,
To think such death is glory!

Oh my little brother
I beg you: do not die in battle.
To add to mother's grief
When she lost father this autumn past,
They took her son
And left her to protect the house.
I hear of "peace" in this great Emperor's reign,
And yet our mother's hair grows ever whiter. . . .

The wretchedness of Korea's roads defies even the specialists. There are more mountain inclines than one can count, and most of them are little more than muddy seas. A horse has a hard time freeing itself if its foot slips off the trail. If an axle sinks in the mud, there is no moving, either forward or backward. The army has to move ahead step by step, through rugged rice fields and uneven mountain terrain, clearing the road as it goes. . . . The real victors in these hardships are the transport soldiers.

—War correspondent Torii Sosen, *Osaka Asahi Shimbun,* May 14, 1904, describing Japanese troop movements in the Russo-Japanese War

Having learned that Japan would get no financial settlement in the Russo-Japanese War negotiations, the newspaper Osaka Asahi Shimbun *declared angrily on September 1, 1905, that it would "not allow the flesh and blood of our slain soldiers to turn to scorched earth." Under the caption "tears of bleached bones," a cartoonist showed the skull of a fallen soldier weeping because he thought his country's diplomats had not secured a good enough settlement.*

A Modern, Urban Society

When a downtown Tokyo auditorium presented Japan's first motion picture in 1897, the hall was packed despite the high one-yen price for first-class tickets—proof that modernity had come to the city. So had great numbers of people. Tokyo's population, which had totaled just 480,000 at the beginning of the Meiji era, passed the two-million mark by 1910, and Osaka grew just as rapidly. The combination of modern ideas, advancing technology, and urbanization produced a kind of society Japan had not known before. Profit-driven factories with low wages, mass production techniques, and long hours spawned urban slums that contrasted markedly with the communal societies in the countryside where workers had been reared. An increase in required schooling and a more effective school system made literacy available to nearly all young people. Inventions such as the wristwatch and the safety razor filled the shelves of a new institution, the department store.

A key element in this development was the appearance, in the 1890s, of Japan's equivalent of the penny press—inexpensive, sensational newspapers aimed at commoners who wanted to be entertained and to know what was going on in the world. One of the most popular of these was *Yorozu Chōhō*, which ran an editorial on November 1, 1892.

Why does *Yorozu Chōhō* publish? It is for one purpose alone: to help the average masses know the times thoroughly at a glance. With this goal in mind, we will strive to keep the price low, to keep the paper small, to make the prose easy to read, and to maintain our editorial independence. . . . High priced papers are not for average people; they provide no benefit to the majority; nor do they concern themselves with the needs of the broader society. We will attempt to keep articles as simple as possible. Long writing wastes time and makes one work hard, taxing the mental powers. It obstructs work in the daytime and consumes lamp oil in the evening; so we will work to keep articles simple. . . . If a paper's prose is not high flown, even the most educated lord of the family will still find pleasure in it. If things are made easy and interesting so that anyone can understand them, everyone will read them: not just the master of the house but the wife, the clerk, the shop boy, the men servants and women servants. There is no better way

I deplore this Russo-Japanese War, because I believe it is in one sense a war between brothers. . . . Are not Russians half-Orientals, and Japanese half-Occidentals? . . . There is nothing sadder in life's experience than misunderstanding between friends and brothers.

—Christian intellectual Uchimura Kanzō, *Kobe Chronicle* column, November 18, 1904

A crowd gathers on a street in
Tokyo's Asakusa entertainment
district around 1903 to watch a
free theatrical performance. In
the background is the Asakusa
Tower, one of the city's most
dramatic symbols of architectural modernity until it toppled
in the 1923 earthquake.

to enable everyone in a household to benefit, for a mere pittance
. . . . Come what may, good or ill, our company will remain independent, steering clear of the government, the political parties—
and above all, those treacherous politicians. Hear us! We will
adhere singlemindedly to truth and integrity. Those who prefer
biased arguments that show favoritism, those who desire wily,
unjust articles, should read another paper.

**The changing currents of late-Meiji society provided an open-
ing for the emergence of women into public life. Although
most women, urged by educators, officials, and establishment writers to be "good wives and wise mothers," still
devoted themselves to traditional household roles, a significant number began entering new fields: as physicians, novelists, and educators. The journalist Hani Motoko describes in
her autobiography the maneuvers she had to perform in
1898 to become the newspaper *Hōchi*'s first woman copyeditor. After her promotion to the reporting staff, she was fired**

for marrying another *Hōchi* employee. Undaunted, she moved on to other careers, and eventually founded a women's magazine and started a school for girls.

On my way to school each morning, I stopped at the main office of the *Hōchi shimbun* to look through their employment guide. Then, passing the *Yamato shimbun* office one day, I found a notice that a copyeditor was wanted. I rushed home to prepare a letter and a resumé and ran back to the *Yamato* office. The sleepy-eyed receptionist informed me that the position had just been filled. My enthusiasm instantly deflated, I nevertheless learned a valuable lesson from the receptionist—his attitude clearly announced that no woman would ever be considered for employment. Thereafter I carried a statement among my application papers explaining why, as a woman, I wished to be a copyeditor. Within a week, the *Hōchi* want-ads announced an opening for a copyeditor at their office. I arrived at the reception desk too early in the morning and was met not by a receptionist but by the head janitor, who said, "Are you applying for the opening yourself? A copyeditor is a man's position you know." "No, I was asked to deliver this to the person in charge," I replied in desperation and handed my papers to him. Since then, I have often tried to convince myself that the lie was forgivable because I had no bad intentions, only a desperate wish. Nonetheless, I was ashamed of having lied to the honest old man.

The following day, I received a postcard from the *Hōchi* summoning me to an interview. My elation was quickly quelled when I entered the shabby, small waiting room to find several men, obviously other applicants for the same position. I was the last to be interviewed. I no longer remember the details of the meeting, except for the impression that the interviewer had apparently read my papers with care and was giving me fair consideration. He proposed a one-day trial. Then and there, I was taken to the copy desk in a corner of the editing room and introduced to the unsmiling middle-aged man who was the chief copyeditor. Without a word, he pushed toward me some copies of an advertisement which he had been busily correcting. I did the best I could on them, discovering the excitement of reading sections of a newspaper before they were printed. Toward evening, the chief dismissed me with a trace of a smile and said, "That's it for today. Come back around ten o'clock in the morning. You'll probably do."

I began work the next morning. . . . At the beginning I heard comments coming from the printers, who worked in a room

The daily schedule of workers in a silk factory in Nagano Prefecture in 1903. Work hours totaled more than fifteen a day.

4:40 AM	Rising
5:10	Starting work
6:30	Breakfast
6:45	Back to work
12:00	Lunch
12:15 PM	Back to work
5:30	Dinner
5:45	Back to work
9:00	Work ends
9:10	Bath
10:30	Lights out

separated from the editing room by a screened window. "Hey, there's a woman in the zoo now," they quipped, using the editing area's nickname. But I was too happy in my new job to mind their teasing and it soon stopped.

Fiction came into its own in these years, too, as writers responded to novelist Tsubouchi Shōyō's call for realistic works in his "Essence of the Novel." Shimazaki Tōson wrote about discrimination against outcastes, Mori Ōgai about sex, Tokutomi Roka about materialism. The era's greatest novelist was Natsume Sōseki, who probed the human psyche and the difficulties of grappling with modern individualism. When the government awarded him the first national award for fiction in 1911, he refused it, saying that acceptance would undermine his ability to write independently. In the novel *Kokoro*, Natsume's protagonist questions a mentor known as "Sensei," or teacher, about why it is so difficult to trust people in the modern era.

Natsume Sōseki, the Meiji period's foremost novelist, at home with his two sons, Noboruku and Jun'ichi, in December 1914. Sōseki's novels captured many of the themes of early twentieth-century Japan: the loss of old traditions, the hypocrisy of the leaders of industry and culture, changing relationships between men and women, and the loneliness that accompanied spreading individualism.

I could hear the cry of a goldfish vendor from the lane on the other side of the hedge. There was no other sound. The house was some distance from the main road, and we seemed to be surrounded by a complete calm. All was quiet, as usual, inside the house itself. I knew that Sensei's wife was in the next room, busy at her sewing or some such work. And I knew also that she could hear what we were saying. but I momentarily forgot this, as I said:

"Then you have no trust in your wife either?"

Sensei looked a little uneasy. He avoided giving a direct answer to my question.

"I don't even trust even myself. And not trusting myself, I can hardly trust others. There is nothing that I can do, except curse my own soul."

"Surely, Sensei, you think too seriously about these things." . . .

"Don't put too much trust in me. . . . I do not want your admiration now, because I do not want your insults in the future. I bear with my loneliness now, in order to avoid greater loneliness in the years ahead. You see, loneliness is the price we have to pay for being born in this modern age, so full of freedom, independence, and our own egotistical selves."

Few novelists did a more vivid job of describing how varied urban society had become than Futabatei Shimei, whose work *Drifting Cloud* (1887–89) is regarded as Japan's first

These charts compiled by government offices in the Meiji years show not just growth but a distinct change in the economy, as Japan began importing more and more raw products and exporting more finished goods. The rise in educational levels suggests one of the underlying causes of this economic growth.

Percentage of School-Aged Children Attending School

	Boys	Girls
1874	48	18
1890	61	28
1900	90	78
1910	94	92

Imports/Exports

1882

Imports (¥29,450,000)		Exports (¥37,220,000)	
cotton yarn	22.3%	silk thread	43%
sugar	15.4	tea	18.2
cotton goods	14.5	marine goods	5.2
woolens	6.2	rice	4.4
petroleum	7.9	other	29.2
iron	4.6		
other	29.1		

1897

Imports (¥219,300,000)		Exports (¥163,140,000)	
raw cotton	19.9%	silk thread	34.1%
rice	9.8	cotton yarn	8.2
sugar	9.0	silk goods	6.0
machines	8.0	coal	5.2
iron	5.6	tea	4.6
cotton yarn	4.4	other	41.9
cotton goods	4.4		
woolens	4.4		
other	34.5		

modern novel. Kanda Gate was in the center of Tokyo, on the northeast side of the imperial castle. Shirokiya, one of the old dry-goods stores, had introduced a Western clothing section in 1886.

It is three o'clock in the afternoon of a late October day. A swirling mass of men stream out of the Kanda gate, marching first in antlike formation, then scuttling busily off in every direction. Each and every one of these fine gentlemen is primarily interested in getting enough to eat.

Look carefully and you will see what an enormous variety of individual types are represented in the huge crowd. Start by examining the hair bristling on their faces: mustaches, side whiskers, Vandykes, and even extravagant imperial beards, Bismarck beards reminiscent of a Pekinese, bantam beards, badger's beards, . . . meager beards that are barely visible, thick and thin they sprout in every conceivable way.

Now see how differently they are dressed. Here is a dandy in a fashionable black suit purchased at Shirokiya set off by shoes of French calfskin. And now confident men oblivious of the ill-fit of their tweeds worn with stiff leather shoes—trousers that trail in the mud like the tail of a tortoise; suits bearing the indelible stamp of the ready-made clothes rack. "I have a beard, fine clothing, what more do I need?" they seem to say. Glowing like embers on the fire, these enviable creatures swagger home, heads erect.

Now behind them come the less fortunate. Pitifully stooped, their hair grey, they stagger along with empty lunch boxes dangling from their waists. Despite their advanced years they still manage to hold a job, but their duties are so negligible they can easily work in old-fashioned Japanese clothes.

The economy grew strongly around the turn of the century. Most economic historians see the 1890s as the time when Japan experienced its first industrial takeoff, a time when production and the number of factory workers soared, when exports and imports tripled to make Japan a major player in world trade.

Unfortunately, rising industrialism also caused an explosion of what journalists called *shakai mondai*, or social problems: slums, crime, political unrest, pollution, and epidemics. The reporter Yokoyama Gennosuke describes his visit to an impoverished area in *Japan's Lower Classes*, an 1899 book based on years of reporting.

Among the poorest of the urban
classes were the ricksha pullers, men
whose bravado made them the stuff
of romance but whose actual living
conditions approached destitution.
Their profession was a short-lived
one, as rickshas did not become
popular until the 1870s and then
were replaced by streetcars and
automobiles in the early 1920s,
a decade after the Meiji era ended.

That unrelated people live together temporarily as one household
is probably the unique feature of slum areas. Only in rare cases so-
called couples have been united through formal, traditional marriage go-betweens. Of the many couples who reside in scores of
houses in any single alley, only two or three are legally married.
There are scores of children in one *nagoya*, "row house," whose
names appear only in a policeman's notebook. But they have not
been registered in the Ward Office. These native-born Japanese
grow up without any of the rights or privileges of formal citizenship. The great number of children without citizenship in slums
results largely from the fact that children are born of common-law
marriages, and women run off, leaving their children behind.
Quarrels between husbands and wives occur most frequently
among families in distress. These quarrels perhaps reflect frustration in their daily lives, as husbands and wives feud for no particular reason. Innocent children become the victims of these parents
and are harshly treated. . . . If one looks at the dark side of life in the
slums, it resembles a picture scroll depicting a scene of carnage. . . .

A worn-out, tired woman with scraggly, unkempt hair sat on
the threshold of her tenement house (or row house) and spoke
despondently of her life. With arms crossed, she was about to continue her narrative when a child of about seven years came running noisily toward the woman, saying, "Mama, it will soon be

One of the darker sides of industrialization was environmental pollution. Tanaka Shōzō became famous in the 1890s as the leader of Japan's first antipollution movement, leading thousands of peasants from the town of Ashio in marches against the Diet in 1898 and 1899. Like so many Japanese leaders, he often expressed his thoughts in poems, including this one, written during the pollution fight.

Die, if you have to.
Kill me, if you must.
In a dead world
What cause for grief
In being killed?
Plants wither,
Men die:
To the Dietmen
It is nothing—
Faces of stone!

noon and time for lunch. Daddy is dead drunk and angry because you are not home." Frowning, she replied, "Is that so?" Then, "I feel utterly at a loss with that drunkard." . . .

We can sympathize with these poor people, however, and find something admirable in them. For example, although they speak ill of other persons behind their backs and quarrel among themselves, they take days off from their work to assist at funerals of their neighbors. These poor people provide assistance to others despite the fact that if they do not work even one day, their livelihood will immediately be in jeopardy. Thus, there is something commendable about the mutual affection they display toward one another.

Two dramatic events in the final Meiji years showed just how complex life in modern Japan had become. The one that captured the greatest public attention was the death of Emperor Meiji, on July 30, 1912. His final illness was covered by the press in a detail that bordered on the macabre, including almost hourly reports on his pulse, his temperature, and his bodily functions. A full 25,000 people marched in the funeral procession, which stretched out for two and a half miles, as hundreds of thousands watched, and warships in Tokyo bay issued 300 cannon blasts.

Almost forgotten in the outpouring of grief and patriotism was the fact that only months earlier, in 1911, the government had executed a dozen people for allegedly attempting to assassinate the emperor. That earlier episode occurred after socialist followers of Kōtoku Shūsui, whose newspaper had been suppressed during the Russo-Japanese War, started arguing that the mystique surrounding the emperor undermined ideas like equality and democracy. When police found materials for making a bomb at the home of one of these men, they charged twenty-six with high treason. A secret trial was held and twenty-four were sentenced to death, though only five could be tied to the plot. In this 1911 prison diary, the one woman in the group, Kanno Suga, discusses her own motives, as well as her reactions when a dozen had their sentences reduced to life in prison.

January 19. Cloudy. . . .
We had sailed into the vast ocean ahead of the world's current of thought and the general tide of events. Unfortunately, we were

shipwrecked. But this sacrifice had to be made to get things started. New routes are opened up only after many shipwrecks and dangerous voyages. This is how the other shore of one's ideals is reached. After the sage of Nazareth was born, many sacrifices had to be made before Christianity became a world religion. In light of this, I feel that our sacrifice is minuscule. . . .

January 21. Clear. . . .
Chaplain Numanami comes and asks me, "How are you?" I reply, "Same as usual." He says, "You have peace of mind because your life is founded on faith in your ism, your cause. Some people may be chagrined about the whole affair, depending on how deeply they were involved in it. You were involved in the affair from the beginning to the end, so you must have been prepared to face anything." What he said pleased me. It was much better than his trying to convert me. . . .

January 23. Clear. . . .
Nowadays, every morning when I get up I think in amazement, "Oh, am I still alive?" That I am still alive feels like a dream.

I heard from Tanaka, chief of moral instruction, that over half of the defendants condemned to death have been given a reprieve. Their sentences were probably reduced one degree to life imprisonment. The verdicts were so unjust that this came as no surprise. Still, it is delightful news. I don't know whose sentences were reduced, but it must be those who had very little to do with the affair; those people who, in my opinion, were completely innocent. They must be overjoyed, since, even though they were condemned unjustly and arbitrarily, they were facing the death penalty.

The authorities first hand down these harsh sentences, then reduce them, touting the action as an act of the emperor's benevolence. They try to impress the people of Japan, as well as those of other nations, that this is an act of justice and mercy. Are we to admire this kind of clever scheming? or condemn it as artful politicking? Still I am really happy that my comrades' lives have been spared. To be fully satisfied I would like to see all others saved except for the three or four of us. If I could take the places of all of them, I would be happy to be broiled to death by being trussed upside down or have my back split open and have molten lead poured into me.

Right after Emperor Meiji's death, General Nogi Maresuke and his wife committed ritual suicide, to follow their lord in death. Though a few writers criticized the sensational act as anachronistic, most Japanese praised its sincerity, calling it an expression of patriotic loyalty. Among the latter was editor Kuroiwa Shūroku, who wrote this poem about Nogi in 1912, for his newspaper, *Yorozu Chōbō*.

Until today
I had thought him
An excellent man.
Now I know he was a god
Born as a man.

Chapter Five

Imperial Democracy: 1912–30

S omething seemed ironic about the fact that the twenty-six-year-old poet Ishikawa Takuboku died of tuberculosis on April 13, 1912—not just the fact that he died so young but that he died three and a half months before the Emperor Meiji did. Ishikawa's life and poetry were not focused and successful like the Meiji era; they were more confused, more troubled than his age had been, more like the era of Meiji's son, Taishō, who reigned from 1912 to 1926. Ishikawa should, by symbolic right, have lived another half year, so that he could have at least tasted the Taishō era for which his tumultuous spirit and writings seemed destined.

Just as Ishikawa was known for tempestuous and frenetic living, the Taishō years were characterized by chaotic pluralism. In the poet's case, the causes were heavy drinking and unorthodox ideas. In the nation's case, everyone commented on the challenges to old values, the new forms of entertainment, changes in gender relationships, gaps between classes, and new literary schools. Automobiles began to fill city streets, talking movies attracted theatergoers, dance halls appeared in city centers, and cafe culture rivaled the old geisha world for young men's attention. *Moga*, "modern girls," wore short skirts and cropped hair and *mobo*, their male counterparts, wore bell-bottoms and straight black hair. Magazines focusing on self-fulfillment sprang up; the radio spread popular culture; and journalists accused young people of being obsessed with three S's: sports, screen, and sex.

In the political and intellectual spheres, this was the heyday of new isms: Marxism and socialism, with their emphasis on class struggle and equality; anarchism, which opposed all forms of government;

Relief workers sort through debris along the waterfront after the earthquake of September 1, 1923—one of the worst in human history—which killed more than 100,000 people and demolished more than 70 percent of the homes in Tokyo and 85 percent of those in Yokohama. Most structures and vehicles along the waterfront were damaged, demolished, or washed away. The destruction triggered malicious rumors that resident Koreans had set the thousands of fires that were caused by the earthquake, and the resultant riots left as many as 6,000 Koreans dead.

American photographer William Rau shot this photo of the busy Nihonbashi Street in the Ginza, Tokyo's most affluent, prestigious shopping district, in 1905. The festive nature of the day is clear from people's formal dress. The electric poles, trolley, and towering background buildings show the district's elite status.

and literary naturalism, which produced novels about the dark side of human nature. It was the time, too, when the Communist Party was formed, the time when ideas of radical professors became part of mainstream political discussion. These years also brought labor and tenant unions into the general public consciousness, with their demands for better pay, fair rents, decent housing, and the right to strike. And more people than ever moved into the civil arena, as political parties increased their power and the right to vote was extended, in 1925, to all males twenty-five and older.

As might be expected, people with radical ideas and activist approaches like Ishikawa's also provoked a negative response from the establishment. Already in the late Meiji years, the government had begun to worry about intellectual diversity. Prime Minister Katsura Tarō had warned that socialist ideas, if unchecked, might turn into an unstoppable wildfire and give Japan its own version of the late-eighteenth-century French Revolution. By the time the cultural explosion was at its hottest in the late 1920s, traditional intellectuals and politicians were decrying it as a crisis, a sign of moral decay where self-centered individualism threatened to destroy the loyalty-based Confucian order—where rigor and hard work were being undermined by laziness and sleaze.

To counter these tendencies, officials instituted numerous measures in the 1910s, both gentle and harsh, to revive the old ethical and intellectual consensus. On the gentler side, school textbooks were revised to encourage patriotism and loyalty to the emperor, while military reserve and veterans associations were strengthened, and youth and women's organizations were created to encourage local identification with the nation's well-being. A series of laws and institutions pressured people to give greater allegiance to the indigenous national faith, Shintō, and an award system was developed to encourage "good" literature. At the same time, officials also strengthened the harsher side of the legal system, to clamp down on moral decay and individualism, as well as on groups that favored communism or socialism. Press laws were tightened to punish editors who pandered to "immoral" tastes and, in 1925, the advocacy of socialism was made illegal. As a result, by the end of the 1920s, thought police had been established to keep watch on groups with subversive ideas.

Taishō Japan was thus the best of times or the worst of times, depending on one's perspective. For those who cherished diversity and pluralism, the years were energizing and hopeful. But for the established elite, Japan seemed in danger of losing its soul. So they set out to revive traditional values by emphasizing patriotism and placing ever more emphasis on the emperor's role as national father and high priest. In the process, they created an atmosphere of imperial democracy—a time when the democratic forces of debate and diversity were almost evenly balanced by imperialism in both of its meanings: loyalty to the emperor at home and pride in Japan's achievements abroad. They also set in motion forces that would lead to a very different decade in the 1930s.

The Energy of Modernity

One reason for Ishikawa Takuboku's influence lay in the fact that his writing caught the Taishō era's spirit of honest, restless probing. His willingness to talk about his own inner self defied the self-effacing stance that writers always had been expected to exemplify. One of his few successful prose works, *Romaji Diary*, encapsulates the self-centered rebelliousness that attracted so many urban readers.

I want only freedom from care. This I realized tonight for the first time. Yes, that's so. Quite definitely so. What I want can't be anything else.

Oh, this freedom from care! The feeling of such peace of mind, what could it possibly taste like? For a long time, ever since I began to comprehend what was going on around me, I have forgotten what peace of mind is.

Few things symbolized Japan's rising material comfort in the 1920s more than the automobile. Boatmen use a traditional ferry to take this modern invention across a river in the middle of the decade.

The man said, . . . "Japan is bigger than Tokyo. And even bigger than Japan. . . . Even bigger than Japan, surely, is the inside of your head. Don't ever surrender yourself—not to Japan, not to anything. You may think that what you're doing is for the sake of the nation, but let something take possession of you like that, and all you do is bring it down."

—Natsume Sōseki, *Sanshiro*, 1908

Nowadays, it's only on streetcars to and from my office that my mind is most at ease. When I'm at home, I feel, for no reason at all, that I must be doing something. That "something" is what bothers me. Is it reading? Is it writing? It seems to be neither. No, reading and writing seem to be only a part of that "something."

Is there anything I can do besides read and write? I don't know. At any rate, I do feel as if I must always be doing something. Even when I'm indulging in idle carefree thought, I always feel as if I am being dogged by that "something." Yet I can't concentrate on anything.

When I'm at the office, I keep hoping time will pass as quickly as possible. It's not that I particularly dislike my work or that I feel my surroundings are unpleasant. It's that I am pursued by the feeling I must get home as soon as possible and do something. I don't know what I'm supposed to do; and still, from somewhere behind me I feel myself pursued by that "something I must do."

I am keenly sensitive to changes in nature in terms of season. When I look at a flower, I feel, "Good heavens, that flower's come out!" That simple experience stabs me as sharply as an arrow.

I feel, furthermore, as if that flower will open in an instant and its petals will fall as I'm looking at it. Whatever I see or hear, I feel as if I'm standing on the brink of a surging stream. I'm not at all calm. I'm not composed. For some reason or other, my mind can't stand still, as if it were being pushed from behind or being pulled forward, and I feel as if I must start running.

Then what is it I need? Fame? No. Projects? No. Love? No. Knowledge? No. . . .

What I am seeking for with all my soul is freedom from care. That must be so!

Ishikawa was known best for his *tanka*, the three- and five-line poems that had dominated Japanese poetry for a thousand years. Part of the appeal lay in his use of a uniquely Japanese form to express the individualistic ideas that characterized modern literature.

When I breathe,
This sound in my chest
Lonelier than the winter wind

All these people
Going in the same direction—
And me, watching them from the side

The last full year of the Meiji era, 1911, offered two sure signs that modernity had replaced tradition for great numbers of Japan's city dwellers: an automobile and a woman chauffeur.

Somehow,
Feel more people than I expected
Think as I do . . .

The Taishō atmosphere gave voice not only to new ideologies but also to groups that previously had not been heard in the public arena. Among the latter were public-minded women. The Meiji years had seen women emerge in the professions, and now their voices became part of the general public discussions, although the majority of women continued in traditional roles, satisfied to exert their power in the home. By the 1920s, Japan had produced a significant number of magazines for women—*Fujin no tomo*, "Woman's Friend," and *Fujin kōron*, "Woman's Opinion," among them—as well as a number of women who wrote for both men's and women's publications. One of the most controversial new journals was *Seitō* (Bluestockings), an opinion journal that provided a forum for heated debates over issues such as chastity, the economic role of women, abortion and birth control, and whether women should enter public life. An article by the feminist editor Hiratsuka Raichō, from *Seitō*'s first issue in 1911, suggests both the magazine's vitality and the intellectual depth that made it influential.

In the beginning, truly, woman was the sun. She was a genuine person.

Today, woman is the moon: a moon with the pale face of a sickly person, one who shines through the light of others, who lives by depending on others.

Now, *Bluestockings* raises a fresh voice—a fresh voice drawn from the work and thought of modern Japanese women.

The day the mountains move has come.
I speak but no one believes me.
For a time the mountains have been asleep,
But long ago they all danced with fire.
It doesn't matter if you believe this,
My friends, as long as you believe:
All the sleeping women
Are now awake and moving.

—Yosano Akiko, first issue of *Seitō*, 1911

Today, the things that women do invite only laughter and ridicule. Knowing that well, I might hide beneath the laughter and ridicule. But I am not afraid. . . .

Earnestness! Earnestness! On that alone we must depend. Earnestness springs from the power of prayer, from the power of volition, from the strength of meditation. Put another way, it comes from the ability to focus the powers of the spirit. Only in that ability to focus our spiritual powers can we grasp the mystery that lies at life's core. When I say mystery, I am not talking about something manufactured, something based on, or separated from, reality, something created by the head or by the hands. The mystery does not come from dreams. This mystery is the reality at the core of our ego; it is the mystery found in the human depths, in the profundity of meditation.

We must seek our natural genius through focusing our spiritual powers. Our natural genius springs from life's mystery. It makes us an authentic person. Natural genius is not a male thing; it is not a female thing. . . . As I look at the world, I do not know what a woman's nature is. I do not know what a man's nature is. I continually see both men and women reflected in my own heart. But I do not see this as male or female.

Japanese education always had a political underpinning, derived from the Confucian idea that the purpose of education was to prepare people to serve the public. In the Taishō period, this traditional view joined with Western philosophy and political science to create exciting discussions about the nature of public life. University professors became major forces in the debates over what direction public life should take. Among these new intellectuals were founders and defenders of Marxism, spokespersons for internationalism, and apologists for a rising right-wing nationalist movement.

Probably the most prominent intellectual was Yoshino Sakuzō, a professor at the University of Tokyo law school who argued that scholars had a responsibility to put their knowledge to work in the world of everyday politics. He played an important role in the heated discussions of what "democracy" should mean in Japan. Though Yoshino eventually grew disillusioned with democracy's many failings, throughout the Taishō years he was its most eloquent defender. In 1916, he argued in "An Essay on Democracy" for a system of rule he called *minponshugi*, in which the people govern themselves

through an honest, popularly elected legislature, under the formal sovereignty of the emperor.

The most important point regarding the relation between the people and the legislators is that the people always occupy the position of master of the house, while the legislators are of necessity transients. The proper maintenance of this relationship is absolutely essential to the functioning of constitutional government. The abuses of constitutional government generally stem from the inversion of this relationship. And it is not just a question of the relation between the people and the legislators. The same truth holds as between legislators and the government. Whenever the legislators, who should supervise the government, are puppets of the government, many evils arise. Likewise, whenever the people, who should supervise the legislators, are instead manipulated by the latter, then the operation of constitutional government is replete with innumerable scandalous corruptions. If the government seduces legislators with offers of gain, if legislators also lead the people astray with offers of gain, then the proper relationships are inverted and the structure of constitutional government is filled with abuses. If we wish to clean up political life and see a normal evolution of constitutional government, the first thing we must do is to pay strict attention to rectifying the relationship between the people and the legislators. There are at least three measures that must be adopted in order to accomplish this.

1. Inculcation of election ethics. . . .
2. Adopting and enforcing strict election regulations. . . .
3. Extending the suffrage as widely as possible. . . .

One of the era's most controversial writers was Minobe Tatsukichi, one of Yoshino's colleagues at the University of Tokyo. A student of constitutional law, Minobe articulated a theory in 1911 that the state was like a living body, and that each component, including the emperor himself, was an organ of that body. This view was accepted by many Japanese scholars in the 1920s, but in the 1930s, as emperor-centered nationalism enjoyed a resurgence, the emperor-as-organ idea came under harsh criticism, as did Minobe for articulating it. Minobe explained his organ theory in 1914 in one of his "Lectures on the Constitution." The phrase *kunmin dōchi*, which means "joint rule of emperor and people," was used widely in early-Meiji political discussions.

University of Tokyo's Political Influence

The influence of political theorists such as Yoshino and Minobe was heightened by the fact that Japan's public life was dominated in the Taishō years by graduates of the University of Tokyo, where the two taught. This chart of the alma maters of Japan's prime ministers and cabinet members from 1918 to 1945 shows their percentages; the University of Tokyo's dominance would be greater yet if the war years had not sent a disproportionate number of military men into the government.

Institution	Percentage of prime ministers from	Percentage of cabinet ministers from
University of Tokyo	26	45
University of Kyoto	4	6
Waseda or Keiō University	4	8
Other Japanese universities	4	8
Foreign universities	4	3
Military cadet schools	52	11
None or unknown	5	20

Kingu (King) was founded in 1925 as a general-interest magazine for Taishō-era pleasure devotees who wanted a menu of romance, fads, sports, current events, and humor. The cover of the first issue gained wide attention for its depiction of the fashion-conscious, sophisticated "modern" woman.

It is a seldom used expression today, but formerly we used the phrase *kunmin dōchi* to express the idea of constitutional government. It states quite simply the flavor of constitutional government, that is, that we, the people, are not only the governed; we are at the same time members of the governing group. While we submit to the authority of the state, at the same time we participate in the government of the state indirectly through the parliament. When the monarch and the people jointly exercise state authority true constitutional monarchy exists. . . .

In the modern idea of the state the monarch does not stand outside the state; he himself constitutes one of the elements of the state. Nor does the monarch possess the state as though it were his personal property; the state itself is a corporation. The monarch does not rule in his own private interest but in the interest of the whole state. In fine, the monarch is an organ of the state and whether or not the term "organ" is used this idea is generally endorsed by all but those who insist on closing their eyes to the truth.

The Taishō-era vitality was reflected vividly in the literary world, which was heavily influenced by the naturalist school, a movement of novelists determined to present human beings realistically, in the most "natural" way. These writers tended to focus on the dark side of human nature, on sexual promiscuity, on violence, on a person's inner demons and the social environment that created them. Their works so often were autobiographical that they came to be known popularly as "I novels."

Tanizaki Jun'ichirō, though not a naturalist, took up similar themes and was known for a rare ability to capture the spirit of restless city youth. A native of Tokyo who moved to western Honshu in the 1920s, he was preoccupied with relationships between men and women, particularly the sometimes mystical, often masochistic way in which men are drawn to women. His 1924–25 novel *Chijin no ai*, literally "A fool's love," and published in English as *Naomi*, was about two young people, Jōji and Naomi, who move from one escapade to another, always seeking fun but never satisfied. Tanizaki succeeded so well in describing the youth of his age that the act of defying convention for the sake of pleasure came to be called "Naomism." Here, Jōji talks with his girlfriend Naomi about the challenge—and joy—of dressing with flair.

"My darling Naomi, I don't just love you, I worship you. You're my treasure. You're a diamond that I found and polished. I'll buy anything that'll make you beautiful. I'll give you my whole salary. . . . You'll be such a lady, you won't even be ashamed to mix with Westerners."

I often used phrases like "mix with Westerners" and "like a Westerner." Clearly this pleased her. "What do you think?" she'd say, trying out different expressions in the mirror. "Don't you think I look like a Westerner when I do this?" Apparently she studied the actresses' movements when we went to the movies, because she was very good at imitating them. In an instant she could capture the mood and idiosyncrasies of an actress. Pickford laughs like this, she'd say; Pina Menicheli moves her eyes like this; Geraldine Farrar does her hair up this way. Loosening her hair, she'd put it into this shape and that.

"Very good—better than any actor. Your face looks so Western."

"Does it? *Where* does it look Western?"

"Your nose and your teeth."

"My teeth?" She pulled her lips back and studied the row of teeth in the mirror. They were wonderfully straight and glossy.

"Anyway, you're different from other Japanese, and ordinary Japanese clothes don't do anything for you. How would it be if you wore Western clothes? Or Japanese clothes in some new style?" . . . .

"How about a narrow-sleeved kimono with an informal sash?"

"That'd be fine. Anything's all right as long as you try for original styles. I wonder if there isn't some outfit that's neither Japanese, Chinese, nor Western . . . ."

"If there is, will you buy it for me?"

"Of course I will."

The most talked-about Taishō political radicals—certainly the ones most worrisome to the conservative establishment— were the socialist and communist groups who looked for leadership to Russia, which had a Communist revolution in 1917. Driven underground by the government after the 1904–5 Russo-Japanese War, these groups reemerged in the energetic intellectual climate of the late 1910s, enlivening intellectual circles with radical, activist tactics and intense debates over nearly every political issue. Two essays illustrate the varying degrees of radicalism that left-wing intellectuals espoused, usually in pursuit of similar goals. Kōtoku Shūsui,

Novelists do write some terrible things, don't they.
—Naturalist novelist Tayama Katai's memoirs, *Thirty Years in Tokyo*, 1917

Mary Pickford, Pina Menicheli, and Geraldine Farrar

Mary Pickford, Pina Menicheli, and Geraldine Farrar were popular American actresses and singers of the 1920s.

The article titles of the February 1, 1914, issue of the popular journal *Seikō*, "Success," illustrate the individualistic concern with self-development that preoccupied café society.

How I Remain Spiritually Vital

The Spirit of Individualism in European and American Young People

The Single Man and the Spirit of Independence

Recollections: My Independent Life of Struggle

The Effect of Zen in Strengthening the Spirit

How to Use Time Efficiently

Kanahara Akiyoshi: Successful Local Farmer

The Most Successful Way to Nurture Young People

How to Start a Billiards Business

A Guide to the February Entrance Examinations

Japanese Labor Disputes in the Taishō Years

One reason that public life seemed stormy at times in the 1910s and 1920s was that the growth of labor and industry prompted a concomitant increase in labor disputes. The entire decade after the Sino-Japanese War had produced about 150 labor struggles. But by the 1920s, each year produced twice that number.

Year	Labor disputes	Participants in disputes
1910	10	2,937
1920	64	7,852
1925	293	89,387
1926	495	127,267
1927	383	103,350
1928	393	101,893
1929	576	172,144
1930	907	191,834

the leading voice of mainstream socialist thought, used an editorial in the newspaper *Heimin Shimbun* to explain why he could not support parliamentary government.

If I were to put in a nutshell the way I think now, it would be along the following lines: A real social revolution cannot possibly be achieved by means of universal suffrage and a parliamentary policy. There is no way to reach our goal of socialism other than by the direct action of the workers, united as one. . . .

As a member of the socialist party there are certain things I believe are important for attaining our end. What we are aiming at is a fundamental revolution in economic organization—the abolition of the wages system, in other words. Now, I believe that, in order to attain this end, it is more important to arouse the consciousness of ten workers than it is to get a thousand signatures on a petition for universal suffrage. I also believe that it is more urgent for us to use ¥10 for promoting the solidarity of the workers than it is to spend ¥2,000 on an electoral campaign and that there is far more merit in holding a single discussion with a group of workers than there is in making ten speeches in parliament. . . .

At a time like this when many comrades are zealously engaged in the movement for universal suffrage, I have been extremely reluctant to say what has been on my mind. . . . But my conscience will not allow me to stay silent any longer. . . . I decided to commit myself to paper in the firm hope that comrades will criticise and comment on what I have to say. I also hope that all comrades will recognise the sincerity of my views.

The anarchist Kaneko Fumiko's cynicism went even farther than Kōtoku's, as she explains in her autobiography. Born in poverty and reared by abusive parents, she was sent to Korea to live with a cruel grandmother. She eventually lost faith in humanity altogether and became a nihilist, a person who believes that life has no meaning. After being tried and convicted in 1925 on trumped-up charges of scheming to kill the emperor, she refused to cooperate with authorities. When her death sentence was commuted to life in jail, she tore up the commutation papers, and on July 23, 1926, hanged herself in her jail cell—at the age of twenty-three.

Although I had once pinned all my hopes on putting myself through school, believing that I could thereby make something of myself, I now realized the futility of this all too clearly. No amount of struggling for an education is going to help one get ahead in this world. And what does it mean to get ahead anyway? Is there any more worthless lot than the so-called great people of this world? What is so admirable about being looked up to by others? I do not live for others. What I had to achieve was my own freedom, my own satisfaction. I had to be myself. . . .

I could not accept socialist thought in its entirety. Socialism seeks to change society for the sake of the oppressed masses, but is what it would accomplish truly for their welfare? Socialism would create a social upheaval "for the masses," and the masses would stake their lives in the struggle together with those who had risen up on their behalf. But what would the ensuing change mean for them? Power would be in the hands of the leaders, and the order of the new society would be based on that power. The masses would become slaves all over again to that power. What is revolution, then, but the replacing of one power with another?

On the streets, the increased democracy sometimes took a disruptive form. In 1912, only months after Emperor Meiji's death, huge demonstrations brought down a cabinet over military interference in the government. In 1914, news that the German firm Siemens had bribed Japanese naval officials to secure contracts prompted six weeks of demonstrations. The largest disruption came in 1918, when fishermen's wives who lived along the Japan Sea coast took to the streets over high rice prices. By September, demonstrations and riots by millions of people had occurred in hundreds of towns and cities, resulting in 25,000 arrests, many deaths, and a great deal of lost property. The government reacted by reducing rice prices, but also put heavy restrictions on press coverage of the riots. An August 26, 1918, article in one of Japan's largest newspapers, the *Osaka Asahi Shimbun*, describes a meeting of more than 200 reporters who criticized the government's efforts to limit their coverage.

Each reporter wore a different countenance, but they all expressed the same spirit. The place was filled with passionate men. Their applause was thunderous, as noisy as fireworks, because they all wanted, each as much as the other, to impeach the cabinet. . . . Matsumoto Muneshige of *Ise Shimbun* stood up, shouting, "Mr. Chairman!" He said that his company's invitation to this rally had been mysteriously opened by some unknown person and that local officials had inquired of each news company whether or

Policeman arresting Nakasone Sadayo, May 1, 1921: What sort of a woman are you! Demonstrating when you should be home looking after your children!"

Nakasone: What sort of man are you! A proletarian who works for the capitalists! Take a look at yourself!

—Socialist leaflet, *Fujin mondai* (Women's problems), June 8, 1921

not it would be attending. No one was surprised at this kind of shady behavior by local officials, given the actions of the central government.

Representatives of each newspaper began to speak, one after another. . . . Their speeches were ardent; the men appeared to be breathing fire.

At one o'clock we took a lunch break. No one could calm down, however. Even though we feasted on meat and drank liquor, everyone was worrying silently about the judgment day coming to our beloved Japan. They had in their minds the evil omen that the ancients used to mutter, "a white rainbow pierced the sun."

When it was time for dessert, Sakai Hiroshi of *Kobe Yūshin* shouted, "Impeach the cabinet!" . . . The last speech was given by Murayama, the chair. The meeting ended at 2:00, with people shouting "banzai."

Among the most effective demonstrations were those calling for universal male suffrage. The suffrage movement waxed and waned through the early Taishō years, then peaked in the 1920s, partly because one of the political parties, the Kenseikai, now embraced the issue quite vigorously, as did journalists, intellectuals, and unions. By mid-decade, even conservative legislators had decided that an expansion of suffrage was needed to prevent revolt from below. As a result, on March 25, 1925, the legislature passed the universal male suffrage law, quadrupling the electorate. A smaller number of activists also demonstrated for women's suffrage, but that would not come for two more decades.

1. Members of the House of Representatives shall establish each election district. They will establish the election district and the number of representatives to be elected from that district on the basis of statistical tables.

5. Japanese male citizens aged twenty-five and above have the right to vote. Japanese male citizens aged twenty-five and above have the right to be elected.

6. The following do not have the right to vote or to be elected:
   1. A person judged incompetent or quasi-incompetent.
   2. A bankrupt person who has not been reinstated.
   3. A person who, because of poverty, receives public or private relief or aid.

white rainbow

The "white rainbow" referred to pre-modern Chinese farmers who would murmur that phrase when contemplating revolution. It prompted the government to act harshly against *Asahi*, threatening to shut it down.

Murayama

Murayama Ryūhei was *Asahi*'s president.

There is a constitutional problem. The elder statesmen have completely disregarded House of Representatives forces in asking Count Terauchi to form a transcendental Cabinet. . . . The question is whether or not our country's politics will follow the people's desires. The question is whether or not popular suffrage will be realized. The question, in other words, is whether the spirit of the constitution will be realized.

—*Tokyo Asahi Shimbun* editorial, October 7, 1916, when the unpopular, military-oriented Terauchi Masatake was selected prime minister.

4. A person who has no fixed place of residence.
5. A person who has been sentenced to more than one year of jail, or has been sentenced to six years of penal servitude.

The lower house of Japan's parliament, called the Diet, meets in its chambers on August 28, 1923, just four days before the Great Kantō earthquake leveled much of Tokyo. The prime minister and his cabinet members are seated on the rear platform.

While Japan remained active abroad during the Taishō years, acting as a colonial power in Korea and Taiwan and working to expand commercial interests in China, its general approach to world affairs was cooperative. When a set of multinational agreements was signed in Washington in 1921 to curb worldwide military spending, Japan was one of the most conciliatory countries, accepting limits on naval spending that undermined its position relative to the other two great naval powers, the United States and Great Britain. Japan signed the 1928 Kellogg-Briand Pact, which renounced war as a way to solve problems. And it followed a peaceful policy toward China. Indeed, Japan's foreign minister through most of the late 1920s, Shidehara Kikujirō, irritated Japanese nationalists several times by supporting tariff

Koreans Living in Japan

One result of Japan's colonialism in Asia during these years was a dramatic increase in the number of Koreans living in Japan.

Year	Korean population
1909	790
1915	3,989
1920	30,175
1925	133,710
1930	298,091

autonomy for China and resisting opportunities to use Chinese weakness for Japan's benefit. This 1929 policy statement of the Minseitō, the political party then in power, captures Shidehara's philosophy.

Improvement of Relations with China. One of the most urgent needs of the day is the improvement of Sino-Japanese relations and the deepening of a neighborly friendship between the two countries. In connection with changes in the "unequal treaties," our policy of friendly cooperation with China has already been demonstrated in a practical way by the holding of the Special Customs Conference and the Extraterritoriality Conference. . . . In their relations each country must understand and give sympathetic consideration to the special viewpoint of the other, and thereby seek a fair and impartial point of balance. To chase about aimlessly after minor interests is not the way to preserve the main interest. To move troops about rashly is not the way to enhance the national prestige. What this administration desires is co-existence and co-prosperity. Especially in the economic relations between the two countries must there be free and untrammeled development. Our country is determined not only to reject an aggressive policy for

The martial ideals of fortitude and physical strength that traditional men valued so highly were instilled daily at elite institutions such as the Peers School for aristocratic boys. The school swim club poses for a group photo in the summer of 1912 at a beach near Kamakura.

any part of China but also to offer willingly our friendly cooperation in the attainment of the aspiration of the Chinese people. . . .

Promotion of Arms Limitation. At this time we must, in cooperation with the other powers, resolutely promote the establishment of an international agreement. The object of this agreement should not be restricted merely to the limitation of arms but should include substantial reduction in arms. The empire's sincere attitude in this matter has already often been demonstrated. Although plans for such an agreement have repeatedly met with difficulties in the past, public demand is more intense, and the time is becoming ripe for the accomplishment of this cherished desire. It is believed that the consummation of this great world undertaking will not be difficult if each power approaches this matter in a spirit of mutual conciliation.

The American representatives, former President Calvin Coolidge, President Herbert Hoover, and Secretary of State Frank B. Kellogg, announce to representatives of other governments their acceptance of the Treaty for Renunciation of War, known as the Kellogg-Briand Pact, in the East Room of the White House on July 4, 1929.

Reining in Diversity

If pluralism, internationalism, and wider involvement in government marked Japan's public face in the 1910s and 1920s, nationalism and a yearning for old values marked its inner reality. This traditionalist core, which made members of the conservative establishment deeply nervous about Western ways, shows up forcefully according to the experience of the feminist Ishimoto Shizue. Reared according to

Founded in 1924, the Women's Suffrage League illustrated the increasing political engagement of women after they were given the right to attend political rallies at the beginning of the decade. By appearing before the league in 1926, Prime Minister Wakatsuki Reijirō made it clear that officials were quite aware of women's growing influence in politics.

traditional, elite values, Ishimoto was encouraged by her husband to become a "modern" woman—educated, self-sufficient, involved in public life. When she followed his advice, however, she discovered that he had another side. When he decided to run for the legislature, or Diet, he found her independence an impediment to his own popularity. In time, Ishimoto was faced with the choice of reverting to the submissive wife's role or leaving him. Painfully, she chose the latter, as she explained in the mid-1930s in her best-selling memoir, *Facing Two Ways.* She was elected to the Diet herself after World War II.

After his long and hard effort to put spirit into a doll-like creature, and just as his labor began to bear fruit, that is to say, just as I learned to express myself, my husband said to me one day that he thought my appearance was losing charm for him.

Now he frankly declared that the beauty of a Japanese woman lay only in her naïveté. He pointed to the delicate feminine figures in the old prints, pronouncing them his ideal. What a contradiction! . . . He who once had undertaken to educate his wife with a view to making her as active and independent as any English or American woman was now gloating over Japanese dolls in the old prints as types to emulate! . . .

When he discussed the proposed entry into the Diet, his friends with one accord insisted that the wife of a candidate for the House of Peers must absolutely conform to the feudal code. She must not talk about women's rights and women's personality. . . .

The women's movement of the future will not demand equality with men, but will plan how men and women can live in harmony and how they can create a wholesome family and home. It is an empty argument to advocate that women should ignore their husbands and children to develop self.

—Yamada Waka, social commentator, *Taiyō* (The Sun), September 1918

To give up all my social interests and maintain a dead silence even within the narrow walls of home was like being sentenced to prison. But my devotion to my husband, my effort to bring him back to his better self, made me pay any price for his sake. However, after paying the heavy costs of this campaign, opportunity for which comes only once in every seven years, he failed to win a seat. . . .

As I spent unhappy days in praying for a bright passage to open for my husband, he proceeded to discover a dark one leading in another direction. His injurious friends led him to shadowy corners. . . . Geisha and the teahouses were the fortresses for these men in this gloomy battle—fortresses which the wife could not assault. . . .

Japan's aggressive side revealed itself often in its relations with nearby Asian neighbors. From 1910 on, it ruled Korea harshly, with an eye to providing resources for Japan itself. And in 1915, well before Foreign Minister Shidehara's conciliatory approach had had a chance to take root, the government decided to take advantage of Europe's preoccupation with World War I by seeking imperialist-style rights along the China coast. The Japanese issued a list of twenty-one demands to Chinese president Yuan Shikai on January 18, demands intended to improve Japan's hold on the Asian giant. The demands were divided into five groups: the first four groups aimed to assure Japanese dominance in China's mining and manufacturing businesses, while the fifth sought to make China into a Japanese protectorate. The weak Chinese government accepted the first four groups in the name of maintaining peace, but insisted on further

Chinese (on the left) and Japanese diplomats sign the document ratifying Japan's Twenty-One Demands in Beijing on May 25, 1915. While China officially agreed to most of the demands, "so that the cordial relationship between the two countries may be further consolidated," anger in Beijing undermined the Chinese government and sparked anti-Japanese reform movements.

I am ashamed of a nation which commits robbery to grow big. . . . Japanese people! Be liberated from the sword, from secret diplomacy, from warships, from greed for new territories, from false history! How long are you going to continue your worship of the sabre?

—Christian social activist Kagawa Toyohiko, *Chūgai Shinpō*, July 11, 1919

discussion of the fifth group. As Japan expected, the Western powers were too preoccupied with World War I to respond effectively. The articles in the fifth group, which never were actualized, show just how bold Japan had become in its approach to China.

1. The Chinese Central Government shall employ influential Japanese as advisers in political, financial, and military affairs.

2. Japanese hospitals, churches, and schools in the interior of China shall be granted the right of owning land.

3. Inasmuch as the Japanese Government and the Chinese Government have had many cases of disputes between Japanese and Chinese police which caused no little misunderstanding, it is for this reason necessary that the police departments of important places (in China) shall be jointly administered by Japanese and Chinese or that the police departments of these places shall employ numerous Japanese, so that they may at the same time help to plan for the improvement of the Chinese Police Service.

4. China shall purchase from Japan a fixed amount of munitions of war (say 50 percent or more of what is needed by the Chinese Government) or . . . there shall be established in China a Sino-Japanese jointly-worked arsenal. Japanese technical experts are to be employed and Japanese material to be purchased. . . .

6. If China needs foreign capital to work mines, build railways and construct harbor-works (including dockyards) in the Province of Fukien, Japan shall be first consulted.

7. China agrees that Japanese subjects shall have the right of missionary propaganda in China.

By the late 1910s, the Japanese controlled every aspect of national life in Korea, managing agricultural policy, administering justice, and running the schools, while suppressing speech and barring Koreans from most political activities. The heavy-handed control was not accepted passively by the Koreans, however. In early March 1919, some 2 million people participated in 3,200 anti-Japanese demonstrations across the Korean peninsula, triggering tens of thousands of arrests and as many as 7,500 deaths. At the heart of the March First Movement, as the episode came to be called, was a "declaration of independence," read at Seoul's Pagoda Park, calling on the world to support Koreans who wanted to retake control of their own country.

We hereby declare that Korea is an independent state and that Koreans are a self-governing people. We proclaim it to the nations of the world in affirmation of the principle of the equality of all nations, and we proclaim it to our posterity, preserving in perpetuity the right of national survival. We make this declaration on the strength of five thousand years of history as an expression of the devotion and loyalty of twenty million people. We claim independence in the interest of the eternal and free development of our people and in accordance with the great movement for world reform based upon the awakening conscience of mankind. This is the clear command of heaven, the course of our times, and a legitimate manifestation of the right of all nations to coexist and live in harmony. Nothing in the world can suppress or block it.

For the first time in several thousand years, we have suffered the agony of alien suppression for a decade, becoming a victim of the policies of aggression and coercion, which are relics from a bygone era. . . .

Alas! In order to rectify past grievances, free ourselves from present hardships, eliminate future threats, stimulate and enhance the weakened conscience of our people, eradicate the shame that befell our nation, ensure proper development of human dignity, avoid leaving humiliating legacies to our children, and usher in lasting and complete happiness for our posterity, the most urgent task is to firmly establish national independence. Today when human nature and conscience are placing the forces of justice and humanity on our side, if every one of our twenty million people arms himself for battle, whom could we not defeat and what could we not accomplish? . . .

Nothing brought out the nationalistic, repressive side of Japanese officials more than the activities of political radicals, particularly socialists. In part because nearby Russia had become communist in 1917, in part because most current leaders remembered the Meiji regime's own revolutionary

The ground campaign in the Russo-Japanese War began on March 14, 1904, when Japanese landed troops at Chemulpo (present-day In'chon), just southwest of Seoul, Korea. Fifteen Japanese soldiers pose in front of a Chemulpo building before beginning the trek north to Manchuria. It was Japan's triumph in that war that set the stage for its control of Korea as a colony.

roots, and in part because they feared the loss of social harmony, officials worked continually to prevent communist ideas from spreading. After the end of World War I, they unleashed a period of increasingly harsh laws and enforcement procedures. When police officers viciously murdered the socialists Ōsugi Sakae and Itō Noe during the chaos following the great 1923 earthquake, the courts let them off with light sentences. Then on April 22, 1925, less than a month after the passage of the universal male suffrage law, the Diet approved a draconian peace preservation law that made both the advocacy of socialist ideas and the criticism of Japan's *kokutai*, "national essence," illegal. The word *kokutai* was a vague term that connoted Japan's traditional ruling system. The word came to be used constantly throughout the next twenty years, with the same patriotic, emotional force as the flag or pledge of allegiance carries in the United States.

1. Anyone who forms, or knowingly participates in, groups whose goal is to deny the system of private property or to change our national essence shall be sentenced to prison or penal servitude of up to ten years. Anyone who attempts to commit this crime also will be punished.

2. Anyone who engages in discussions intended to carry out the aims of Article One, Clause One shall be sentenced to prison or penal servitude of up to seven years.

3. Anyone who instigates actions by others intended to carry out the aims of Article One, Clause One, shall be sentenced to prison or penal servitude of up to seven years.

4. Anyone intending to carry out the aims of Article One, Clause One who instigates crimes resulting in riots or violence that cause damage to property, bodily injury, or destruction of life, shall be sentenced to prison or penal servitude of up to ten years.

5. Anyone who, intending to carry out the aims of Article One, Clause One or of the crimes described in the three previous clauses, gives money, goods, or other financial benefits to others, or makes promises of such for that same purpose, shall be sentenced to prison or penal servitude of up to five years. Anyone who knowingly demands or receives such remuneration, or makes a commitment for such remuneration, shall be given the same punishment.

6. Anyone guilty of the offenses in the five preceding articles who surrenders voluntarily to the police shall receive a lighter sentence or be exonerated.

The newspaper Tokyo Nichi Nichi Shimbun *devoted an entire page on February 11, 1914, to stories, photos, and sketches of the tumultuous demonstrations that had occurred the previous day, after the public revelation that Japanese officials had taken bribes as inducements to purchase naval supplies from the German firm Siemens. The bandaged man at the top is a* Nichi Nichi *reporter, Hashimoto Shigeru, who was beaten up by henchmen of Home Minister Hara Kei when he went to the minister's residence to inquire about the scandal. The incident presaged the government's broader crackdown on opposition voices that would occur in the 1920s.*

7. This law shall apply to anyone who commits these crimes, even if that person lives outside the regions where the law has jurisdiction.

The seriousness with which administrative officials took the left-wingers' threat to public order is obvious in Home Ministry figures on the number of publications warned or temporarily banned from publishing in the late 1920s for printing materials deemed likely to "disturb public order." Several more were banned each year for "disturbing morals."

Domestic periodicals punished under the newspaper law, 1925–32

Year	Total number of press organs	Total number of daily newspapers	Total banned for endangering public order	Post-publication warnings
1925	6,899	1,012	154	789
1926	7,600	1,035	251	884
1927	8,350	1,093	331	773
1928	8,445	1,150	345	558
1929	9,191	1,221	374	998
1930	10,130	1,215	504	1,127
1931	10,666	1,280	832	1,546
1932	11,118	1,330	2,081	4,348

During the second half of the 1920s, as the Home Ministry developed administrative procedures to enforce the peace preservation law, the crackdown on leftist students and intellectuals became severe. The Justice Ministry created a "thought section," with special "thought police" to deal with radicals. On the night of March 15, 1928, police raided more than 120 places across the nation, ferreting out supporters of the Japan Communist Party, which had reorganized itself after the passage of universal male suffrage. Nearly 1,600 were arrested that night, and by year's end several political parties and organizations had been banned. Public life remained lively in these years—cafes, shops, and dance halls still attracted young people, intellectuals continued to discuss public policy vigorously, and elections proceeded smoothly.

But for those on the left, the age turned dark, as the memoirs of the labor activist Tanno Setsu make clear. Tanno was living in a home with other socialists when the March 15 raid occurred; though she was not apprehended then, she was jailed later in 1928 and spent most of the next year in prison. Tanno's friend Kokuryō Goichirō, a member of the Japan Communist Party's central committee, died in prison. Watanabe Masanosuke, also a Communist, was Tanno's husband. Having been released from jail, he went to Shanghai for a trade conference in 1928, then apparently was killed by police in Keelung, Taiwan, though officers said he committed suicide. Kobayashi Takejirō, a stockbroker, provided shelter for many of the radicals, though he was not himself an activist. Tanno spent most of the 1930s in jail, but survived the war and became involved in health care until her death at age eighty-five in 1987.

"The gentleman is talking socialism, aren't you?"

"I am. So what?" I challenged him back.

"It's socialism, so you're under arrest. Come with me."

"This is humorous! I'll go wherever you want." I shoved the policeman's hand away and rushed into the Nihonzutsumi police station, which was just across from us.

—Autobiography of the socialist activist Ōsugi Sakae, written in 1922, a year before he was murdered by police.

Kokuryō and I were arrested when the authorities were tracking down those of us who had escaped in the mass arrests of March 15, 1928. . . . After I was questioned and tortured severely for three days, the questioning suddenly stopped. I thought it was strange but decided that the authorities wanted to take their time with the investigation. A week later an official from the national police headquarters came and escorted me to a room different from the interrogation room. The officials were sitting in the room with some sushi prepared for me. I thought it was odd.

As soon as I sat down one of the officers said, "Tanno-san, you mustn't lose heart." I said, "Watanabe was killed, wasn't he?"

They were taken aback and asked, "How did you know?"

I replied, "I can tell by the way you are treating me."

The political police said, "Take it easy today. Relax and eat."

"I don't feel like eating," I replied.

I didn't cry while I was with them, but as soon as I returned to the detention cell I burst into tears. The guard was baffled and asked, "What's the matter? You're usually tough. You weren't tortured today, were you? Your face isn't even swollen. People cry like that only when their parents die." . . .

After I spent twenty-nine days in the Tomizaka police station jail, the landlord of the Asakusa hideout insisted that I move our things out of his house. So I asked the police to transfer me from the Tomizaka police station to the Zōgata station. When I arrived in the Zōgata police station and was placed in the detention room at the end of the hallway, I saw Kobayashi come out of his cell, wearing a dark blue, patterned kimono. . . . I can't describe how seeing him shocked me. We had gotten this kind man in trouble. I didn't say a word about Kobayashi, and the police did not even ask me about him. . . . I couldn't let it be known that I knew Kobayashi, so I pretended not to recognize him. I didn't want him to recognize me either, so I kept out of his sight. His wife, Hagino Osaka, brought him his meals, and at every mealtime, three times a day, he was brought out from his cell. He was treated better because he was merely a sympathizer. Whenever I saw him go back and forth I felt relieved because he was looking well.

Eventually Kobayashi was released. I was shocked to learn later that because he was arrested as a sympathizer his relatives held a family council and declared him legally incompetent to hold property. He could not endure the poverty that followed, and he committed suicide.

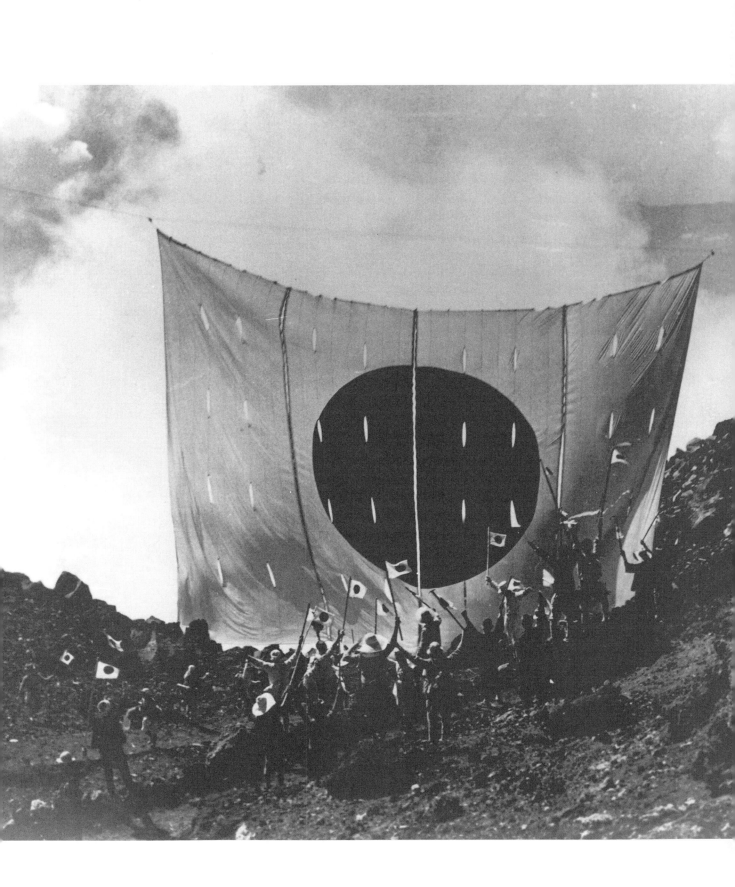

Chapter Six

The Dark Era: 1930–45

F ew nations boast a more peaceful history across the centuries than Japan. For the nation's first thousand years, fighting was so scattered and sporadic that its cities did not need the walls that Asia's other urban centers required. And for nearly 300 years after 1600, Japan avoided wars completely, experiencing the "Tokugawa peace" that provided such rich education and culture. The common narrative of outsiders, however, tells a different story, describing the Japanese as a people of war. The reason for the error lies partly in the dramatic legends that grew out of Japan's one long warring period during the medieval centuries when the samurai class ruled, and it lies even more in the brief but devastating years of 1931–45, when Japan took on much of the world in World War II.

The 1920s came to a close with Japan in conflict, torn between the forces of pluralistic democracy and authoritarian imperialism. Some historians argue that the latter was dominant, while others contend that the forces were in balance, or that momentum lay with pluralism and diversity. Whoever is right, a series of events occurred at the turn of the decade to stop movement toward openness and push Japan in a darker, more aggressive direction. One of these was the worldwide depression, which followed on an already tumultuous economic decade, throwing the country's finances into disarray and undermining confidence in the internationalist policies of big business. Farmers were hit especially hard, particularly after bad harvests in 1931 and 1932, and workers by the hundreds of thousands lost their jobs, creating widespread anger and malaise.

A second development that propelled the national mood in a chauvinist direction was the Manchurian Incident of September 18, 1931. On that night, Japanese military officers in the Manchurian city of Mukden, known today as Shenyang, secretly bombed a segment of track on their own South Manchurian Railway, hoping to push Japan

The rising spirit of nationalism was exemplified on August 12, 1934, by a group of patriots who carried Japan's flag up the 12,000-foot Mt. Fuji and hung it above the crater at the summit.

The 1918 agreements ending World War I allowed Japan to station troops and set up garrisons in territories formerly occupied by Germany in northeastern China. One of those sites was Jinan in Shandong province, where Japanese residents welcomed their national troops in 1928.

into a more aggressive stance in northeastern China. The bomb did little damage, but the plot worked. Defying the Tokyo government, Japanese troops in China took control of Mukden, alleging that they had to protect themselves against potential Chinese terrorists, and by the next year, Japan had turned Manchuria into a puppet state called Manchukuo. Perhaps the most important result was the impact on the Japanese public. Frustrated by the depression and a decade of conciliatory foreign policies on the one hand, and convinced, on the other, that Chinese zealots had blown up the track, the press responded with loud demands for greater military activity on the continent.

The years that followed saw a steady, rapid movement toward ultranationalism: ever-increasing support for more aggressive foreign policies, and less and less tolerance for dissident political views. The Japanese social fabric never unraveled during these years. Elections continued as usual, with liberals winning as often as conservatives. Constitutional government remained strong, as did the rule of law. Dissent still was heard, though less often and within narrower bounds. But the general mood turned threatening, as ultranationalist rhetoric became the norm. Right-wing groups became not only louder but more mainstream. Several terrorist incidents resulted in a period when prime ministers were chosen largely from the lists of generals and admirals. Slogans such as "white peril," "Japanese Monroe Doctrine," and "Asia for the Asiatics" were heard everywhere. And not long after another military incident occurred near the Marco Polo Bridge near Beijing on July 7, 1937, the government committed Japan to a general war in China. The Pacific War had begun.

That war was a disaster in almost every way. Although Japan took Shanghai after several months of fighting, its troops soon became bogged down in China, and near the end of 1937 they committed brutal atrocities in the Nanjing area, including the massacre of perhaps 100,000 civilians. In 1940, the Japanese signed a Tripartite Alliance drawing them close to Germany and Italy. And when the United States began cutting off rubber and oil sales to Japan after negotiations failed in 1940 and 1941, Japan's leaders decided to launch a surprise attack on Pearl Harbor, a naval base in Hawaii. It was a brilliant blunder that wreaked havoc on America's Pacific fleet but assured Japan's eventual defeat in World War II, due to the technological and material superiority of the Western power. Although Japan won a number of early victories, while the Americans geared up for full-fledged conflict, the tide had turned by May of 1942. By the time the war ended a little more than three years later, Japan had lost its empire, a quarter of its wealth, and nearly 3 million people. Some sixty-six cities had been bombed, two of them by atomic bombs, and only 35 percent of Tokyo's homes remained standing. The war had left the country humbled and destitute.

The Militarist Turn

It is hard to imagine a document that better captures the transition from the 1920s to the 1930s than the Christian pacifist Fujii Takeshi's poem "Go To Ruin!" published in July 1930, the month of his death. Disturbed by declining morals, rising talk of military expansion, and corruption in the government, Fujii employed Biblical images to call his beloved land to account. Although his words describe the country's imperialistic turn, his passion illustrates the continuing willingness of many dissenters to speak up.

I know not whether Japan is growing or declining,
Whether my beloved country is blessed or cursed.
I believed she was growing; I saw her as blessed.
But I cannot find a single statesman in this country
Who loves righteousness and acts justly.
I leave no stone unturned, but still I find not one soul
Who seeks after truth for its own sake.
Young men stick close to the ground, like chickens, forgetting
    eternity;
Young women pursue the foolish and the shameful, trampling
    on pearls—like swine. . . .

Surely, Japan is falling, like flesh peeling from lepers.
The name of Japan, my beloved fatherland, soon will be
    removed from the earth;
The Great Crocodile will devour her.
Be ruined, you country of disgraceful young women, you country of spineless young men!

The Great Crocodile

The Great Crocodile refers to the United States.

You country of insects and beasts who neither know nor love
    truth: Be ruined!

I wholly agree with my teacher who said on his deathbed:
"You tell people that I am leaving
This disgraceful country with no regrets."
To the people, the country, that betrays truth: Cursed be you!
To my Heavenly Father: Thy will be done!

**Right-wing organizations with names such as Black Ocean
Society and Black Dragon Society had advocated patriotism
and military expansion since the middle Meiji years. Now, at
the beginning of the 1930s, they became more active,
encouraged by the restless public and the government's
attempts to restrict socialist and left-wing thought. The
event that roused them more than any other was Japan's ratification of the London Naval Treaty in the fall of 1930. Japan
had gone into the conference hoping to increase its spending
on large warships to 70 percent of what the British and
Americans spent—10 percent more than was allowed under
the treaties then in effect. After intense negotiations,
Japan's representatives had compromised, however, maintaining the 60-percent limit on most items. The reaction in
Japan was much like that at the end of the Russo-Japanese
War. Although both sides actually had compromised in the
negotiations, conservative groups thought their diplomats
had bowed to imperialist bullying.**

**Prime Minister Hamaguchi Osachi came in for particular-
ly harsh criticism as the one whose administration ratified
the treaty, and in November 1930 he was shot by a right-
wing youth at Tokyo station. He died the following August.
The memoirs of Harada Kumao, political secretary to Japan's
former Prime Minister Saionji Kimmochi, indicate that moderate officials realized the danger ultranationalist groups
posed to democracy. In this 1930 diary entry, Harada has just
traveled to Saionji's villa at Okitsu, some 125 miles southwest of Tokyo, to report on the Hamaguchi shooting. Ogawa
Heikichi, railways minister from 1927 to 1929, was a well-
known supporter of rightist organizations, and he had been
jailed for bribery during his time in office. The Kokuhonsha,
or National Foundations Society, had been formed by right-
wing bureaucrats in 1924 to oppose democracy, which they
saw as leading to a decline in traditional values.**

My teacher

Fuji's teacher was the
era's most prominent
Christian intellectual,
Uchimura Kanzō.

Today we witness the burial of the "ideal" of
our beloved Japan. In fact, it may be the
burial of the Japan that has lost its ideals. This
tragedy reduces mere human anger and grief
to futility. . . . Let us bury this country in order
to revive the ideal Japan.

—Tokyo University professor Yanaihara
Tadao, in a commemorative lecture for Fujii
Takeshi, October 1, 1937, shortly after Japan
had gone to war with China

Prime Minister Hamaguchi is carried down from a Tokyo railway station platform after being shot on November 1, 1930, by an ultranationalist who blamed him for compromising too much with the Western powers in the London Naval Treaty. Though Hamaguchi lived until the following August, he never recovered from the wounds and never again took an active part in politics.

I pointed out to the Prince that Hamaguchi's assailant was a member of the Aikokusha, a right-wing organization, and that he was tied up with Iwata Ainosuke, the henchman of Ogawa, the former Railways Minister. There's talk of various reasons for the action—the treaty, the depression, and the like; but the fact remains it is sheer gangsterism. The Prince commented,

"Well, when the public is treated to the spectacle of admirals and vice-admirals, and similar presumably well-informed persons, issuing statements that 'the supreme command has been contemned' or that 'the London Treaty is against the nation's interest,' of course such statements are an incitement to young ignoramuses. . . .

On my return to Tokyo I met with both the Railways Minister and the Foreign Minister. Then, curious about the results of investigation of Hamaguchi's assailant, I called at the Justice Ministry to talk with the Vice Minister. Since he was out, I talked with . . . the Chief Secretary, who had no notable new developments to report. It seemed to me that while the courts are vigorous in inquiring into left-wing activities, as far as right-wing activities are concerned the courts are not only lenient but seem intentionally inclined to be more or less protective. . . . The criminal in this case is affiliated with the Kokuhonsha. The facts, further, are that he had been staying in the home of an influential member of the Kokuhonsha, . . . that the pistol which he used in his assault of Hamaguchi belonged to a certain Aikokusha member . . . , and that he had spent the night before his crime in a drunken carouse with a number of friends. These are all facts. Where the money came from we can well imagine. When a case like this is investigated thoroughly, it invariably develops that someone is behind it all.

On November 22, 1932, the New York World ran a cartoon titled "The Grabber's Answer," criticizing Japan's creation of the state of Manchukuo out of Manchuria after a League of Nations commission headed by the Earl of Lytton had condemned Japan's aggression. The cartoon shows a group of Western leaders in Geneva, where the League of Nations was headquartered. A gun with a bayonet, labeled "Japan's Plea of 'Self Defense,'" has been thrust through the "Lytton Report on Manchukuo."

South Manchuria Railway

Changchun lay on the South Manchuria Railway, about 175 miles north of Mukden; Kirin is some 60 miles east of Changchun.

Japanese refer to World War II in Asia as the Great Pacific War, or *Taiheiyō Sensō,* and they regard the Manchurian Incident of 1931 as the beginning of that war. In the months after the takeover of Mukden, the Japanese forces in Manchuria, known as the Guandong Army, took control of nearly all of southern Manchuria through a series of military and political maneuvers. Although the government in Tokyo officially opposed the Guandong Army's aggressive approach, it was unable to curtail it, partly because many middle level officials supported what was going on in Manchuria and partly because public opinion was so vociferous in favor of Japanese expansion on the Asian continent.

By 1932, the puppet state of Manchukuo had been created, and in 1933, when the League of Nations criticized Japan as the aggressor in Manchuria, Japan left the League, creating a rift that would increase with each passing year. Despite these realities, Japan's official stance—following the Manchurian Incident articulated in a 1932 "progress report" prepared by the South Manchurian Railway Company, was that Chinese had attacked the railway and Japan was acting in self-defense.

September 24, 1931.

1. The Japanese Government has constantly been exercising honest endeavors, in pursuance of its settled policy, to foster friendly relations between Japan and China and to promote the common prosperity and well-being of the two countries. Unfortunately, the conduct of officials and individuals of China for some years past has been such that our national sentiment has frequently been irritated. In particular, unpleasant incidents have taken place one after another in the regions of Manchuria and Mongolia in which Japan is interested in an especial degree, until the impression has gained strength in the minds of the Japanese people that Japan's fair and friendly attitude is not being reciprocated by China in a like spirit. Amidst an atmosphere of perturbation and anxiety thus created, a detachment of Chinese troops destroyed the tracks of the South Manchuria Railway in the vicinity of Mukden and attacked our railway guards at midnight on September 18. . . .

2. The situation became critical, as the number of the Japanese guards stationed along the entire railway did not then exceed ten thousand four hundred, while there were in juxtaposition some two hundred and twenty thousand Chinese soldiers. Moreover,

hundreds of thousands of Japanese residents were placed in jeopardy. In order to forestall an imminent disaster, the Japanese army had to act swiftly. . . .

4. The Japanese Government, at the special cabinet meeting of September 19th, took the decision that all possible efforts should be made to prevent the aggravation of the situation, and instructions to that effect were given to the Commander of the Manchurian Garrison. It is true that a detachment was despatched from Changchun to Kirin on September 21st, but it was not with a view to military occupation but only for the purpose of removing a menace to the South Manchuria Railway on its flank. As soon as that object has been attained, the bulk of our detachment will be withdrawn. . . .

5. It may be superfluous to repeat that the Japanese Government harbours no territorial designs in Manchuria.

Calls for expansion into Asia grew more intense as the 1930s progressed. The number of ultranationalist organizations grew too. Some of them conspired to bring down the government, arguing that it was too conciliatory toward Western powers and overly tied to the decadent values of the political parties and big business. On May 15, 1932, for example, some naval officers associated with rightist groups assassinated Prime Minister Inukai Tsuyoshi in an unsuccessful effort to get the military to take over the government. The extremist organizations had various visions about the shape Japan's government should take, but all wanted more activism in Asia: some groups called for Japan to help Asia become independent from Western imperialism, others wanted Asia as a place for Japan's own growth. Hashimoto Kingorō, an army officer who helped to form the ultranationalist soldiers' group, called the Cherry Blossom Society, expresses the desire for Japanese expansion on the Asian continent in his 1930 "Address to Young Men." His resentment of Western hypocrisy and anti-Japanese attitudes is typical; like most Japanese, he felt bitter about both rising protectionism abroad and the U.S. Congress's racist National Origins Act of 1924 that prohibited all Japanese and Chinese immigration to the United States.

We have already said that there are only three ways left to Japan to escape from the pressure of surplus population. We are like a great crowd of people packed into a small and narrow room, and

I do not applaud our quitting the League. The people act as if by withdrawing we have achieved something great, or they believe our achievement is withdrawal itself. . . . This shows the shallowness of thought in the Japanese public.

—Makino Nobuaki, elder statesman, in his diary, February 20, 1933

In the 1930s activists produced a plethora of slogans to publicize their issues. These included:

Yamato damashii ("spirit of Yamato," Japan's ancient name)

Shōwa Restoration (a call for the emperor to actually rule, free from the corrupting control of politicians and businessmen)

Greater East Asia Co-prosperity Sphere (the dream of an Asian economic bloc led by Japan, free of the Western colonial powers)

Japanese Monroe Doctrine (an effort to apply to Asia the American idea that it should be responsible for the defense of its own hemisphere)

White peril (a vision that saw "white" Westerners as threatening Asian independence and peace)

Hakkō ichiu ("eight cords, one roof," an ancient phrase denoting Japanese control of the "eight directions"—that is, the world)

Ichioku isshin ("a hundred million hearts beating as one," heralding national unity behind the war effort)

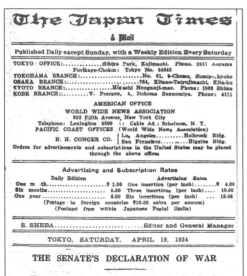

The Japan Times
& Mail

Published Daily except Sunday, with a Weekly Edition Every Saturday

TOKYO OFFICE:............Shiba Park, Kojimachi. Phone. 2617 Aoyama
    Furikaye-Chokin: Tokyo No. 64848
YOKOHAMA BRANCH:....................No. 61, 6-Chome, Sumiyoshi-cho
OSAKA BRANCH:..................784, Kitano-Taiyujimachi, Kita-ku
KYOTO BRANCH:..................Higashi Honganji-mae. Phone: 1063 Shima
KOBE BRANCH:.......V. Pearson, 4, Itchome Sannomiya. Phone: 4111

AMERICAN OFFICE
WORLD WIDE NEWS ASSOCIATION
803 Fifth Avenue, New York City
Telephone: Lexington 6500 :: Cable Ad.: Schelsom, N. Y.
PACIFIC COAST OFFICES (World Wide News Association)
H. H. CONGER CO. { Los Angeles..........Holbrook Bldg.
    { San Francisco..........Higgins Bldg.
Orders for advertisements and subscriptions in the United States may be placed
through the above offices

Advertising and Subscription Rates
Daily Edition
One month......₹ 1.00 One insertion (per inch)......₹ 4.00
Six months......5.00 Three insertions (per inch)....10.00
One year......8.00 Six insertions (per inch) ... 18.00
(Postage to foreign countries ₹10.00 extra per annum)
(Postage free within Japanese Postal limits)

S. SHEBA....................Editor and General Manager

TOKYO, SATURDAY, APRIL 19, 1924

THE SENATE'S DECLARATION OF WAR

There is no denying that the adoption by the American Senate of the exclusion amendment to the Immigration Bill has given a shock to the whole Japanese race such as has never before been felt and which will undoubtedly be remembered for a long time to come. The wonder is, rather, that the shock has not found expression in a louder outburst of indignation than is the case. The knowledge that Senators Johnson, Shortridge and company do not necessarily represent the entire American nation in offering an unnecessary affront, is largely responsible for the spirit of forbearance which seems to be generally ruling the mind of the nation for the present. The country is aware, also, that the Immigration Bill as a whole has yet to be passed by the Senate, to be put through a joint conference of the two Houses and then to receive the signature of President Coolidge before it becomes a law, and it is unquestionably thought unwise to destroy, by ill-measured utterances, the only possible chances that might prove favorable to the Japanese in the meantime.

The adoption by the U.S. Senate on April 16, 1924, of a proposal to bar all Japanese from immigrating prompted a dismayed outcry in Japan, including the charge in Japan's leading English-language newspaper, the semi-official Japan Times, which editorialized that "the Senators were looking for some excuse to get angry" and that the act amounted to a "declaration of war."

there are only three doors through which we might escape, namely emigration, advance into world markets, and expansion of territory. The first door, emigration, has been barred to us by the anti-Japanese immigration policies of other countries. The second door, advance into world markets, is being pushed shut by tariff barriers and the abrogation of commercial treaties. What should Japan do when two of the three doors have been closed to her?

It is quite natural that Japan should rush upon the last remaining door.

It may sound dangerous when we speak of territorial expansion, but the territorial expansion of which we speak does not in any sense of the word involve the occupation or the possessions of other countries, the planting of the Japanese flag thereon, and the declaration of their annexation to Japan. It is just that since the Powers have suppressed the circulation of Japanese materials and merchandise abroad, we are looking for some place overseas where Japanese capital, Japanese skills, and Japanese labor can have free play, free from the oppression of the white race.

We would be satisfied with just this much. What moral right do the world powers, who have themselves closed to us the two doors of emigration and advance into world markets, have to criticize Japan's attempt to rush out of the third and last door?

If they do not approve of this, they should open the doors which they have closed against us and permit the free movement overseas of Japanese emigrants and merchandise. . . .

If it is still protested that our actions in Manchuria were excessively violent, we may wish to ask the white race just which country it was that sent warships and troops to India, South Africa, and Australia and slaughtered innocent natives, bound their hands and feet with iron chains, lashed their backs with iron whips, proclaimed these territories as their own, and still continues to hold them to this very day?

A central concern of Japanese intellectuals in the 1930s was Western hypocrisy, particularly the way Great Britain and the United States opposed Japan's advances in Asia while they held tightly to their own colonies and restricted trade and immigration. Even the more internationalist writers often found common cause with the nationalists on this point. The highly respected Quaker Nitobe Inazō, an undersecretary of the League of Nations, refused to visit the United States after it passed the 1924 immigration Act. And

Kawakami Karl Kiyoshi, who lived in the United States and wrote widely in support of cooperation between Japan and America, worried about the contradictory facets of U.S. policy, which undermined allies in Japan who worked for fairness. In *The Real Japanese Question*, a 1921 book written in response to American immigration policies, Kawakami argues that Caucasians control more than 83 percent of the earth's land while making up only 36 percent of its population. This situation, he argues, undermines the work of those who seek peace.

It was the good luck of the Anglo-Saxon race to gather in its lap most of the desirable colonies in the world. Those European nations that came after it in the race for colonial expansion have had to be contented with territories whose value is often doubtful. And the Asiatic nations, which came still later, not only cannot find any overseas territory available for colonization, but have had to offer their own lands upon the altar of Western ambition. The so-called colonies of Japan, Korea, and Formosa are in reality not colonies at all, for they are already so well populated that they offer no room for Japanese settlers.

Here, in a nutshell, is a condition which should not be ignored in any consideration of international problems affecting the peoples of Asia. It is obvious that the great Powers of the West have accumulated more land than they should rightly own—than they can hold without doing injustice to the smaller nations, which find themselves in a sad plight, due to the impossibility of finding room for their surplus population. The injustice of holding such vast territories would not be so obvious, if they were to recognize, in favor of the small nations, the principle of unhindered immigration and of unrestricted enterprise within those territories. It is when they erect insurmountable walls around themselves and adopt a hidebound policy of exclusion that they become a menace to the welfare of the human race.

It seems to me that any proposition for permanent peace which fails to take into consideration the present inequitable distribution of territory, cannot be carried out without trampling upon the just claims of the smaller nations. An attempt to build permanent peace upon the *status quo* of the world seems as futile as an attempt to rear a Tower of Babel upon a foundation of sands. . . .

And yet any proposition to alter the *status quo* along the line I have suggested would at once be condemned by the opulent,

Formosa

Japan had taken over the island of Taiwan, also known as Formosa, after defeating China in war in 1895.

The August 15, 1938, cover of Shōnen Kurabu (Children's Club) captures the patriotic, military spirit of children's training at the time: the fatherly general, the little boy with rifle and sword, and the simple, military-style attire of the children. The characters at the bottom proclaim: "Interesting! Interesting! Expanded Summer Edition."

Japan must be victorious, not for the sake of her own national interest, but for the salvation of the world.

—1927 essay by Army Staff College instructor Ishiwara Kanji, arguing that Japan must prepare for a coming "final war"

contented Powers as a disturbance of the peace. In their eyes a small nation that should dare raise a finger against the present order of things would be a disturbing element, a rebel and an outlaw.

While the intellectuals focused on international inequities, 1930s schoolchildren were reared increasingly in the virtues of patriotism and loyalty to the emperor. In addition to repeating the Imperial Rescript on Education, students made visits to shrines, took part in military training, and read textbooks that glorified the country and taught reverence for the emperor. In 1937, the Ministry of Education published a document, *Kokutai no hongi* (Cardinal Principles of Our National Entity), which outlined in classical prose what it meant to be a citizen. The book's focus is on the inviolability of the imperial family, the uniqueness of Japanese culture, and the need for citizens to sacrifice themselves for the country. Distributed widely to officials and educators, it was intended to guide teachers in inculcating traditional ethics in their students. *Ohmitakara* is an ancient word for the emperor's subjects that means "great treasures." The last example of benevolence refers to Emperor Meiji.

Evidences of the Emperor's endless love and care for his subjects are constantly seen throughout history. The Emperor graciously treats his subjects as *ohmitakara*, loves and protects them as one would sucklings, and, depending on their cooperation, diffuses his policies widely. With this great August Will the successive Emperors directed their August minds towards the happiness of their subjects, not merely encouraging them to do what is right but pitying and putting aright those who had gone astray. . . .

Such historic facts as the following move us subjects to tears: namely, how on a cold night the Emperor Daigo (898–930 CE) took off his robes to think over the conditions of his subjects—how the Emperor Go-Daigo (1318–38 CE), hearing of the famine throughout the country, said, "if there is anything for which We are to blame, may Heaven punish Us alone. Through what fault are the subjects meeting with this calamity?"—and how he went without his breakfast in order to give to the famished and those stricken with poverty. . . .

And when we read in one of the Emperor's poems:

O that Our subjects were sound in health
Who each in his own sphere toils!

we respectfully witness the Emperor's August compassion which exceeds a parent's love for his child. The Emperor's deeds that remain with us are so many as to defy enumeration when we cite such things as how he enshrines as deities in Yasukuni Shrine those loyal subjects that have sacrificed their lives for the nation . . . , lauding their meritorious deeds without regard to standing or position, and how he poured out his great August heart in giving relief in times of natural calamities. . . . So endlessly great are the Imperial virtues, who is there that cannot but be deeply impressed!

The climax of radical right-wing activity came on February 26, 1936, a snowy Wednesday when some 1,400 troops attempted a coup d'état in Tokyo. When the Young Officers' Movement, a group demanding expansion in China, learned that many of its supporters would be transferred soon to Manchuria, it rose in rebellion. The insurgents took over much of central Tokyo and killed three top officials, including the finance minister. Prime Minister Okada Keisuke escaped only because the rebels confused him with his brother-in-law. The mutineers held parts of the city for two days, demanding, as a condition for giving in, a new cabinet sympathetic to their cause. The authorities refused to budge, however, and the emperor, angry over the murders, demanded that the movement be destroyed. The diary entries of his chief aide, Honjō Shigeru, recall the emperor's reaction to the uprising. The rebellion collapsed on February 29, and nineteen of its leaders were executed after a secret trial. Although this episode marked the end of terrorist-style turbulence, it also led to increased military influence in the government.

The First Day (February 26, 1936). . . . I presented myself before His Majesty and reported that I was mortified at the outbreak of this extraordinary incident. His Majesty was extremely upset and said the incident must be quashed as quickly as possible and a way must be found to turn the disaster into a blessing. He also recalled that I had expressed fears about such an incident breaking out.

I left his presence with a profound sense of mortification. . . .

Around 9:00 AM War Minister Kawashima appeared at the court. He did not express any opinion but merely reported on the current state of affairs. (He read to His Majesty the young activist officers' manifesto.) He said that he was mortified that an incident

Yasukuni Shrine

The Yasukuni Shrine in Tokyo has served since 1869 as the place where spirits of Japan's war dead are memorialized.

of this kind had taken place. In response His Majesty ordered him to quash the incident as quickly as possible. . . .

On this day His Majesty summoned me every 20 or 30 minutes and asked about the course of events and urged that the troops be subdued. Because the lord privy seal had been attacked and was in hiding and the grand chamberlain was seriously injured, and because the incident involved the activities of military men, I, the chief aide-de-camp, alone was in a position to respond to his questions. I realized the gravity of my responsibilities. Even at night, as late as 2:00 AM, His Majesty summoned me. So I assume he did not go to bed until after 2:00 AM. . . .

The Second Day (February 27). . . . During my audience with His Majesty on this day I said that the conduct of the officers who moved the troops cannot be forgiven because they used His Majesty's troops without permission. They have violated the supreme command. But from the standpoint of the spirit that moved them to action, because they were thinking of the good of the nation they should not necessarily be condemned.

His Majesty summoned me later and said, "How can we not condemn even the spirit of these criminally brutal officers who killed my aged subjects who were my hands and feet?" He also said on another occasion, "To kill the old subjects whom I trusted the most is akin to gently strangling me with floss-silk." . . .

Also on this day His Majesty grew impatient with the army authorities for not executing with greater dispatch the measures designed to subjugate the activist troops. He told me that he would "personally lead the Imperial Guard Division and subdue them."

On the third day of the crisis, the rebel leaders, who still were holding out, said they would commit suicide if the emperor would not send a representative. The division commander in Tokyo hesitated to attack them, however, saying he could not bear having his own troops fight their fellow soldiers. Honjō's diary records the emperor's response.

His Majesty was highly displeased at this and said, "If they wish to commit suicide, let them do so as they please. It is out of the question to dispatch an imperial agent to such men." He also said that if the division commander is unable to take any positive action it means that he does not understand his responsibility. I have never seen His Majesty display such anger. He ordered me to dispatch strict orders that the troops must be subjugated at once.

Official troops marched to the army general headquarters in Tokyo, attempting to restore order following the February 26, 1936, uprising by 1,400 ultranationalist soldiers. Demanding that Japan take more aggressive action in China, the rebels had assassinated three leading officials and held central Tokyo for three days.

Needless to say, I withdrew from his presence unable to utter a single word.

On the night of July 7, 1937, unidentified troops fired shots at Japanese soldiers who were on maneuvers near the Marco Polo Bridge southwest of Beijing. The fighting that ensued resulted in an all-out conflict between Japan and China, conflict that would eventuate in World War II. China proved a far more difficult opponent this time than it had been in 1894, and after a hard-fought Japanese victory in Shanghai, followed by a massacre of Chinese civilians in Nanjing, the war bogged down. Although Japan conquered large areas and forced President Chiang Kai-shek to set up a temporary capital in mountainous Chongqing, which then was known by Westerners as Chungking, Japan's troops were never able to topple the government. Prime Minister Konoe Fumimaro's speech to the Diet in September of that year, explaining the situation in China, says much about both Japan's eagerness to win international acceptance of its actions and the Japanese view of world affairs.

Since the outbreak of the affair in North China on July 7th, the fundamental policy of the Japanese Government toward China has been simply and purely to seek the reconsideration of the Chinese Government and the abandonment of its erroneous anti-Japanese

Japan launched an all-out assault on Shanghai in August 1937, thus launching World War II in Asia. In this rare photograph, citizens of Shanghai flee the incoming Japanese troops, carrying their belongings in any kind of makeshift cart or vehicle they can find.

policies, with the view of making a basic readjustment in relations between Japan and China. This policy has never undergone a change; even today it remains the same. The Japanese Government has endeavored to save the situation by preventing aggravation of the incident and by limiting its scope. This has been repeatedly enunciated; I trust that is fully understood by you.

The Chinese, however, not only fail to understand the true motives of the Government, but have increasingly aroused a spirit of contempt and have offered resistance toward Japan, taking advantage of the patience of our Government. Thus, by the outburst of uncontrolled national sentiment, the situation has fast been aggravated, spreading in scope to Central and South China. And now, our Government, which has been patient to the utmost, has acknowledged the impossibility of settling the incident passively and locally, and has been forced to deal a firm and decisive blow against the Chinese Government in an active and comprehensive manner.

At the present moment, . . . the sole measure for the Japanese Empire to adopt is to administer a thoroughgoing blow to the Chinese Army so that it may lose completely its will to fight. And if, at the same time, China fails to realize its mistakes and persists in its stubborn resistance, our Empire is fully prepared for protracted hostilities.

Although public rhetoric had become overwhelmingly nationalistic by the late 1930s, the country was not without

voices of dissent. Yanaihara Tadao, forced to resign from Tokyo University for criticizing Japan's invasion of China, published a private journal calling for justice. The journalist Kiryū Yūyū asserted that same spirit in a private magazine named *Tazan no ishi* (Stones from Other Mountains), after his attacks on the military forced him out of mainstream journalism in 1933. In a 1935 essay entitled "A Second World War," he worries about what will happen if hostilities came.

The thing we fear so greatly is that the second world war will be more cruel, more inhuman, even than the first one, that it will involve noncombatants, that it will be a hopeless war involving the people of literally every country. It is conceivable that people in every civilized country will come to know the tragedy of death.

I am an optimist, however. Because we have developed such frightening weapons, this second world war may lead to a time when war is impossible, to a time when people, at the least, will feel deeply that war must not be allowed.

When the February 26 uprising created such chaos in 1936, Kiryū reacted in *Tazan no ishi* by recalling an angry essay he had written when Prime Minister Inukai was killed on May 15, 1932. Titled "The Emperor's Army Has Become a Private Force," the article calls for an aroused public to stop military extremism. Kiryū died in the fall of 1941, not long before the attack on Pearl Harbor.

Did I not say it before? If too many of us close our eyes and blindly praise the May 15 criminals, we will not be able to block the military.

Did I not say it before? If we do not check the reckless actions of the military, the harm they do will be beyond imagining.

Have I not been censored several times as a result of my warnings against the army and the government? The public may finally have awakened, but it is too late. Only a part of the army may have been involved, but their sins are grave; they engaged in the most hateful national acts, showing themselves without scruples in turning the emperor's army into their own private force. There is no shame greater than dishonoring the imperial army. They did not use their weapons or the emperor's valiant troops against the enemy but to murder their own fellow countrymen. What is more, those fellow countrymen were high officials, men in important national positions, elder statesmen responsible for giving the emperor counsel on matters internal and external—and now we have lost them. How this must grieve our august emperor's spirit. The criminals should receive the harshest punishment.

Although the time is late, it is better that the Japanese wake up now than not at all. Listen, army officials, to the people's newly awakened voice! They will not overlook the officers' crimes this time. If the people have not brought them to task physically, it is because they have not had the "military weapons" to do so, but they already are questioning them spiritually.

The chief characteristic of the years between the 1937 Marco Polo Bridge Incident and the attack on Pearl Harbor was the tightening of control in all areas of life by the military and the mobilization of the public for war. By 1940, the political parties had been dissolved, and the government had created an Imperial Rule Assistance Association designed to bring the citizenry into one overarching political organization. Although the association never was an effective political society, its local and regional branches served as powerful tools for publicizing the government's war agenda and suppressing opposition. The organization was launched in October 1940, and its goals were articulated in a "basic outline" that December.

At a turning point in the world history today our Imperial country, which advocates the realization of the principle of extending the benevolent rule of the Emperor, is destined to become the glorious moral leader of the world. Toward this end, we, the nation of 100 million, must with singleness of mind dedicate our all to the Emperor and establish a national system with unity of spiritual and material things. This Association, being an assemblage of His Majesty's subjects, shall promote mutual assistance and mutual encouragement and become the vanguard of our nation. We shall maintain a relationship of close cooperation with the government at all times and endeavor to let the will of those who are above be transmitted to those who are below, and to let the desires of those who are below be known to those who are above. In this way we shall work toward the realization of a nation highly organized for national defense. . . .

We shall cooperate in the establishment of a new cultural order. We shall nurture a new Japanese civilization based on the spirit of our national polity and endowed with majestic, elegant, brilliant, and scientific qualities. Internally we shall promote our racial and national spirit and externally we shall encourage the formation of a Greater East Asian civilization.

The government also worked hard in the late 1930s at tightening its control of Japan's colonial empire, which now included Manchuria. Officials developed an extensive program to induce Japanese farmers to move to that region, mobilizing village elites, writers, and government agents to publicize the colonization cause. It succeeded in getting more than 140,000 to emigrate to Manchuria between 1937 and 1941. Officials also created large training centers for those who had agreed to go, where they instilled in young recruits a sense that they were headed out to render heroic service to their nation, to bring the fruits of Japanese civilization to far-flung peoples in need. The poet Tatsumi Seika expresses the spirit that imbued the colonial trainees at Uchiwara Center northeast of Tokyo in his 1930s poem "Morning in the Sun-Shaped Barracks."

By 1941, Japan was in control of nearly all of coastal China and fighting for interior areas. Here, Japanese soldiers stand at attention during a military drill.

Through the dew-drenched leaves
You can see the sun-shaped barracks . . .
Those sun-shaped barracks
Looking like conical Mongolian hats,
Those perfectly round roofs
Thatched with cedar.
Inside them young men
Silently reading, writing,
Earnestly preparing themselves.
These boys of tender years
Gather from throughout the nation,
Wishing to give to their country,
Burning with the bold and valiant
Colonial spirit.

War

Controversies abound over the maneuvering that preceded Japan's attack on Pearl Harbor in Hawaii on December 7, 1941. Who knew what—and when? Could the U.S. have been better prepared? Did the Japanese intentionally fail to provide the warning required by international rules? What never will be disputed is the monumental nature of the event. In mere hours, more than 3,000 men were killed, nineteen ships were

Foreign Minister Tōgō Shigenori: I would like to include the following in the final diplomatic communication we will send to the United States Government: The American position, Japan's response to this, and the contents of the Imperial Rescript announcing the declaration of war. In this way we will bring things to an end and sever diplomatic relations.

Someone: State it in such a way that it will not be the final word, but that there will be some room for negotiations.

Navy Chief of Staff Nagano Osami: There is no time for that. . . .

Someone: As for the time when it should be delivered to them: if it is too early, it will allow them time to get ready; on the other hand, if it is too late, there will be no point in delivering the note. At any rate, the most important thing now is to win the war.

—Notes from December 4, 1941 liaison conference, when the decision was made to notify America about the attack on Pearl Harbor, from *Japan's Decision for War: Records of the 1941 Policy Conferences*

Yesterday, December 7, 1941— a date which will live in infamy— the United States of America was suddenly and deliberately attacked by naval and air forces of the Empire of Japan.

—U.S. President Franklin D. Roosevelt, addressing Congress, December 8, 1941

sunk or severely damaged, and the United States was pulled into world war.

The decision to attack the United States was based on a conviction that Japan desperately needed the resources that America had blocked by freezing Japanese assets in the United States and embargoing exports to Japan. Even so, meeting at an imperial conference on November 6, 1941, Japan's top officials decided that if negotiations with the United States had reached no conclusion by the beginning of December, Japan would commence bombing. The resolution adopted by the imperial conference set Japan on its fateful course.

Essentials for Carrying Out the Empire's Policies

I. Our Empire, in order to resolve the present critical situation, assure its self-preservation and self-defense, and establish a New Order in Greater East Asia, decides on this occasion to go to war against the United States and Great Britain and takes the following measures:

1. The time for resorting to force is set at the beginning of December, and the Army and Navy will complete preparations for operations.

2. Negotiations with the United States will be carried out. . . .

3. Cooperation with Germany and Italy will be strengthened.

4. Close military relations with Thailand will be established just prior to the use of force.

II. If negotiations with the United States are successful by midnight of December 1, the use of force will be suspended. [Japan already had allied itself with the Axis powers through the September 1940 Tripartite Pact, a military alliance that recognized German/Italian leadership in Europe and Japanese leadership in Asia.]

The imperial declaration of war, made in Tokyo on December 7, 1941, might have seemed cynical and unrealistic to Japan's enemies in the West, who saw ulterior motives behind every idealistic statement. The truth was that most Japanese fully believed both its ideals and its optimistic predictions about the future.

We hereby declare war on the United States of America and the British Empire. The men and officers of Our Army and Navy shall do their utmost in prosecuting the war. Our public servants of var-

```
                           U. S. S. RANGER
                      NAVAL DISPATCH
Heading:   NSS NR 977 Z 0F8 1B30 0F3 0F4 0 BT



        AIR RAID ON PEARL HARBOR X THIS IS NOT DRILL




                            EXECUTIVE
From:   CINCPAC                        Date 7 DEC 41  ED
To:    CINCLA NT  CONAF  OPNAV              SUPR  CWO
```

The Commander in Chief Pacific (CinCPAC) sent this message to Washington from Honolulu at 7:58 AM on December 7, 1941, announcing Japan's surprise attack on Pearl Harbor.

ious departments shall perform faithfully and diligently their appointed tasks, and all other subjects of Ours shall pursue their respective duties; the entire nation with a united will shall mobilize their total strength so that nothing will miscarry in attainment of our war aims.

To ensure the stability of East Asia and to contribute to world peace is the farsighted policy which was formulated by Our Great Illustrious Imperial Grandsire and Our Great Imperial Sire succeeding Him, and which We lay constantly to heart.

To cultivate friendship among nations and to enjoy prosperity in common with all nations has always been the guiding principle of Our Empire's foreign policy. It has been truly unavoidable and far from Our wishes that Our Empire has now been brought to cross swords with America and Britain.

More than four years have passed since China, failing to comprehend the true intentions of Our Empire, and recklessly courting trouble, disturbed the peace of East Asia and compelled Our Empire to take up arms. . . .

Eager for the realization of their inordinate ambition to dominate the Orient, both America and Britain, giving support to the Chungking regime, have aggravated the disturbances in East Asia.

Moreover, these two Powers, inducing other countries to follow suit, increased military preparations on all sides of Our Empire to challenge us. They have obstructed by every means our peaceful commerce, and finally resorted to a direct severance of economic relations, menacing gravely the existence of Our Empire. . . .

This trend of affairs would, if left unchecked, not only nullify Our Empire's efforts of many years for the sake of the stabilization of East Asia, but also endanger the very existence of Our nation.

Imperial Grandsire and Sire

The Imperial Grandsire and Sire refer, respectively, to the Meiji and Taishō emperors.

The situation being such as it is, Our Empire for its existence and self-defense has no other recourse but to appeal to arms and to crush every obstacle in its path.

The hallowed spirits of Our Imperial Ancestors guarding Us from above, We rely upon the loyalty and courage of Our subjects in Our confident expectation that the task bequeathed by Our Forefathers will be carried forward, and that the source of evil will be speedily eradicated and an enduring peace immutably established in East Asia, preserving thereby the glory of Our Empire.

For nearly six months after the attack on Pearl Harbor, Japan experienced a string of victories in the Pacific, driving the Americans out of the Philippines, the Dutch out of the Dutch East Indies, and the British out of Singapore, Burma, Malaysia, and Hong Kong. They also took several Pacific island groups. Accompanying the victories was an overwhelming popular dedication to the war effort, a belief in the rightness of Japan's cause and the inevitability of its victory. The Buddhist priest Itabashi Kōshō makes clear the attitude of the Japanese in a late-1980s interview with an American historian.

I felt as if my blood boiled and my flesh quivered. The whole nation bubbled over, excited and inspired. "We really did it! Incredible! Wonderful!" That's the way it felt then.

I was brought up in a time when nobody criticized Japan. The war started for me, in the brain of this middle-school student, as something that should happen, something that was natural. Every day, we sent warriors off with cheers of *"Banzai! Banzai!"* War was going on in China. "Withdraw your forces," America ordered Japan. If a prime minister with foresight had ordered a withdrawal, he probably would have been assassinated. Even I knew that withdrawal was impossible! There was the ABCD encirclement— the Americans, British, Chinese, and Dutch. They wouldn't give us a drop of oil.

The Japanese had to take a chance. That was the psychological situation in which we found ourselves. If you bully a person, you should give him room to flee. There is a Japanese proverb that says, "A cornered mouse will bite a cat." America is evil, Britain is wrong, we thought. We didn't know why they were encircling us. In Japan, nobody was calculating whether we would win or not. We simply hit out. Our blood was hot! We fought. Until the very

Tōjō Hideki, a Tokyo native and a career military officer, was prime minister when Japan made its decision to go to war with the United States in 1941. Known for his focus on military technology, he was removed from office in 1944 and was hanged in 1948 after being convicted of crimes against humanity in the Tokyo War Crimes trials.

Flames rage at the U.S. naval air station at Pearl Harbor on the morning of December 7, 1941, hours after Japan's attack. This assault drew the United States into war and turned the European conflict into a world war.

end, no one considered the possibility that Japan could lose. . . .

The objective of war is always these things. No wars have ever been fought for any other reasons. . . . For Japan, that was a sacred war. Japan claimed it would unite the eight corners of the world under one roof. If Japan had declared it was fighting only to add territory, I don't believe we ever could have gone as far as Borneo.

By the middle of 1942, defeats had replaced the early triumphs and Japan's military was on the defensive. In June, the Americans crushed the Japanese fleet when it attempted to take the Pacific island of Midway, destroying four aircraft carriers and killing more men than had died at Pearl Harbor. From that point on, Japan's war was largely defensive, as the Allied troops retook island after island in the Pacific, at a staggering price in lives. When Japan lost the Marianas in July 1944, Tōjō resigned as prime minister. And when General Douglas MacArthur's troops landed in the Philippines that fall, prescient Japanese knew that their country's defeat was inevitable. Much of the populace remained uninformed about that fact, however, because heavy censorship blocked negative news. That things were not going well was obvious from the dire economic straits and from the fact that battles were being fought closer and closer to home. But news reports still focused on the troops' gallantry and the country's eventual victory.

WHEREAS the successful prosecution of the war requires every possible protection against espionage and against sabotage to national defense material, national defense premises, and national defense utilities . . . :

I hereby authorize and direct the Secretary of War, and the Military Commanders whom he may from time to time designate, . . . to prescribe military areas . . . from which any or all persons may be excluded. . . . The Secretary of War is hereby authorized to provide for residents of any such area who are excluded therefrom, such transportation, food, shelter, and other accommodations as may be necessary . . . to accomplish the purpose of this order. . . .

—Franklin D. Roosevelt, Executive Order 9066, February 19, 1942, sending 112,000 Japanese Americans, two-thirds of them U.S. citizens, to internment camps

Both Japan and the United States carried out full-fledged propaganda wars against each other during World War II. This Japanese cartoon from about 1941, produced for distribution in the Philippines, shows Japan saving Asia from the dangerous waters of American imperialism and racial prejudice.

After early 1945, however, even those reports could not conceal the country's dismal situation. In March, Allied forces began bombing Japan's cities, incinerating huge po tions of Tokyo, Osaka, Nagoya, and more than sixty other cities, leaving 13 million people—more than a sixth of the total population—homeless. The Japanese by then were living in desperate conditions, nearly all of the country's resources having been poured into the war effort. When Okinawa fell to the Allies in June, 1945, at a cost of 50,000 American and 100,000 Japanese casualties, few could have held hope for an upturn in Japan's fortunes. People continued to support the war, however, sometimes motivated by hatred for the enemy, sometimes because there was no choice, and sometimes for philosophical reasons. The diary entries of a twenty-three-year-old University of Tokyo law student, who died on a human torpedo mission in late July 1945, provide a glimpse into the motivation that kept one soldier fighting in the war.

April 13, 1945. . . . Exactly one more month, then we will be sent to the front to face our enemy. I am going to get after our enemy, and aside from this particular feeling, I have no thought of death.

We are lucky, we need not be bothered with questions like "what is life?" or "what is death?"

I cannot talk like a sub-lieutenant by the name of N who exaggerates everything. Every word that comes out of his mouth is full of patriotism. In my placid mind now, all such thoughts are consigned to the depth of quiet reflection. Some people may say that this type of inner reflection is unwarranted at a time like this. However, we have discovered the meaning of thinking, and this is a burden we have to bear. . . .

My comrades in arms have said to me that my face has betrayed my weariness for the past several days.

I know during the same period I have been trying to give meaning to my own death.

I have been absorbed in the task of making an angle-of-fire chart so that I can make my human torpedo hit the enemy for sure. . . .

May 15. Yesterday I was granted my furlough. . . . I did not send a telegram home. When I arrive tonight, how surprised all of them will be! My suitcase is full of cookies, shirts, whiskey, and cigarettes.

I am not sure of myself. When I see my parents face to face, I may not be able to hold back anything and tell them everything. What will they think and what will they say?

May 29. I came to the front only yesterday, but what I have in mind is the desire to give my life seven times over to annihilate my enemy. I have this ever growing hostility toward the enemy.

June 20, the final entry. A person who is truly enlightened is said to be able to meditate on the question of life and death and eradicate it from his mind. . . . My life has been one of vanity and at the same time one that lacked moral courage. Yet to me this one month of quiet meditation has been a significant period in my life in more than one way. However, the fruition of this month is yet to come. . . .

Now I am claiming that I have discovered my own answer to the question of life and death. Maybe it is another manifestation of my desire to put on an act. I know I must keep on reflecting on my own shortcomings and work hard toward finding an answer.

Despite the high-flown rhetoric and noble sentiments, Japanese troops were guilty of terrible atrocities during the war, including the 1937 massacre of civilians in Nanjing, the brutal treatment of Chinese war prisoners in southeast Asia, the use of chemical weapons, the torture and rape of civilians throughout China, and Unit 731's conduct of biological experiments on Manchurians, several thousand of whom died after being injected with typhoid, bubonic plague, and other diseases. Among the most notorious programs was the systematic use of thousands of Asian and European women to serve the sexual needs of Japanese troops. Maria Rosa Henson, a Filipina captured by Japanese soldiers and forced to serve as a comfort woman, or sex slave, for nine months at age fifteen, recollects her experience in a 1999 memoir.

The guard led me at gunpoint to the second floor of the building that used to be the town hospital. It had been turned into the Japanese headquarters and garrison. I saw six other women there. . . .

The following day was hell. Without warning, a Japanese soldier entered my room and pointed his bayonet at my chest. . . . He used his bayonet to slash my dress and tear it open. I was too frightened to scream. And then he raped me. When he was done, other soldiers came into my room, and they took turns raping me.

Twelve soldiers raped me in quick succession, after which I was given half an hour to rest. Then twelve more soldiers followed. They all lined up outside the room waiting for their turn. I bled so much and was in such pain, I could not even stand up. . . .

During the war, everything was National Defense Color. That was the army's color, the color of uniforms. . . . It was the safest color, fine anytime, anyplace. The streets were full of army color.
—Dressmaker Koshino Ayako in 1988, recalling the pervasiveness of khaki clothes during the war, quoted in Haruko Taya Cook and Theodore F. Cook, *Japan at War: An Oral History*, 77–78

We began the day with breakfast, after which we swept and cleaned our rooms. Sometimes, the guard helped. He fixed my bed and scrubbed the floor with a wet cloth and some disinfectant. After cleaning, we went to the bathroom downstairs to wash the only dress we had and to bathe. The bathroom did not even have a door, so the soldiers watched us. We were all naked, and they laughed at us. . . .

I felt that the six other women with me also despised the Japanese soldiers. But like me, there was nothing they could do. I never got to know them. We just looked at each other, but were not allowed to talk. Two of the women looked Chinese. They always cast their gaze downward and never met my eye.

Seeking resources such as oil and rubber, Japanese troops advance into Southeast Asia, then commonly referred to as Indo-China, in mid-1941. Japan's move came after it became bogged down in China and after relations with the United States turned frigid, depriving Japan of many of the materials it needed for its military efforts.

Support for the war was not universal among the Japanese people. Life in the homeland surely was difficult; it also was complex, as people's attitudes ranged from total support to quiet opposition. Those who opposed the war effort typically did so in subtle, highly personal ways. Hatano Isoko wrote a note to her son Ichirō in October 1944, explaining why she is defying official regulations and working so hard each day to secure more than the bare food necessities for her family. Her situation is particularly difficult because the family has had to leave its Tokyo home, to escape the danger of bombing, and has taken up residence in a village where they are regarded as outsiders.

I didn't really resist the war. I was simply chased after by the police. I only wanted to keep from doing what the military ordered me to do. I gave opportunities to former Communists and others as often as possible, but they weren't writing Communist propaganda. Had they, I'd have cut them. . . . I abhor military men. I consider them a separate race of humanity because of education. . . . Theirs is childish, simple-minded thinking.

—1988 reminiscence, in interview, of historian Hatanaka Shigeo, whose journal *Chūō Kōron* was shut down by the authorities on July 19, 1944

There are only two possible courses nowadays; one can either live at a bare subsistence level on the official rations, or use every possible means to try to find provisions and eat a little better. I imagine that you, who are just getting into adolescence, would prefer the first course and want to have it observed by everyone.

But with the official rations only, we couldn't get enough to eat: it would be absolutely impossible! Particularly since rationing is even more limited here than in Tokyo. Perhaps this is because we are new arrivals. If such is not the case, the rations are fewer than in Tokyo probably because they assume there is more opportunity of getting supplementary food from friends and relatives. But if one has no such connections, isn't one obliged to seize every opportunity for getting food for oneself and one's family? Your father says it would be a complete absurdity to die in such a war as this. I don't fully understand what he means by that, but I do know that it would serve absolutely no purpose for children like you to die and that you must be kept alive at all costs. If you are not to die, the important thing is that you be in good health. Do you understand?

With the armies losing and the economy disintegrating, Japan's leaders spent June and July 1945 debating whether and how to end the war. In late June, the Supreme Council for the Direction of the War asked the Soviets to help set up negotiations with the Allies, since a 1941 neutrality pact meant that the USSR and Japan were not, technically, at war with each other. While the Soviets delayed their response, the Allies issued the Potsdam Declaration on July 26, 1945, demanding that Japan surrender unconditionally or be subject to "prompt and utter destruction."

(1) WE—THE PRESIDENT of the United States, the President of the National Government of the Republic of China, and the Prime Minister of Great Britain, representing the hundreds of millions of our countrymen, have conferred and agree that Japan shall be given an opportunity to end this war. . . .

(5) Following are our terms. We will not deviate from them. There are no alternatives. We shall brook no delay.

(6) There must be eliminated for all time the authority and influence of those who have deceived and misled the people of Japan into embarking on world conquest, for we insist that a new order of peace, security and justice will be impossible until irresponsible militarism is driven from the world.

(7) Until such a new order is established and until there is convincing proof that Japan's war-making power is destroyed, points in Japanese territory to be designated by the Allies shall be occupied. . . .

(8) . . . Japanese sovereignty shall be limited to the islands of Honshu, Hokkaido, Kyushu, Shikoku and such minor islands as we determine.

(9) The Japanese military forces, after being completely disarmed, shall be permitted to return to their homes with the opportunity to lead peaceful and productive lives.

Allied leaders met at the Potsdam Conference in July 1945 to determine the conditions for a Japanese surrender. Winston Churchill of Great Britain is at the upper left, with a cigar; the Soviet Union's Joseph Stalin is at the right, holding a cigarette; and U.S. President Harry Truman is at the bottom, looking right with his back to the camera. British, Soviet, and American flags sit in the middle of the table.

I was greatly moved. I . . . said to the group of sailors around me, "This is the greatest thing in history. It's time for us to get home."

—Harry S. Truman, recalling his reaction on August 6, 1945, when handed a message about the Hiroshima bombing on the ship *Augusta*, en route home from Potsdam Conference (from *Memoirs, 1: Year of Decisions* [1955])

(10) We do not intend that the Japanese shall be enslaved as a race or destroyed as a nation, but stern justice shall be meted out to all war criminals, including those who have visited cruelties upon our prisoners. . . .

(13) We call upon the government of Japan to proclaim now the unconditional surrender of all Japanese armed forces, and to provide proper and adequate assurances of their good faith in such action. The alternative for Japan is prompt and utter destruction.

Neither the threat of the Potsdam Declaration nor the devastation on the battlefields was enough to end the late-July division in Japan's Supreme Council, where diehards held out for assurances that the imperial institution would be maintained. A rush of shocks early in August settled the issue: on August 6, 1945, the United States dropped the world's first atomic bomb on Hiroshima; on August 8, the Soviets announced they were entering the war against Japan; and on August 9, the United States dropped another atomic bomb on Nagasaki. After the Nagasaki bombing, the emperor, who had supported the war from its beginning, said it was time to bring the devastation to an end, and began the chain of events that led to Japan's formal surrender on September 2, 1945.

Nothing in the entire war made such an impression on the human psyche as the atomic bombs. The physical destruction at Hiroshima and Nagasaki was no greater than in other bombed cities. But the implications were apocalyptic—more than 200,000 people killed, two cities reduced to rubble, 7,000-degree Fahrenheit temperatures that impressed human shadows onto concrete walls—and all by just two bombs, neither of them more than twelve feet long. Hiroshima doctor Hachiya Michihiko describes in his journal the day the atomic bomb hit Hiroshima.

6 August 1945. The hour was early; the morning still, warm, and beautiful. Shimmering leaves, reflecting sunlight from a cloudless sky, made a pleasant contrast with shadows in my garden as I gazed absently through wide-flung doors opening to the south.

Clad in drawers and undershirt, I was sprawled on the living room floor exhausted because I had just spent a sleepless night on duty as an air warden in my hospital.

Suddenly, a strong flash of light startled me—and then another. So well does one recall little things that I remember vividly how a stone lantern in the garden became brilliantly lit and I debated whether this light was caused by a magnesium flare or sparks from a passing trolley.

Garden shadows disappeared. The view where a moment before all had been so bright and sunny was now dark and hazy. Through swirling dust I could barely discern a wooden column that had supported one corner of my house. It was leaning crazily and the roof sagged dangerously.

Moving instinctively, I tried to escape, but rubble and fallen timbers barred the way. By picking my way cautiously I managed to reach the *rōka* and stepped down into my garden. A profound weakness overcame me, so I stopped to regain my strength. To my surprise I discovered that I was completely naked. How odd! Where were my drawers and undershirt? . . .

Blood began to spurt. Had my carotid artery been cut? Would I bleed to death? Frightened and irrational, I called out . . . : "It's a five-hundred-ton bomb! Yaeko-san, where are you? A five-hundred-ton bomb has fallen!"

Yaeko-san, pale and frightened, her clothes torn and blood-stained, emerged from the ruins of our house holding her elbow. Seeing her, I was reassured. My own panic assuaged, I tried to reassure her.

"We'll be all right," I exclaimed. "Only let's get out of here as fast as we can."

She nodded, and I motioned for her to follow me.

The shortest path to the street lay through the house next door so through the house we went—running, stumbling, falling, and then running again until in headlong flight we tripped over something and fell sprawling into the street. Getting to my feet, I discovered that I had tripped over a man's head.

"Excuse me! Excuse me, please!" I cried hysterically.

There was no answer. The man was dead. The head had belonged to a young officer whose body was crushed beneath a massive gate.

We stood in the street, uncertain and afraid, until a house across from us began to sway and then with a rending motion fell almost at our feet. Our own house began to sway, and in a minute it, too, collapsed in a cloud of dust. Other buildings caved in or toppled. Fires sprang up and whipped by a vicious wind began to spread.

rōka

A *rōka* is a small veranda facing onto the home's garden.

Yaeko-san

Yaeko-san is Hachiya's wife.

Asia's largest cathedral, the Urakami Catholic Church, was destroyed by the bombing of Nagasaki, and its bell tower fell into the river on the north side of the cathedral. This photo was taken shortly after the bombing.

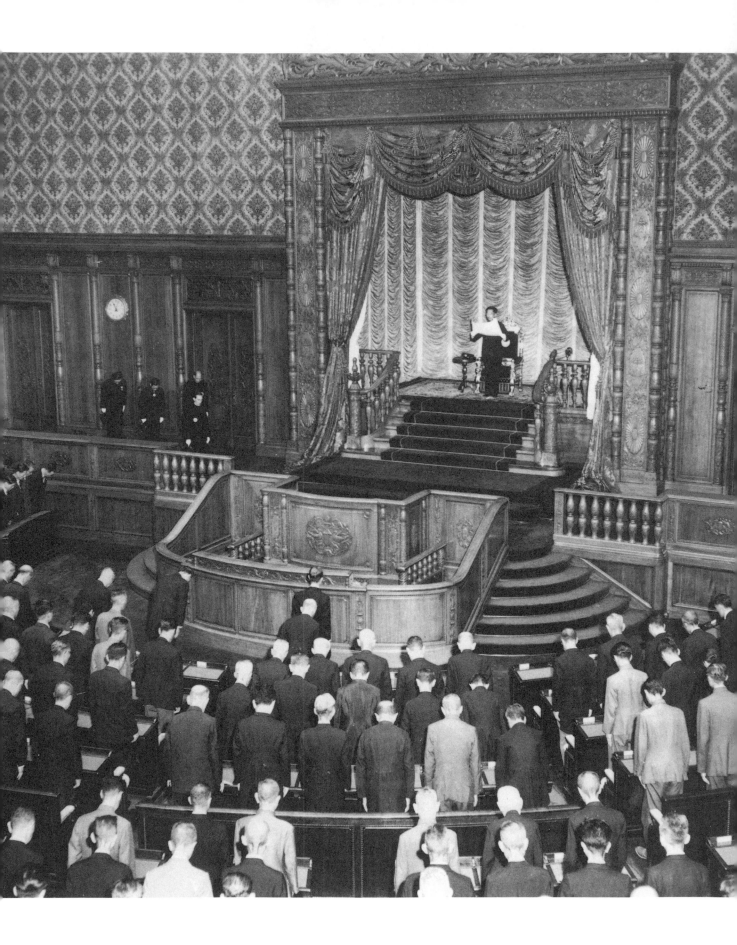

Chapter Seven

The Reemergence: 1945–70

Destitution reigned in Japan at the end of World War II. The major cities were fields of rubble. Nearly 10 percent of the population had been killed or injured in the war, and some 9 million people were homeless. Food and resources were nearly gone, with steel production at one-tenth of what it had been a year earlier and food sharply rationed by the government. Almost everyone was buying even basics on the black market, and Yamaguchi Yoshitada, a conscience-bound judge who ate only what the regulations allowed, died of starvation. Inflation had begun soaring too; in the first year after hostilities ceased, prices rose 539 percent! Survival seemed questionable, recovery perhaps impossible. However, only a generation later, in 1969, Japan had become the world's third-largest economy, worthy of the label "superstate" by Western economists. It was as if the Meiji era had occurred once again: a desperate state had overcome all predictions of doom, utilizing native astuteness and Western assistance to become an economic giant with a global shadow. How did it happen? And with what effects?

The first seven years after the war were, on one hand, among the most humiliating in Japanese history and, on the other, the most impressive. The humiliation came from occupation by a foreign power. For the first time ever, Japan was run by outsiders, primarily the Americans who dominated the Allied Occupation government. They were hard years, as inflation persisted, the economy continued to sputter, and people wondered whether good times ever would return. But they also proved Japan to be one of the world's most adept countries at transcending crises. To a degree that surprised almost everyone, the Japanese people cooperated immediately with the invading forces and threw themselves into the task of rebuilding. Perhaps most important, although some of the old elites resisted, the country as a whole enthusiastically supported the Allies' two main goals for the country: demilitarization and democratization. Working alongside the offices of the Supreme Commander of the Allied Powers (or SCAP, headed by U.S. General Douglas MacArthur), the Japanese government adopted a new, more democratic constitution, encouraged the growth of labor unions, made the school system more democratic, broke up several of the old economic cartels, and even reformed the land system to turn tenants into farm owners. The enthusiasm for that kind of democratization cooled a couple of years into the period, as SCAP turned its energies away from bringing militarists to trial and toward creating a state strong enough to support the democratic West against Soviet and Chinese communism in the emerging Cold War. But with militarism and heavy-handed government so thoroughly discredited, democratic institutions had taken firm root by the time the occupiers left in 1952.

During the remainder of the 1950s, Japan developed the approaches and structures that would characterize its public life for the second half of the twentieth century. Its economy also moved back to prewar levels. The dominating person—in a country whose myths say it has no dominating individuals—was Prime Minister Yoshida Shigeru, who served for more than seven years between 1946 and 1954. Besides presiding over the 1952 peace settlement, he helped create a structure that would enable his conservative party (called the "Liberal Democratic Party" or LDP) to dominate Japanese political life until well into the twenty-first century. And he gave shape to a philosophy that has come to be known as the Yoshida Doctrine, under which Japan focused on economic growth (especially trade), while depending on the United States for a major part of its military defense. Under that system, Japan saw the reemergence of a consumer society in the 1950s, as income levels finally passed those of the prewar period and people began to shop once more, especially for the "three sacred

U.S. army troops drive down a walkway to a Shintō shrine in Osaka, surveying the devastation of war in September 1945. Troops were used to restore order, maintain the peace, and help rebuild Japan's devastated infrastructure. They also helped administer the Occupation government.

pieces of equipment" that symbolized the period: refrigerators, washing machines, and television sets.

Building on that base, Japan became an economic giant again in the early 1960s, in sync with Prime Minister Ikeda Hayato's promise to double the economy in a decade. Unfortunately, Ikeda did not live to see the full fruits of his policies, as cancer took his life in 1965, but by the late 1960s the economy had soared far past his goals. Equally unfortunate, though probably inevitable, was the fact that in the mid-1960s, just as the world was beginning to talk about Japan's second economic miracle, the darker results of development also began to be apparent. Urbanization and new industries created overcrowding and forced people to live in cramped quarters and take long, crowded commutes to work. Pollution filled the skies and waters—and sickened or killed Japan's people. Money scandals rocked the political world. And students erupted by the hundreds of thousands in protests against everything from the Vietnam War to ineffective education, shutting down scores of colleges for months on end. Few would have gone back to earlier days, but by 1970, few saw economic growth as an unalloyed good.

An Occupied Land

The way in which World War II ended set the tone of Japan's postwar years. People had been ordered to turn their radios on at noon on Wednesday, August 15, 1945, for an important message. Most were stunned to hear the message delivered by Emperor Hirohito himself, a man whose voice had never been heard in public. A few months later, Hirohito would be required by Occupation officials to issue a rescript denying his divinity, but the scratchy, high-pitched voice that came over the airwaves that Wednesday already had made that clear. Ōe Kenzaburo, a boy of ten living in a mountain valley on Shikoku island, recalled in a newspaper essay half a century later what kind of impact Hirohito's radio announcement had. Ōe later won a Nobel prize for literature.

Because of the poor reception in our valley in the forest, particularly during the day, there was no point in listening to anything but a high-performance radio. On that day, people gathered at the manor houses of wealthy families, where radios were tuned and ready. At the house where I went to listen, the radio had been installed on the porch facing the front garden. . . .

As life returned to normal after World War II, people began once more to participate in festivals and public ceremonies. In 1948, Culture Day was established as a national holiday held on November 3. Some 30,000 people took part in this Lantern Dance at the Imperial Palace Plaza in Tokyo.

Japanese prisoners in an Allied war prison in Guam stand with bowed heads on August 15, 1945, after hearing the radio broadcast of Emperor Hirohito's surrender message. Japan surrendered officially on September 2.

The war has lasted for nearly four years. Despite the best that has been done by everyone—the gallant fighting of military and naval forces, the diligence and assiduity of Our servants of the State and the devoted service of Our one hundred million people, the war situation has developed not necessarily to Japan's advantage, while the general trends of the world have all turned against her interest. . . . Should We continue to fight, it would not only result in an ultimate collapse and obliteration of the Japanese nation, but also it would lead to the total extinction of human civilization. Such being the case, how are We to save the millions of Our subjects; or to atone Ourselves before the hallowed spirits of Our Imperial Ancestors? This is the reason why We have ordered the acceptance of the provision of the Joint Declaration of the Powers. . . . We have resolved to pave the way for a grand peace for all the generations to come by enduring the un-endurable and suffering what is insufferable. . . .

—Emperor Hirohito, announcing surrender, August 15, 1945

The Emperor speaking to us in a human voice was beyond imagining in any reverie. The Emperor was a god, the authority of the nation, the organizing principle of reality. The military and the police, our system of social classes—the Emperor as a god was at the source of all things. And all the laws and systems under our Constitution had erected hard, high barriers of reality to keep the Emperor at a distance from us. We had even prayed at our shrines for victory in war to the Emperor who was a god. . . .

After a dazed silence following the broadcast, the adults tried without confidence to decipher the Emperor's words: the war is over—Japan has been defeated—you must now endure your suf-fering and survive. Some had different interpretations, but were unable to assert them with any conviction. The radio's owner put the precious device away inside the house and saw his guests to the door; the people who had been standing in the garden went their separate ways, mostly in silence. But among the children there were a few with the rebellious courage to imitate the Emperor's voice: *bearing the unbearable, enduring the unendurable*. The children lift-ed their voices in laughter and then fled the angry voices of the adults who emerged from the house to yell at them. In truth, they were running in fear of their own laughter. I was among them. But I didn't return home: I went to the river, took off my clothes in the bamboo grove and submerged my body in the inlet.

Lying in the lukewarm water, I rubbed my body against the soft clay on the bottom and gazed upward at the brilliance of the mid-day summer sky. I discovered that I was feeling a curious freedom. Until now, I had feared that I was too young to become a soldier and would miss the opportunity to die in battle for the Emperor. At the same time, I wanted desperately to be too late, a shameful desire that tore at me. Now I had been released from that agony.

Though Japan was devastated, its people showed remarkable resiliency. The democratically oriented decisions of the Occupation may have helped Japan recover, as did economic aid from the United States. But more than anything else the efforts of the Japanese themselves brought on their success. Credit belongs partly to good leadership, partly to the effectiveness of bureaucratic structures set up before and during World War II—and above all to the Japanese spirit. Fed up with militarism, imbued with intelligence, humor, and a willingness to work hard, commoners and elite alike committed themselves to the task of rebuilding. The eighty-five-year-old journalist Miyake Setsurei captures this forward-looking spirit in an essay titled "Creating Culture Through Truth, Beauty, and Virtue," published posthumously in January 1946.

We may be a small country that has lost its independence, but we belong to one huge family of 75 million people nurtured since ancient times by our forefathers. We must do whatever is necessary to recover the people's power and expand our influence to the world. When and how that will happen, we do not know. One answer lies in gradually recovering our strength and, increasing the numbers of people diligently devoted to the effort, reaching the place where we once again contribute to the good of the world. Although the way of accomplishing this may not yet be clear, it is not hard to conjecture from the experiences of our distant past that we will, again, create a special culture and spread it to the whole world. The world is not what it once was. Today, airplanes fly in the sky, freeing us from old ways of travel. A bomb of the sort once unimaginable has been invented. There is no limit to where human knowledge will take us. Although Japan is relatively far removed from the world's culture today, though we are weak in the spirit of study, if we take part in the world's creations and discoveries, we can hope, through the stimulus of others as we make contact with the rest of the world, to produce many people who will make great contributions.

Where will our national strength take us? We must carry out successful, valuable enterprises as individuals. The military clique must not return. . . . Truth, virtue, and beauty were the ideals in ancient Greece, while in Japan we had the three imperial treasures,

The first meeting between Emperor Hirohito and General MacArthur conveyed multiple meanings to the Japanese: American informality, Occupation authority, and MacArthur's intention to work with the Japanese.

the mirror, the sword, and the jewel

From ancient times, Japanese had taken the mirror, sword, and jewel to symbolize the imperial family's legitimacy and authority.

Japan's destitution in the fall of 1945, following the end of the war, was exemplified by the hundreds of homeless people who slept each night in underground subway stations, often on newspapers or dirty clothing.

the mirror, the sword, and the jewel, and in China's Zhou Dynasty the *Golden Mean* spoke of knowledge, human heartedness, and courage. These values accompany progress everywhere, and at all times. It matters not whether it is the first century, the tenth century, or the hundredth century, truth will become increasingly true; virtue will be ever more virtuous; beauty will become more beautiful still. And they will lead us to a state no one yet has been able to imagine.

Not all Japanese people were always as optimistic as the journalist Miyake; most had neither his age nor his affluence to make them philosophical. For the vast majority, times were too dire, particularly in the early months of the Occupation, to allow anything but survival. If grit and determination made up one of the postwar period's unique features, destitution constituted another. A November 7, 1945, worker's letter to *Asahi Shimbun* in Osaka makes clear that more than a few people were driven beyond hope, imbued more with contempt for officials and concern about their loved ones than by high-flown ideas about Japan's directions.

I am a mere common laborer. I write this now standing at the dividing point between life and death. My mind has become empty. There is only resentment toward our incompetent government. With five children, I worked hard and even managed to meet the responsibility of saving a little in these hard times, but the government's incompetence regarding food supplies kept getting worse and finally I became unable to work even half the month. I felt sorry for the children, though, and thinking that even our children may be useful for the country in the future, I fed them by buying food on the black market. That couldn't go on forever, however, and we reached our limit. In the end, I even borrowed money at high interest to get food, but I can no longer do this and so we have not eaten for four whole days. My wife collapsed yesterday, and two of the children are losing spirit. The government just talks and does nothing. I understand that high officials are filling their stomachs, but there is nothing we can do. On the other hand, evil merchants involved in the black market—

there are two or three of them in this neighborhood alone—make what amounts to 50,000 or 60,000 yen a year.

At last, I have resolved to commit suicide. I am going to die, reproaching the incompetent, merciless government. Indirectly, I've asked neighbors and the head of the neighborhood association to look after my wife and children. . . . High officials—get rid of your indifference and willingness to let others suffer for years, and show some human heart! . . . When this letter reaches you, I may already be dead. I have written this gathering up all the spirit I have left.

The Supreme Commander of the Allied Powers (SCAP) made democratization the cornerstone of its early policies, on the theory that a democratic country would resist militarism and serve as a dependable ally. To that end, officials created a host of new programs and institutions. Elections were held in 1946 under a new law, and more than 80 percent of the 466 Diet members, including 38 women, were elected for the first time. Much of the old political leadership was purged, with the major wartime leaders tried in the 1948 War Crimes Trials, which resulted in seven executions and life imprisonment for sixteen others. Land reform turned vast numbers of tenant farmers into property owners—and political participants. And the push for labor unionization spurred workers to become active voters and campaigners.

The cornerstone of democratization was the new constitution, which took effect on May 3, 1947. Convinced that a new fundamental law was needed to prevent a return of autocracy, General MacArthur told the Japanese to draw up a new constitution. When their proposals hewed closely to the old Meiji constitution, he told SCAP's Government Section to write its own draft, and gave them roughly a week to do it. As a result, a committee of twenty-four Americans drafted Japan's new constitution in English, had it translated into Japanese, and presented it to a group of stunned Japanese officials who reluctantly guided it through to ratification. The two most controversial features of the document deal with the emperor and the military. At MacArthur's behest, the drafting committee decided to retain the emperor, though as a "symbol of the state" rather than as a sovereign. Also at his urging, the constitution outlaws war and the military, in human history's most sweeping peace clause. The constitution also calls for a British-style, bicameral legislative

yen
Changing dollar-yen exchange rates make accurate comparisons across time impossible, but 60,000 yen then would equal at least $500,000 in early-21st-century terms.

I am over my head in thoughts and impressions of . . . seeing Japan after ten years, of seeing it as a countryside devastated by a terrific storm and the people coming out to look at the damage, like farmers at their wheat knocked down, only their looking continues longer. . . . Tokyo, the first war casualty I've seen, is a devastated, immodest mess, but the silence is what gets me most; no honks, yells, clangs—none of the stuff you hate in a town but come to expect. . . . Everybody is still staring in that god-awful silence.

—Sherwood Moran, U.S. naval officer and son of former Japan missionaries, in letter to Donald Keene, September 26, 1945

Prior to elections in January 1949, a female candidate speaks to families in a Tokyo neighborhood. Women's suffrage came to Japan in 1946, and during the late 1940s relatively large numbers of women were elected to both local and national legislatures.

system, an independent judiciary, local autonomy, and a set of rights that not only guarantees freedoms but also assures equality of the sexes, academic freedom, and the right to a basic living standard.

We, the Japanese people, acting through our duly elected representatives in the National Diet, determined that we shall secure for ourselves and our posterity the fruits of peaceful cooperation with all nations and the blessings of liberty throughout this land, and resolved that never again shall we be visited with the horrors of war through the action of government, do proclaim that sovereign power resides with the people and do firmly establish this constitution. . . .

1. The Emperor shall be the symbol of the State and of the unity of the people, deriving his position from the will of the people with whom resides sovereign power. . . .

9. Aspiring sincerely to an international peace based on justice and order, the Japanese people forever renounce war as a sovereign right of the nation and the threat or use of force as means of settling international disputes.

In order to accomplish the aim of the preceding paragraph, land, sea, and air forces, as well as other war potential, will never be maintained. The right of belligerency of the state will not be recognized. . . .

The trial of the vanquished by the victors cannot be impartial no matter how it is hedged about with the forms of justice.
—U.S. Senator Robert A. Taft, October 6, 1946, quoted in John F. Kennedy's *Profiles in Courage* (1955)

11. People shall not be prevented from enjoying any of the fundamental human rights. . . .

13. All of the people shall be respected as individuals. Their right to life, liberty, and the pursuit of happiness shall, to the extent that it does not interfere with the public welfare, be the supreme considerations in legislation and in other governmental affairs.

14. All of the people are equal under the law and there shall be no discrimination in political, economic or social relations, because of race, creed, sex, social status or family origin.

15. . . . Universal adult suffrage is guaranteed with regard to the election of public officials. . . .

23. Academic freedom is guaranteed.

25. All people have the right to maintain the minimum standards of wholesome and cultured living. . . .

27. All people shall have the right and the obligation to work. . . . Children shall not be exploited.

28. The right of workers to organize and to bargain and act collectively is guaranteed.

41. The Diet shall be the highest organ of state power, and shall be the sole law-making organ of the State. . . .

59. A bill becomes a law on passage by both Houses, except as otherwise provided by the Constitution. . . .

76. The whole judicial power is vested in a Supreme Court and in such inferior courts as are established by law. . . .

96. Amendments to this Constitution shall be initiated by the Diet, through a concurring vote of two-thirds or more of all the members of each House and shall thereupon be submitted to the people for ratification, which shall require the affirmative vote of a majority of all votes cast thereon, at a special referendum or at such election as the Diet shall specify.

The education system was a major focus of the government's attention during the Occupation. Convinced that the schools' emphasis on loyalty to the emperor had undermined freedom in the prewar decades, the new educational officials and SCAP authorities worked hard to democratize the schools. They rewrote textbooks (after having students themselves black out ultranationalist passages in books until new texts could be produced), gave local communities control over schools, and urged teachers to encourage students to think for themselves. Subjects that came in for special scrutiny were geography, history, and ethics, all

Mr. Prima Donna, Brass Hat, Five Star MacArthur. He's worse than the Cabots and the Lodges—they at least talked with one another before they told God what to do. Mac tells God right off.

—President Harry S. Truman, discussing General Douglas MacArthur's ego in a June 17, 1945, memo

Tokyo University professor Kawashima Takeyoshi interviewed members of a farming community near Tokyo in 1950 about their views of the emperor:

42-year-old lawyer. It is sheer nonsense to think that people in modern times ever believed the emperor was really a god. I respect him and I support him absolutely as a human being.

71-year-old landlord. He's the mainstay of our people, their center and pillar.

16-year-old boy. If he should cease to exist, our lives would lack direction.

42-year-old landlord. I think the emperor is descended from the gods.

Extreme deconcentration of industry . . . may . . . postpone the day when Japan can become self-supporting. . . . I can assure you that our decisions will be made with realism and with a firm determination of doing all possible to prevent Japan from again waging unprovoked and aggressive and cruel war against any other nation. We hold to an equally definite purpose of building in Japan a self-sufficient democracy, strong enough and stable enough to support itself and at the same time to serve as a deterrent against any other totalitarian war threats which might hereafter arise in the Far East.

—U.S. Army Secretary Kenneth C. Royall, in a January 6, 1948, speech to the Commonwealth Club of San Francisco

mainstays of nationalist thought. In the early months after the war, a SCAP-appointed mission of twenty-seven educators spent three weeks examining Japan's schools, then recommended a host of changes in the system. Though many of their recommendations were abandoned after the Occupation, those dealing with textbooks had a lasting impact. The 1946 *Report of the United States Education Mission to Japan* shows the reasoning behind the reformers' focus on ethics, which resonated with many Japanese educators.

The course in morals as taught in the Japanese schools of late years was aimed at an obedient citizenry. This effort at order through loyalty proved so effective, upborne as it was by all pillars of society, that the means became identified with malicious ends. So the course on morals has been suspended. But a democratic system, like any other, requires an ethics to match and to perpetuate its own genius. . . .

The Japanese tradition has borrowed largely from the French, and there appears to be an expectation on the part of both parent and student for a special course in ethics. Let it be so, beginning the course with what the Japanese have—good manners. Japanese civilians, at least, are noted the world over for their formal gentility. Persons that come to laugh at the consummate art of face-saving may well pause to pray that they knew as well how to save human feelings from daily hurt. . . .

Boys and girls alike should . . . grow up knowing their national constitution, for it is the institution under which majority rule

Girls at the Futaba Catholic School in Tokyo study in a classroom they helped rebuild after their school was bombed near the end of World War II. The school was named Futaba, meaning "two leaves," to symbolize the coming together of Eastern and Western cultures. Many alumni sold personal belongings to finance the school's reconstruction.

prevails. They should know something, too, of other constitutions. They should have elections to determine the officers of their own organizations as a preparatory step for later citizenship. If they must imitate, let them imitate the Diet, having miniatures of it in every school.

Above all, pupils should be introduced to the heroes of civil life, so that the virtues of peace may become as personalized as the vices of war. Literature that glorifies civic heroism is a contribution to ethics, wherever it may appear in the curriculum. . . .

If ethics is to be taught as a single and separate course, we recommend (1) that every effort be made to save for its content such Japanese manners as are consistent with genuine equality, (2) that the good sportsmanship of daily give-and-take, including the constitutional machinery which makes such accommodation possible, be studied and taught comparatively, and (3) that whatever variety of work there is in Japan, and whatever contentment of spirit the practice of skill has achieved, be celebrated in the curriculum.

Educational reforms offered new opportunities for many Japanese children after World War II, including Tomita Hiroko (left) and Atoguchi Tadami (right), orphans whose parents were killed by the atomic bomb in Hiroshima on August 6, 1945. Their teacher is at center.

Although the Japanese made swift progress toward instituting democratic ideas, they had less success in the economic sphere. War had so devastated the economy that gargantuan efforts seemed for a long time to have little effect. SCAP's initial plan of punishing Japan by breaking up its old business conglomerates put an additional burden on the economy. Although MacArthur took a "reverse course" and began after 1946 to emphasize recovery over democracy, the economic indicators remained disastrous throughout the 1940s. When a conservative American banker, Joseph Dodge, was brought in to impose economic discipline in 1948, his measures cut inflation but triggered higher unemployment, a drop in production, and public unrest. Not until the Korean War of 1950–53 brought a massive demand for Japanese products and supplies did the economy finally begin to get back on its feet. The 1950 yearbook of the newspaper *Asahi* captures the frustration most Japanese felt.

Under the drastic methods of the Dodge Line, the majority of enterprises, centering on the basic industries, were virtually strangled. Trade was the last resort, but foreign demand for commodities

In 1945 and 1946, Tokyo citizens were forced by the wartime devastation to set up makeshift food shops outside the tents that they used as temporary living quarters—and alongside their equally makeshift clotheslines.

The winter wind has gone
and long-awaited spring has arrived
with double-petalled cherry blossoms

—Emperor Hirohito, April 29, 1952, welcoming peace on his fifty-first birthday

was also affected by the global recession, and thus bankruptcy occurred throughout middle and small enterprises as a result of rapid increases in inventories, accumulated goods, and unpaid accounts. Industry was being driven into an historic recession. More specifically, the shock was especially severe on those key industries in the Japanese economy such as heavy industry, machinery, and chemicals, which carried the burden for the future. Personnel readjustment and rationalization on the labor front for the purpose of strengthening labor had reached its ultimate limits. The only remaining possibility whereby Japan could meet international price levels lay in the improvement of plant and equipment and introduction of technology, but with the exception of certain enterprises, there was little progress in this direction for both financial and international reasons. By June 1950, among the holdings in these sectors on the Tokyo and Osaka stock exchanges there were scarcely any which exceeded par value, thus presenting a pitiable spectacle.

The Return to Normal Life

Although American officials had predicted an occupation of as many as twenty-five years, things went so well in all areas but the economy that within a few years they were making plans to end it. The Occupation officially ended on April 28, 1952, three years before the formal end of occupation in Japan's wartime ally Germany. Taken as a whole, it had been a remarkable period, a time when idealistic Americans used both democratic and totalitarian methods—including purges, censorship, and war crimes trials that ignored international legal norms—to nurture an open, egalitarian society. The Japanese people had responded by throwing themselves into the effort to restore normal life. The widely admired MacArthur fell into some disfavor with the Japanese when he described them as "child-like" (and thus teachable) after returning to the United States. But the impact of his time would be felt for decades, mostly in positive ways. The end of the Occupation was marked by two international agreements, both concluded on September 8, 1951, in San Francisco: a forty-eight-nation peace treaty that declared a formal end to hostilities and the U.S.-Japan Security Treaty, which allowed the United States to keep military bases in Japan in exchange for providing military protection.

Security Treaty between the United States and Japan,
September 8, 1951

Japan has this day signed a Treaty of Peace with the Allied Powers.
On the coming into force of that Treaty, Japan will not have the
effective means to exercise its inherent right of self-defense
because it has been disarmed. There is danger to Japan in this situation because irresponsible militarism has not yet been driven
from the world. Therefore, Japan desires a Security Treaty with
the United States of America to come into force simultaneously
with the Treaty of Peace between the United States of America
and Japan. . . .

Accordingly, the two countries have agreed as follows:

I. Japan grants, and the United States of America accepts the
right, upon the coming into force of the Treaty of Peace and of
this Treaty, to dispose United States land, air, and sea forces in and
about Japan. Such forces may be utilized to contribute to the
maintenance of the international peace and security in the Far East
and to the security of Japan against armed attack from without,
including assistance given at the express request of the Japanese
Government to put down large-scale internal riots and disturbances in Japan, caused through instigation or intervention by an
outside Power or Powers.

II. During the exercise of the right referred to in Article I,
Japan will not grant, without the prior consent of the United
States of America, any bases or any rights, power, or authority

*Though many Japanese were
critical of General Douglas
MacArthur, particularly after
he began outlawing some strikes
and tightening press censorship
after 1947, many others praised
him as the person who brought
Japan democracy and ended
militarism. These men express
the hope, in April 1948, that
the general will be elected
President of the United States.*

whatsoever, in or relating to bases or the right of garrison or of maneuver, or transit of ground, air, or naval forces to any third Power.

III. The conditions which shall govern the disposition of armed forces of the United States of America in and about Japan shall be determined by administrative agreements between the two Governments.

IV. This Treaty shall expire whenever in the opinion of the Governments of the United States of America and of Japan there shall have come into force such United Nations arrangements or such alternative individual or collective security dispositions as will satisfactorily provide for the maintenance by the United Nations or otherwise of international peace and security in the Japan Area. . . .

Although the Japanese generally cooperated with the Americans and appreciated their idealism, relations between the two nations were not always smooth. Many Japanese resented what they saw as American arrogance and condescension, and millions of them were skeptical about the way the new relationship tied Japan to American foreign policies. On May 1, 1952, only three days after the Occupation formally ended, more than a million Japanese demonstrated against the continuing presence of U.S. military bases in Japan and America's general dominance in Japanese life. And when a Japanese fisherman died in 1954 following U.S. hydrogen-bomb tests at the Bikini atoll of the Marshall islands, more than 30 million Japanese signed protest petitions. Strategically, however, most thought Japan was better off to remain disarmed except for a relatively small Self-Defense Force, which consumed about 1 percent of the annual gross national product (GNP). Prime Minister Yoshida explains the reasons for maintaining the Self-Defense Force in his 1958 memoirs, reflecting on a 1954 visit to West Germany, which still was under Allied occupation.

During a demonstration at the Imperial Plaza on May 3, 1951, trade unionists are dragged away by police. By the early 1950s, many on the left felt betrayed by the swing in Occupation priorities away from many democratic policies and toward programs aimed at rebuilding the economy and preventing the rise of communism.

What I have said might, perhaps, lead people to think that I found myself in agreement with the leaders of West Germany about everything, but there was one point on which I could not see quite eye to eye with them. This was on the issue of rearmament. They expressed interest in Japan's attitude towards this question. I told them that, for the present, rearmament for Japan would have the opposite effect to that desired—that it was obviously necessary

A mushroom cloud forms over Bikini Atoll in the Pacific Ocean, after the United States tested a hydrogen bomb in 1954. The test resulted in the death of a Japanese fisherman and a massive antibomb petition movement in Japan.

and desirable to possess a certain amount of armed strength, but to go beyond that point, on a scale that warranted the name of rearmament, would place too great a burden upon our people, would provoke national unrest and only serve to aid Communist propaganda and infiltration. The West German leaders did not seem disposed to agree with this contention: they stated that they were paying 9,000,000,000 marks annually for Occupation expenses, which was enough to maintain an army of half a million men, and that they were going to rearm as soon as the result of the Nine Power Conference in London had been made clear. My visit to them took place shortly after the conclusion of that conference in London, held to reach decisions on the question of German rearmament; . . . the rearmament of West Germany became a fact in 1956.

On the question of the attitude of the German people towards the various armies in occupation of West Germany, someone summed it up this way: the Americans were liked, the British known for their stolidity, and the French liked least of all. This appeared to express prevailing feeling in West Germany most succinctly.

The economic boom, fueled by the Korean War and increasing exports, continued throughout the 1950s, with GNP growth rates ranging between 6 and 14 percent a year. The Japanese people became consumers again, sometimes with

To do business by making cunning use of others is a clear principle of economics.

—Diary entry of Yamasaki Kōji, University of Tokyo student who grew wildly wealthy in 1950 through illegal loans a passion. After a decade and a half of austerity, people began to spend on everything from books and magazines to the refrigerators and television sets that symbolized the new prosperity of the era.

Not everyone looked on the new consumerism happily, though. With improved income levels came a growth in what some commentators saw as decadence and spiritual discontent, with many young people turning to money-making and hedonism. Society was shocked when it learned of a University of Tokyo student who had loaned money at 10 percent interest for ten days, then used his wealth to live like a playboy. Many were even more disturbed when the young writer Ishihara Shintarō won a major literary award for his 1955 novel, *Season of Violence*, which depicts young people, led by the protagonist Tatsuya, consumed by drinking, sex, and the pursuit of pleasure.

The return of prosperity in the 1950s dramatically increased the number of automobiles on city streets, leading to traffic jams like this one in Tokyo's Ginza district in 1957. Some drivers reportedly abandoned their cars during this traffic snarl and began walking.

Up till then Tatsuya had only been interested in sensual pleasure. The women he knew best were those of the red light districts. In the confusion of modern life, love was out of the question for Tatsuya. . . .

Among his friends, emotions, and love in particular, came to be looked at from a materialistic point of view; the word "love" was only used with contempt. To them it was a word used to tease or ridicule someone ignorant of women. A popular remark was: "He's in love, so we know he hasn't had a woman yet." . . .

All the group were very good friends, but theirs were not the generous friendships each had had in his high school days. There was no element of self-sacrifice in their relationships, but instead a carefully balanced system of debit and credit. If the debit column grew too long, the friendship would break up. . . . Their conception of friendship was that of being accomplices in crime. There was a common bond formed by their savage or immoral acts—acts which were not wholly attributable to their youth— and this welded the bonds of their friendships.

This group of young men was mixed up in all sorts of sleazy doings—with women, questionable businesses, fights, and even blackmail. These involvements occurred frequently and were always considered the result of youthful mistakes. Their elders would either ignore their faults or else excuse them because they were "young." . . .

The young unconsciously tried to destroy the morals of their elders—morals which always [were] judged against the new generation. In the young people's eyes, the reward of virtue was dullness and vanity. . . . Tatsuya was no exception. He behaved like a spoiled child.

By the late 1950s, Prime Minister Yoshida's "doctrine" was firmly established, and his party, the LDP, looked to increase its popularity by getting the Americans to revise the U.S.-Japan Security Treaty in a way that recognized Japan's growing strength. In contrast to the 1952 treaty, the proposed revision provided for more consultation between the two countries and allowed either party to withdraw from the arrangement unilaterally after the passage of ten years. The Americans also agreed, in writing, to interpret the new treaty as meaning that the United States must secure Japan's agreement before introducing new "equipment" (that is, nuclear weapons) onto Japanese soil.

Unfortunately for the ruling party, the revisions revived discussion of the basic U.S.-Japan relationship, and the ratification process triggered powerful opposition by those who wanted Japan to be more independent in world affairs. When the LDP-led government used strong-arm tactics to ram the revision through the Diet on May 19, 1960, massive demonstrations resulted, some of them involving up to 6 million people, and Prime Minister Kishi Nobusuke was forced to resign, even as the revised treaty took effect. The antitreaty forces insisted for another decade that the security treaty was unconstitutional, as Tabata Shinobu, president of the prestigious Dōshisha University in Kyoto, argued in this 1966 declaration.

It was not by mere chance that we, the Japanese people, surrendering after the atomic bomb attacks on Hiroshima and Nagasaki, have established a Constitution with peace and freedom clauses.

Article 9 of the Japanese Constitution renounces war, an idea that originated with the late Prime Minister Kijūrō Shidehara. The resolution of Premier Shidehara, which succeeded in convincing General MacArthur, was based on the political consciousness of the Japanese people, who believe that armament is futile in the atomic age. . . .

However, the Security Treaty, which was concluded in 1951 between Japan and the United States, contradicts the people's desire and the Constitution; it has turned Japan into a warlike power state based on a military alliance with America. . . . The

The Income of an Average Japanese Family

The contours of the economic changes in the 1950s show up in two sets of economic data, the first on savings rates, the second on what percentage of a family's income went to food, clothing, rent, and personal expenses such as recreation and leisure. As income increased, the percentage spent on food decreased, leaving more money available for housing and personal expenses.

Year	Percentage of Income Saved
1953	7.8
1955	13.4
1957	15.6
1959	16.7
1961	19.2

Year	Percentage of Income Spent on	
	Food/clothing	Housing/recreation/education/leisure
1950	71.0	8.9
1952	69.7	9.0
1954	66.3	10.2
1956	54.3	18.8
1958	51.3	20.4
1960	48.7	21.9

If we sanction the events of the night of May 19–20, it is tantamount to admitting that the authorities are omnipotent in the sense that they can use any forceful methods they wish. If you admit that the authorities are omnipotent, you cannot at the same time accept democracy. . . . This is the choice that has been placed before us.

—Maruyama Masao, one of Japan's most respected scholars, addressing a meeting to demand Prime Minister Kishi's resignation, May 24, 1960

Security Treaty in 1960 added a marked degree of unconstitutionality, which is clearly revealed in the state function that we label "Security Treaty System." The contradiction between the Constitution and "System" has become the cause of many troubles and of anxiety about war, including the problems of the military bases, the entry into Japan of nuclear-powered submarines, and the Vietnam War.

This contradiction and many consequent difficulties should be corrected and solved in accord with the Japanese Constitution. Regarding this solution, there is no alternative left but for the Japanese people or the Diet to declare perpetual neutrality and to establish a neutral state. . . .

The policies of a country, of course, should accord with its Constitution. Unconstitutional politics, at the least, will deprive the people of happiness. However, the present foreign policy, forcibly executed by the Government, embodies partisan diplomacy based on the Security Treaty, which implies subordination to the United States. This policy is fundamentally wrong because of its contempt for and neglect of the Constitution. . . .

The Reemergence

Along with the ministries of foreign affairs and finance, the Ministry of International Trade and Industry (MITI) was considered one of Japan's three most powerful cabinet departments in the early postwar decades. It was significant then when MITI Minister Ikeda Hayato began in 1959 to use a journalist's chance phrase, "income doubling," in his speeches. When he became prime minister after Kishi's 1960 resignation, he made the phrase an official government goal: national income would be doubled within ten years. In actuality, it was a conservative goal, because the country's income had been increasing 10 percent a year since the mid-1950s. But the phrase caught on, and when the goal was reached by 1964, "income doubling" became a catchword for the rapid return of national prosperity. The cabinet adopted the formal plan on December 28, 1960.

Objectives of This Plan
The plan to double the individual income must have as its objectives doubling of the gross national product, attainment of full employment through expansion in employment opportunities,

and raising the living standard of our people. We must adjust differentials in living standard and income existing between farming and non-farming sectors, between large enterprises and small and medium-sized enterprises, between different regions of the country, and between different income groups. We must work toward a balanced development in our national economy and life patterns.

Targets to Be Attained

The plan's goal is to reach 26 trillion yen in GNP (at the fiscal year 1958 price) within the next ten years. To reach this goal, and in view of the fact that there are several factors highly favorable to economic growth existing during the first part of this plan, including the rapid development of technological changes and an abundant supply of skilled labor forces, we plan to attain an annual rate of growth of GNP at 9 percent for the coming three years. . . .

Points to Be Considered in Implementing the Plan and Directions to Be Followed

. . . We must act flexibly and pay due consideration to the economic growth actually occurring and other related conditions. Any action we undertake must be consistent with the objectives described above. To do so, we shall pay special attention to the implementation of the following:

(a) Promotion of Modernization in Agriculture . . .

(b) Modernization of Medium and Small Enterprises . . .

(c) Accelerated Development of Less Developed Regions . . .

(d) Promotion of Appropriate Locations for Industries and Reexamination of Regional Distribution of Public Sector Projects . . .

(e) Active Cooperation with the Development of the World Economy. Raising productivity means strengthening our export competitiveness. Bearing in mind that an important key to the success of this plan is in the expansion of our exports and an increase in revenues in foreign currencies, we must promote a viable export strategy accompanied by other measures increasing nontrade revenues such as tourism and maritime transportation. We shall actively seek cooperation with other countries in promoting economic development in less-developed countries and raise their income levels.

Trains symbolized Japan's economic recovery in the late 1950s. The first luxury trunk line, the Kodama, took to the rails in November 1957, providing eight cars and carrying 420 passengers. Its 100-mile-per-hour speed presaged the world's first high-speed bullet train, the Shinkansen, which would begin running in Japan just seven years later.

Japan's World Ranking, 1969, in Industrial Products

Product	Rank
Aluminum	second
Cameras	first
Cement	second
Commercial motor vehicles	first
Computers	second
Cotton yarn	second
Crude steel	second
Motorcycles	first
Plastic resin	second
Radio sets	first
Shipbuilding	first
Television sets	second

Symbols can affect people's spirits as much as reality does, particularly when they are consistent with that reality. One symbol of Japan's reemergence was the 1964 Olympics, held in Tokyo. As the first games ever staged in Asia, they showcased Japan as a peaceful power. The Shinkansen, the world's first bullet train, made its initial run ten days before the games started; several art exhibits brought an unprecedented level of culture to the Olympics; and the sports venues won raves for architectural excellence. Japanese efficiency was apparent in the nearly errorless conduct of the competitions. And the country's rising affluence enabled 2 million spectators to spend $40 million on tickets. Even in the competition, Japan won more medals than it ever had before, ranking third in golds and fourth overall. On the day after the closing ceremonies on October 25, the *Japan Times* reported that its editor, Hirasawa Kazushige, had found Olympic president Avery Brundage brimming with praise—and still pleased about the effect of his own efforts to speak in Japanese at the end of his address opening the games.

This official poster promoted the October 1964 Olympics, held in Tokyo. The highly successful games were heralded in the press as evidence that Japan had once more become a peace-loving international leader.

In the interview held at Brundage's Imperial Hotel suite, Hirasawa counted three factors which he thought have made significant contributions to the success of the Tokyo Olympics.

They were the Japanese speech Brundage made at the end of his remarks at the Games opening ceremony in requesting the Emperor to officially open the 18th Olympiad, the arts exhibitions and demonstrations, and the five structures built for the games.

Brundage agreed with Hirasawa's view but added that there was a fourth factor, which he said was the most important.

"The most important factor," he said, "was the fact that the Japanese Organizing Committee has converted the whole 95 million people of Japan to the idea of the Olympic movement.

"Your primary school children have sent me *senbazuru* [1,000 folded paper cranes] and everywhere I went, children came up to me, tried to speak to me and asked for my signature. Not just sports people but all the people—that was never done before."

In a message he issued Friday, Brundage called Japan the "Olympic nation No. 1 in all the world."

As for the Japanese speech he made, Brundage accepted Hirasawa's praise with a smile. He said he had originally planned to make part of his closing ceremony remarks in Japanese again but thought better of it because his Japanese in the opening remarks had made a good impression and he didn't want to spoil it.

The phrase "timid colossus" often was used to describe Japan in the 1960s. The nation's economic clout had grown rapidly, but its political profile remained slight. Although Japan had begun to be more active in Asia, the security treaty with the United States kept it from developing an independent approach to foreign policy. The war in Vietnam exacerbated the sense that Japan was not its own master diplomatically, when the government consistently supported America's war and allowed U.S. troops to deploy from Japan despite widespread public opposition to the war. Contrasting essays in 1966 by the playwright Fukuda Tsuneari and the political scientist Fukuda Kan'ichi illustrate the debates over Vietnam policy, and over Japan's broader approach to world affairs. In "Let's Not Make the United States Stand Alone," Fukuda Tsuneari argues that Japan has no choice but to be a follower on the international scene.

If a jet fell on Little Ei's home,
Little Ei would surely will die.
Then, he would regret that
We signed the Japan-U.S. Security Treaty.

—Song by peace demonstrators in the late 1960s

In writing this essay, I wish to make absolutely clear my belief that Japan, as a member of the free world, must follow the lead of the United States. I believe that the Japanese people must awake to a sober realization of this fact and strive to rid their minds of the now obsolete 19th-century concept of nationalism. However noble a concept it may have been in the past, 19th-century European-style nationalism is no longer valid in our time. . . .

The world today is at the threshold of a new era, an era in which no country can be truly independent in the classic sense of the term. One country's interference in another's internal affairs should no longer be condemned as a violation of international law. It is rather the obsoleteness of today's international law and the anachronistic thinking of the people who cling to it that should be condemned. We must wake up to the fact that every country in the world has to choose between communism and America's new internationalism. Every underdeveloped country must decide whether to modernize itself according to America's formula or join the forces of communist "internationalism" in order to carry out a nationalistic struggle against American "imperialism." When a country fails to choose, the two types of internationalism inevitably clash within its borders. This is exactly what has happened in Vietnam. . . .

Japan must cooperate fully with the United States in carrying out the latter's policy of world management. . . . A country such as ours cannot begin to formulate its foreign policies until it has determined which internationalism it will follow. My suggestion would be for all Japanese to take a definite stand for one or the other, for American internationalism or for communist internationalism. We should once and for all abandon the illusion that there is a third choice we can make.

Fukuda Kan'ichi, a professor at the University of Tokyo, disagrees with the "follow America" approach, arguing in "Japan's Reaction to the Vietnam Crisis" that Japan has to act more independently, deciding on its own which approach is right, then acting according to conscience.

One would naturally like to think that even within the limited framework of the mutual security treaty Japan might make some diplomatic gesture to help bring about a peaceful settlement in Vietnam, a concrete proposal designed to produce some tangible effect on American policy and action. . . . My proposal is that the Japanese government follow the lead of France, which on March 9, 1965, notified the United States that French support would not be available should the Vietnam conflict develop into a military showdown between China and America. Japan should make it absolutely clear that she will never allow the U.S. to use its bases in Japan for attacking mainland China or North Korea. . . .

Of course, Japan does not actually possess sufficient military power to prevent the U.S. from employing its bases in Japan for operations against China or North Korea; we can nevertheless exert moral pressure, and we can threaten to withdraw all services and facilities now provided for maintenance of the bases. . . .

For Japan to assume the role of an observer with a do-nothing attitude toward limiting U.S. action in Vietnam is tantamount to her cooperating in America's war efforts. Any act of cooperation with brute military power is clearly incompatible with the spirit of our Constitution as expressed in the Preamble: "We have determined to preserve our security and existence, trusting in the justice and faith of the peace-loving peoples of the world."

Japan's intellectual life was as turbulent in the 1960s as its economic life was vibrant. By the middle of the decade, people around the world were taking notice of Japan's success in producing some of the world's best-educated, most productive workers. Within Japan itself, however, there was increasing criticism of how this success was achieved, and particularly of a university entrance-exam system that put

inhuman pressures on students and, according to critics, produced conformists. That, along with anger about Japan's
support of the Vietnam War, environmental pollution, and
the poor quality of university education, led to massive student protests in the latter years of the decade. A professor at
the University of Tokyo shares selections from essays that his
students were writing in 1967 on what had come to be discussed as the "test hell."

1. Tests, tests, tests. . . . They have dominated our student days.
They have kept us from taking the time to think about our society
or the meaning of our own lives. . . . An education stressing com-
petition and inculcating false values has, unawares, created a kind
of person who thinks only of himself and is uninterested in others.

2. All those who study for the college entrance exams certainly realize how differences in class rank become absolute walls
between students. Those on top of the heap have their superiority confirmed by those on the bottom, and those on the bottom
see those on the top as symbols of authority. . . . It is absolute nonsense to determine the worth of a person on the basis of fine differences in test scores.

3. Up till now, I had never once thought about what it *meant* to
go to college. For me, I suspect that *getting into* the university was
my ultimate objective. I didn't know why, I just gave up everything
else and decided I wanted to get into Tōdai.

4. The fate of those dedicated to preparing for the college
entrance exams is clear: if one puts up too much resistance to the
system it's "curtains."

Another source of widespread frustration in the late 1960s
lay in the inability of social systems to keep up with rapid
urbanization and industrialization. Landscapes were rav-
aged to make way for industrial plants. Housing could not
keep up with the pouring of people into the cities. And
industrial pollution became a major problem, with great
numbers of people affected by air pollution, noise, and poi-
soning from mercury, PCBs, and cadmium. The worst pollution case was in Minamata, a fishing town on the island of
Kyushu where hundreds died and thousands experienced
incurable illness from wastes that the Chisso carbide company discharged into the harbor. Known as Minamata Disease,
which caused mental disorders, deformity, and shaking, the

*Formal goals adopted by Japan's major teacher's union,
Nikkyōso, in 1966 include:*

1. Intensify the joint struggles of all public servants for the early attainment of a large salary
increase.

4. Oppose education controlled by the central
government. . . .

5. Oppose the "invasion" of Vietnam, destroy
the United States-Japan Security Treaty, prohibit the nuclear rearmament of Japan, return
Okinawa from American control, and intensify
the People's Movement for Peace.

Tōdai

Tōdai is the abbreviation
used universally in Japan
for Tokyo Daigaku, or the
University of Tokyo.

Many victims of Minamata Disease, a pollution-induced illness named for the southern industrial city where it occurred most frequently, suffered from gnarled fingers and painful joints. It often attacked the central nervous system, leaving victims with mental defects and plunging families into both psychological stress and serious financial difficulties.

illness became a worldwide symbol for the evils of industrial pollution. In a 1972 memoir, *Paradise in the Sea of Sorrow*, Ishimure Michiko, a Minamata resident, describes its effects on a fifty-six-year-old fisherman named Tsurumatsu.

It was the old fisherman's eyes, glaring at me with intense hatred, and the little comic magazine he held fast with both hands in front of him like a shield, which had attracted my attention, compelling me to stop abruptly in front of his room. . . .

Tsurumatsu looked at me with undisguised hostility. His booklet suddenly slipped down to the floor. The hatred in the fisherman's eyes died out like a candle in the wind, and his look became moist, sad, and forlorn, like that of a young, mortally wounded deer.

Because of the Disease, Kama Tsurumatsu, the fifty-six-year-old fisherman with his broad, sunburnt cheeks covered with an irregular growth of beard, and his sharp, penetrating glance, had lost the ability to speak. In all probability he was not aware of the fact that he was a victim of Minamata Disease, that unheard-of, manmade disease of the central nervous system caused, to put it scientifically, by ingestion of fish and shellfish contaminated by organic mercury. . . .

Tsurumatsu certainly realized that he had been stricken by an evil curse and that his death was imminent. He fell into the sea so often while fishing that his family became worried and had him admitted to the hospital. His condition deteriorated rapidly: he could no longer articulate words, and his convulsions became increasingly violent. He would fall out of bed and lie on the floor for hours, unable to climb back into bed by himself. In spite of his hopeless condition, Tsurumatsu had preserved enough dignity to be ashamed of his appearance. Even more than shame, he was consumed with anger: with himself, for having become a helpless wreck; with society, because it either ignored or laughed at him; and with medical science, because of its inability to cure his disease.

A less tragic but more universal result of rapid growth of city residents was inadequate housing and transportation that forced millions to live in tiny apartments (derided by critical observers as "rabbit hutches") or in huge and impersonal housing complexes, and to commute on Japan National Railways (JNR) trains for as much as two hours each way to work. A 1974 diary-style essay by an American resident in Japan, called "The Work-to-Rule Struggle," describes what the conditions on Tokyo's rush-hour trains could be like, particularly when intensified by a labor slowdown.

8:23. More people jam on at . . . Asagaya. Still more, how is it possible!—at Koenji. At Nakano we half-shove, are half-carried by the human flow toward the door. The ubiquitous, anonymous hand in the small of the back propels me out of the car. Salmon swimming upstream . . . to the company. . . . [The Japanese names denote successive train stations on Tokyo's Central Line. The rider here transfers at Nakano, just west of the line's hub at Shinjuku Station.]

8:55. Sendagaya Station. I try to count the number of passengers between us and the door. There are too many. The density of bodies is amazing. The doors open, and I start to force my way through, my boy following close in my wake. People do not move aside (they cannot) and it's difficult to step without treading on someone. I am bigger than they are, I remember triumphantly, and lower my shoulder and hit the line. No semblance of a gracious exit now, every man for himself before that door closes. . . . Storming ahead I forget to bend at the doorway . . . crack! My head hits the doorframe and my knees buckle at the sharp pain. I manage to avoid falling and regain my balance. Embarrassed, a pounding crease on top of my skull, rage . . . at the JNR, the unions, the politicians who never ride the trains, at the public that tolerates these wretched conditions.

Commuters pack the Shinjuku Station in central Tokyo on a typical weekday morning in 1962. Trains arrive every two or three minutes, but the process of transit workers pushing riders into the cars to make space enough that the doors can shut is necessary each time. The crowding—and the pushing—have continued to the present day.

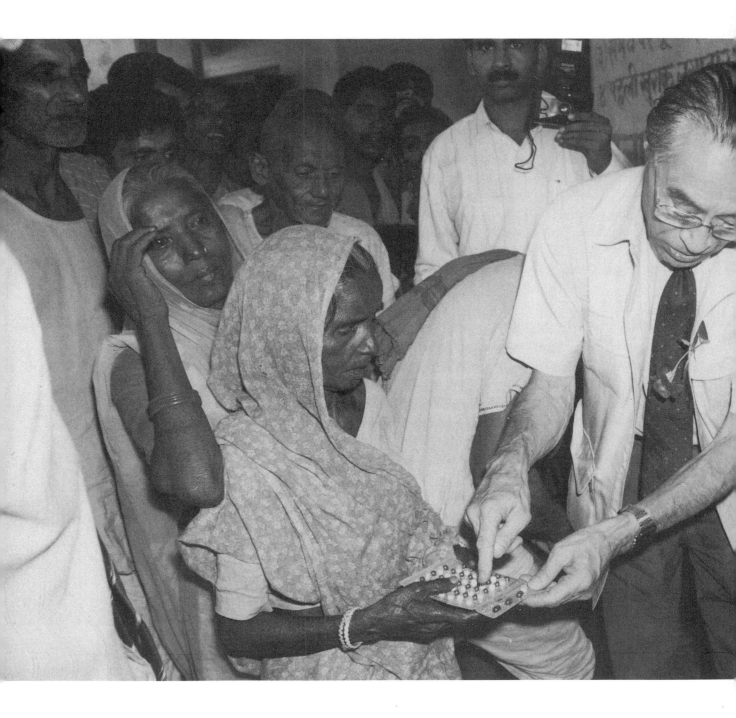

Chapter Eight

Japan as a World Power: After 1970

Contemporary periods always plague historians trying to create a cohesive narrative. Full of conflicting currents, they are too recent for a consensus to emerge about the "big picture." It seems safe nonetheless to say that two features dominated the last third of Japan's twentieth century. On the one hand, there were the sharp, roller-coaster ups and downs of the economy characterized by inflation and economic turbulence followed by a long period of abundance, and followed again by economic troubles. On the other hand, there was the consistent vitality of life for most Japanese. Personal living standards remained among the highest in the world, even during the economic downturns of the 1990s. Japanese cities were accessible and safe. Public transportation was efficient and reliable. The country's popular culture exported video games and animated films, internationally known as *anime*, to the rest of the world. Japan also continued to set standards for efficiency and innovation in areas as varied as computer software and automobile manufacturing. From the late 1980s, the Japanese government gave more foreign aid than any other country in the world. And its Japan Exchange and Teaching Program, popularly known as JET, set benchmarks for internationalization-in-action by bringing in thousands of foreigners each year to teach English.

The 1970s began with the country in a tailspin, as the troubles of the late 1960s seemed to intensify with each passing month. The environmental problems continued, even after the Diet began passing antipollution legislation. The worldwide energy crisis that occurred when oil prices quadrupled in 1973 hit Japan particularly hard, because oil accounted for three-fourths of its energy and had to be almost

During the last two decades of the twentieth century, Japan became the world's largest provider of foreign assistance. Here, Dr. Yuasa Yo explains the use of pills to a patient at a Hansen's disease (leprosy) clinic supported by the Nippon Foundation in Vaishali, India. The foundation is working to eradicate leprosy worldwide.

Forced to deal with intense population pressures, Japan has developed some of the world's most innovative technologies in recent years: everything from swimming pools heated by garbage incineration to small electric cars that save both fuel and space.

completely imported. And in the middle of the decade, a series of political scandals toppled a prime minister and sent the LDP reeling. Even in the midst of these troubles, however, the hallmark of the decade was vitality. As if following the script of the early postwar years, the leaders responded to the difficulties with sensible and visionary programs that quickly restored economic health. Inflation was curbed, wage increases were moderated, and industry cut its dependence on oil, so that by the end of the decade, oil made up only 55 percent of Japan's energy use. When a second oil crisis hit the world late in the 1970s, the impact on Japan was relatively slight.

The result was that in the 1980s Japan basked in material wealth and self-confidence such as it never had known before. In many ways, that decade was symbolized by Nakasone Yasuhiro, prime minister from 1982 to 1987. A World War II naval officer who wanted to increase Japan's self-reliance and military spending, he approached both politics and the world aggressively, addressing U.S. President Ronald Reagan as "Ron." Japan became the world's largest creditor nation in these years. It had thirty banks in London alone, and its trade surplus with the United States soared to the point that "Japan bashing" became a favorite pastime of some American congressmen. When the emperor died in 1989, bringing to a close Asia's longest imperial reign, it was hardly surprising that 164 countries sent representatives to Tokyo for his funeral. Riches may have caused jealousies and resentment in other nations, but they also attracted those who wanted to benefit from Japan's generosity, influence its policies, or win its cooperation.

In many ways, the last decade of the millennium was a repeat of the 1970s, in more serious form. When the country's hyper-

No country in the world has a livelier popular culture than Japan. In the late 1970s, its restaurants and bars introduced the world to karaoke, pictured above, and at century's end adults and children alike were devouring millions of manga, *or comic books, every year. Particularly popular were educational comics for children.*

inflated land prices began to decline, the economy fell with them, as large companies that had used unrealistic land values to secure loans found themselves unable to repay, and banks went bankrupt. The bubble of the 1980s had burst; the stock exchange plummeted; the economy grew at the slowest rate since the war, then began to fall during the second half of the decade. The country also experienced a host of political and social difficulties that sapped its people of self-confidence: a succession of scandal-plagued, weak cabinets; criticism from Asia and the rest of the world over a failure to accept responsibility for World War II crimes; a devastating earthquake in Kōbe in 1995; a gas attack on Tokyo subways by religious extremists the same year; worries about nuclear activity in nearby North Korea; and a rush of social criticism about the self-centered younger generation. Despite all of this, Japan's general dynamism remained undeniable—and unstoppable. The Japanese continued to travel widely and consume voraciously; they remained among the world's best educated, most widely read people, and maintained impressively high levels of savings. By the early 2000s, their culture, goods, and people—everything from sushi, ramen noodles, karaoke, videos, *anime*, and automobiles to major-league baseball players—had come to pervade the world as a part of the common international heritage.

Surmounting Crises

The Japanese were stunned on November 25, 1970, when the renowned novelist Mishima Yukio committed *seppuku,* ritual suicide, disemboweling himself after a speech before cadets at the eastern headquarters of the nation's Self-Defense Forces (SDF) in Tokyo. After the act, one of Mishi-

Though Japan's military remains small in proportion to its population and economic might, the Self-Defense Forces maintain state-of-the-art technology and take part regularly in ceremonial occasions.

ma's aides decapitated the writer, then committed *seppuku* himself. The Japanese press and intellectual world discussed the meaning of the act endlessly. Did it represent a revival of 1930s-style military activism, which was what Mishima—who himself never was in the military—demanded in his speech just prior to the suicide? Was it a sign of the spiritual emptiness of the postwar generation? Or was it simply the mad act of a fanatic, as the majority concluded? Whichever line of reasoning one followed, everyone agreed that Mishima's suicide was symbolic of the problems that had been plaguing Japan for the previous several years. Mishima made it clear in his speech to assembled SDF troops immediately before his death that he thought Japan's difficulties lay in spiritual flabbiness, which kept people from rising up against their leaders and demanding that the constitution be revised to allow Japan to have an army and navy. The constitution's prohibition of armed forces, he said, made the very existence of the Self-Defense Forces a sham. The listening troops paid little attention to him.

The purpose of Mishima's paradoxical action was to focus critical attention on such problems as war guilt, the emperor system, modernism, postwar democracy, pacifism and mass society. Seen from the vantage point of intellectual history, his act was a collision of "modernization and nationalism."

—Political analyst and editor Kano Tsutomu, writing early in 1971 in *Japan Interpreter*, soon after Mishima's death

We have seen postwar Japan stumble into a spiritual vacuum, preoccupied only with its economic prosperity, unmindful of its national foundations, losing its national spirit, seeking trivialities without looking to fundamentals, and falling into makeshift expediency and hypocrisy. Gnashing our teeth, we have had to watch politics serve the glossing over of inconsistency, the protection of individual status, thirst for power, and hypocrisy. We have had to stand idly by while the policies and the future of the nation were entrusted to foreign powers, while the humiliation of our defeat was merely evaded and not effaced, and while the traditions of Japan were being desecrated by the Japanese themselves.

We dreamed that today the real Japan, the real Japanese, and the real *bushi* spirit exist nowhere else but in the Self-Defense Forces. In the meantime, it seems patently clear that under the theory of law, the Self-Defense Forces are unconstitutional, and defense, the nation's basic problem, continues to be evaded by opportunistic legal interpretation. We see the Self-Defense Forces being an army but not being called an army. Such fundamental inconsistencies are bound to cause a deterioration of the Japanese people's spirit and a corruption of their morals. The army, which should hold honor in the highest esteem, has tolerated neglect under the most pernicious deception. . . . We are angered by postwar Japan's overlong sleep. We believe that Japan will awaken precisely when the Self-Defense Forces awakens. We believe that unless the Self-Defense Forces itself wakes up, sleeping Japan will not awaken. And we believe that we, as Japanese, have no greater duty than to exert ourselves to the utmost for the day when, through constitutional revision, the Self-Defense Forces can stand on the principle of founding an army and in fact become a real army. . . .

We will wait no longer. There is no reason to wait for those who debase themselves. But we will wait for thirty more minutes, a last thirty minutes. . . . We will show you that there is a value higher than reverence for life.

It is neither freedom nor democracy. It is Japan. Japan, the country whose history and traditions we love. Is there no one who will die by hurling his body against the constitution which has mutilated her? If there is, let us rise together even now, and let us die together. It is in the fervent hope that you who are pure in spirit will once again be men and true *bushi* that we have resorted to this act.

The timing of Mishima's suicide was tied to America's return of Okinawa to Japan in 1972, an event that, in the words of Prime Minister Satō Eisaku, brought the postwar era to a close. Okinawa Prefecture encompasses the Ryūkyū island chain, of which Okinawa is the largest set of islands. The

bushi

Bushi is another word for samurai, widely used in Japan's medieval era. Both words mean warrior.

chain, which extends for about 800 miles southwest of Kyushu, came under the authority of the United States when Japan was defeated in 1945. During the student unrest of the late 1960s, Mishima had envisioned a nationalistic uprising against Japan's reliance on the United States. The popularity of Okinawa's reversion, however, made him see how unrealistic that vision was and convinced him that his struggle to revive Japan's militant spirit was futile. For the Ryūkyū islanders themselves, reversion was a complex blessing. While most preferred an end to American control, they had ambivalent feelings about the relationship with Japan, which had taken control of Okinawa forcibly less than a century earlier. The fact that more than half of America's Japan-based military forces were stationed in Okinawa also angered many Ryūkyūans. On November 21, 1969, U.S. President Richard Nixon and Prime Minister Satō put together the communiqué that laid the groundwork for reversion. It takes note of Japan's opposition to nuclear weapons and of both nations' concern about growing trade problems.

5. In light of the current situation and the prospects in the Far East, the President and the Prime Minister agreed that they highly valued the role played by the Treaty of Mutual Cooperation and Security in maintaining the peace and security of the Far East including Japan, and they affirmed the intention of the two governments firmly to maintain the Treaty on the basis of mutual trust and common evaluation of the international situation. . . .

6. The Prime Minister emphasized his view that the time had come to respond to the strong desire of the people of Japan, of both the mainland and Okinawa, to have the administrative rights over Okinawa returned to Japan on the basis of the friendly relations between the United States and Japan and thereby to restore Okinawa to its normal status. The President expressed appreciation of the Prime Minister's view. The President and the Prime Minister also recognized the vital role played by the United States forces in Okinawa in the present situation in the Far East. As a result of their discussion it was agreed that the mutual security interests of the United States and Japan could be accommodated within arrangements for the return of the administrative rights over Okinawa to Japan. They therefore agreed that the two governments would immediately enter into consultations regarding specific arrangements for accomplishing the early reversion of

Okinawa without detriment to the security of the Far East including Japan. They further agreed to expedite the consultations with a view to accomplishing the reversion during 1972 subject to the conclusion of these specific arrangements with the necessary legislative support. . . . The President and the Prime Minister agreed also that the United States would retain under the terms of the Treaty of Mutual Cooperation and Security such military facilities and areas in Okinawa as required in the mutual security of both countries.

8. The Prime Minister described in detail the particular sentiment of the Japanese people against nuclear weapons. . . .

12. In their discussion of economic matters, the President and the Prime Minister noted the marked growth in economic relations between the two countries. . . . In this regard the President stressed his determination to bring inflation in the United States under control. He also reaffirmed the commitment of the United States to the principle of promoting freer trade. The Prime Minister indicated the intention of the Japanese Government to accelerate rapidly the reduction of Japan's trade and capital restrictions. . . .

Several shocks came to Japan in rapid succession early in the 1970s. U.S. President Richard Nixon had won favor with his agreement to return Okinawa to Japan, but he also disturbed the Japanese several times by sending the message that Japan really was not important to him; he failed to consult with Japan before deciding to visit China in 1972, even though successive American leaders had promised to discuss any changes in their China policy with Japan. A year later, he imposed a worldwide embargo on American soybean sales. It was a move directed at the Soviet Union that failed to take into account that Japan got much of its protein from American soybeans. These problems had hardly passed before the Arab countries formed a cartel called the Oil Producing Export Companies (OPEC) and quadrupled the price of oil, sending Japan's economy into crisis. And while the Japanese still were dealing with that problem, they were confronted with their biggest postwar political scandal, which ousted a popular prime minister from office.

The popular politician Tanaka Kakuei, a can-do political outsider with only an eighth-grade education, had gotten rich by corrupt means and had become prime minister in 1972 after bribing other politicians. Press coverage of his

Generally seen as one of the most popular politician of the 1970s, even after his fall from the prime minister's post in a 1974 corruption scandal, Tanaka Kakuei greets well-wishers during a rain shower.

One reason for the quickness of Tanaka's fall lay in the rise in the early 1970s of more than 3,000 citizens' movements, made up of groups of housewives and other commoners who formed local organizations to fight against everything from corrupt politics and pollution to high commodity prices and inept public services. The editor of the Japan Quarterly *assesses their revolutionary impact on Japanese thinking, in 1973:*

The consciousness of the citizens of Japan has changed greatly. . . . The people, who once regarded politics as "a world apart" and somehow impenetrable, are now actively jumping up onto the political stage. Direct democratic thought has blossomed. . . . The idea of "a sovereign people" has at last begun to have real meaning.

the restoration

Ishihara refers here to the Meiji Restoration, the watershed event of 1868, which often is talked about by popular commentators as the beginning of Japan's modern era.

illicit behavior drove him from office late in 1974. A few months before that, his success-at-all-costs approach and inability to see the need for moral leadership prompted an essay titled "Japan's Moral Principles" by Ishihara Shintarō, the novelist who had riveted the nation with his descriptions of youthful self-absorption in the 1950s. Ishihara worried that Tanaka's moral failings reflected those of the broader Japanese society.

The outlook and basic sensitivity of contemporary Japanese, whichever generation, are the same. The core of that outlook is an unqualified belief in the absolute effectiveness of economic rationality. The emotional framework of the wartime generation may be colored by a few cosmetic differences, but economics remains their spiritual and psychological absolute. . . .

Tanaka Kakuei is to me the symbol of the ruin and confusion in Japanese affairs. I know of no other example of a politician whose character so epitomizes the society or so affects it. Sociologists like to say that during the century after the restoration the social and economic hierarchy was superseded by the urban bourgeois elite, which is typified by the man who moved from one of the poorest areas in Japan to success in the big city. This is Tanaka Kakuei himself. . . . The failure to see his own responsibility for a mismanaged government is only natural in a person who cannot recognize the basic changes that have taken place in society. When he should feel a heavy burden of responsibility, all he can feel is chagrin. Perhaps his reluctance to take responsibility is because he has no conscious sense of being the first one who should.

Japanese economic and industrial success after the war is a result of rationality and good fortune, combined with lucky speculation. Tanaka's genius would be spectacular in the circumstances of a few years ago, precisely because of his ability to make the right guess. But the time has passed and his genius cannot provide a foundation for the moral principles necessary today.

Japan's leadership, both inside and outside the government, responded forcefully to the political and economic crises of the early 1970s. When Nixon snubbed the Japanese in his decision to go to China without consulting Japan's leaders, the Japanese immediately opened full diplomatic relations with China—well before the Americans did. When oil prices soared, Japan began to cooperate more with Arab countries,

Japan's mountainous terrain makes its rivers short but rapid. As a result, hydroelectric plants dot the country, providing a rich supply of energy for massive urban centers and industrial complexes.

cut back on the use of electricity, and eliminated industries that used energy inefficiently. And when Tanaka was forced to resign, the Diet turned to a surprise choice, the impeccably clean Miki Takeo, as prime minister. One result was that by the end of the decade the economy was vibrant again and the public sense of pride was palpable. This 1976 response to the oil crisis and recession by one of Japan's industrial giants, National/Panasonic founder Matsushita Kōnosuke, illustrates the kind of long-range thinking that, though not always practical or in tune with environmental concerns, kept Japanese economic development vibrant during these years. Matsushita is concerned not just with the oil crisis but with Japan's lack of space for development.

The current recession is unlike anything we have hitherto experienced. Yet, as with any unfortunate experience, some good can emerge. . . . I often wonder if the present recession might not be a momentary lull before the emergence into a new age in which mankind will achieve a balance between material and spiritual needs and a harmony between mind and matter. Perhaps more than ever, we have been provided the opportunity to ask ourselves, "now, where should we go from here?" . . .

I propose that the solution to Japan's territorial restrictions lies in levelling about 20 percent (75,000 sq. km) of the total land space presently occupied by mountains. In any other country, the earth and rocks would have to be hauled some distance to the ocean to be dumped; Japan, with the ocean close at hand, has just the set-up for this kind of project.

The plan I have in mind, however, involves much more than an ordinary reclamation project for converting coastal areas into usable land; it proposes the creation of a whole new island, about the size of Shikoku. Not only would the 20 percent of our area presently taken up by mountains be made available for use but new land will actually be created, a new island equivalent in size to the newly levelled area. This would add 40 percent more to the 30 percent of Japan's area now in use, more than doubling the available area for development and providing in one project the secret to self-sufficiency in food production. . . .

Is it folly to embark upon such a scheme? I believe not. Japan is uniquely suited for this project, and it can be successful. If we were talking about a hot, tropical region, there would be little value in such a scheme, but Japan's temperate climate and topography are favorable. Moreover, being an island country, we do not face the problems of a change in national borders that a land-bound nation does. We infringe upon no other nation's territory by adding another Shikoku just off Kōchi; we merely create another Inland Sea.

A centuries-old Japanese tendency toward self-reflection turned into a craze in the 1970s, as writers praised Japan's postwar successes and debated the sources of Japanese culture in a discourse called *Nihonjinron*, "discussions of Japaneseness." Although their analyses differed, they all agreed on one thing: Japanese culture was unique. Some writers focused on the tendency to organize society into small, hierarchical groups; many discussed the uniqueness of the Japanese language, or of a culture shaped by rice planting; some wrote about the "island mentality," others about a propensity for hard work. One expression of *Nihonjinron* came in the many writings about former soldier Onoda Hiroo. After spending thirty years in the Philippine jungles, sure that World War II was still underway because no commander had ordered him to quit fighting, he was finally persuaded in 1974 to come home to Japan. An intelligent man, Onoda was seen as typifying that loyal, never-give-up quality that made Japanese "unique." He explains in *No Surrender*, a 1974 memoir, how he and a then-surviving comrade named Kozuka Kinshichi interpreted newspapers left in the jungle by an unsuccessful search team that came from Japan in 1959, trying to find him.

Shikoku

Shikoku is Japan's fourth-largest island, lying across the Inland Sea from Hiroshima and Kōbe. Kōchi Prefecture makes up its southern half. It has a land area of 7,254 square miles, slightly less than that of New Jersey.

Japan as Number One: Lessons for America. The very title will blow the minds of many Americans. But unquestionably Japan today has a more smoothly functioning society and an economy that is running rings around ours. Vogel's fascinating book will help explain this best organized and most dynamic of all major modern nations.

—Former U.S. Ambassador to Japan Edwin Reischauer, on dust jacket of Harvard sociologist Ezra Vogel's *Japan as Number One: Lessons for America* (1979)

For fifteen years, I had been outside the flow of time. All I could be sure of was what had been true in late 1944 and what I had sworn at that time to do. I had kept my vow rigidly during those fifteen years.

Reading the 1959 newspapers in this same frame of mind, the first thought I had was, "Japan is safe, after all. Safe and still fighting!"

The newspapers offered any amount of proof. Wasn't the whole country wildly celebrating the crown prince's marriage? Didn't the pictures show a lavish wedding parade through the streets of Tokyo, with thousands of cheering Japanese lined up along the way? There was nothing here about 100 million people dying. Japan was obviously thriving and prosperous.

Who said we had lost the war? The newspapers proved this was wrong. If we had lost, our countrymen would all be dead; there would be no more Japan, let alone Japanese newspapers.

Kozuka agreed with me completely. As we were reading the papers, he looked up and remarked, "Life in the home islands seems to be a lot better than it was when we left, doesn't it? Look at the ads. There seems to be plenty of everything. I'm glad, aren't you? It makes me feel it has been worthwhile holding out the way we have."

How could we even dream that Japan's cities had been leveled, that Japan's ships had nearly all been sunk, or that an exhausted and depleted Japan had indeed surrendered? As to the details of the defeat, such as the invasion of Manchukuo by the Soviet Union or the dropping of the atomic bomb on Hiroshima, the newspapers of 1959 gave not an inkling.

Awash in Capital

No single fact characterized Japan in the 1980s better than the economic boom. It was as though Prime Minister Ikeda's promise two decades earlier of "income doubling" had become a permanent feature of the country. By the late 1980s, four of the world's ten largest auto makers were Japanese, as were seven of its ten largest banks. Japanese companies were buying well-known American firms and landmarks. Japan had an annual trade surplus of more than $100 billion (half of it with the United States), $200 billion in foreign assets, and the largest per-capita GNP of any of the world's powers. People were spending lavishly too—on foreign trips, hyper-inflated homes or land, and even on children's Christmas parties where the entrance fee was roughly

One facet of *Nihonjinron* was a constant comparison of Japan with Western nations. Kato Shūichi, well-traveled sociologist, published a list of comparative national strengths in the newspaper *Asahi Shimbun* on January 5, 1976.

Seven Plusses for USA

Low price of beef
Western calendar
Space
Love of nature
Use of language
Vanguard of the arts and sciences
Personal courage

Seven Plusses for Japan

Better beer
Metric system
Excellent, clean public transportation
Low crime rate
Absence of nuclear weapons
Ancient cultural traditions
Job security

Household Gender Relationships

Japan's Management and Coordination Agency compiled a chart on who made household decisions in 1992. The researchers found that affluence led to only a limited change in gender relationships. Most husbands continued to make the majority of the household decisions, with the exception of the daily budget. The figures indicate percentages.

Matter to be decided:	Husband	Wife	Both	Other
Land or house purchase	53.2	1.9	31.5	13.3
Furniture, large electric-appliance purchase	23.2	20.1	43.7	13.1
Control of daily household budget	9.7	70.5	15.0	4.8
Overall decision-making power	61.7	11.6	20.5	6.3

$100. Deficit spending by the government continued in these years, but few worried because the economy was so robust.

One of the more unusual forums for talking about the bustling economy was the comic book, a serious medium read by people of all ages and educational levels in Japan. In the popular 1986 *Manga Nihon keizai nyūmon* (Comic Book Introduction to Japanese Economics), two workers, one of them named Kudo, discuss Adam Smith's idea of the "hidden hand" in the operation of the world's economic system. A noted eighteenth-century economic philosopher, Smith argued that if individuals were free to seek profits, God's "hidden hand" would guide humankind to prosperity.

In *Wealth of Nations*, Adam Smith says that economic self-interest led by the unseen hand of God enriches the world.

Growing confidence in diplomacy accompanied the affluence. Prime Minister Nakasone in particular pushed for Japan
to be less subservient in dealing with other nations. He
moved to increase defense spending; developed a personal
relationship with U.S. President Ronald Reagan; upset critics
who claimed he was violating the separation of church and
state when he visited Yasukuni Jinja, the national Shintō
shrine to Japan's war dead; and nurtured cooperation among
Asian countries. Japan's new pride frequently came off as
arrogance toward Asian neighbors, however, and served
to complicate rather than lubricate relations. Particularly
problematic were official efforts to make history textbooks
more patriotic.

Win or lose—
what matter?
we fight
for
freedom of spirit.

—Ienaga, 1974, composing
poem for supporters during
court fight over his textbook

Under the Japanese system, only books approved by the Ministry of Education may be used in public schools, and for years the Ministry had been pressuring authors to revise passages that painted Japan in a negative light, particularly in sections on World War II. When reporters brought the Ministry's pressure to light in 1982, China and Korea issued diplomatic protests, saying Japan was whitewashing its wartime record. Ienaga Saburō, a textbook writer who had fought against the Ministry's revisions for decades, provided the transcript of his 1981 debate with officials about a passage on the Xi'an Incident of 1936, when Chinese President Chiang Kai-shek was kidnapped by his own troops who wanted him to fight against the Japanese, not against fellow Chinese. The debate focuses on Ienaga's use of the word *shinryaku,* "aggression," to describe Japan's presence in China, in contrast with the term *shinshitsu,* "advance," which Ministry officials preferred. The officials questioned forty-one such sections.

Ienaga's text: In China, the Xi'an Incident gave rise to a united front between the Kuomintang government and the Communist Party against Japan and to a firm determination to resist Japan's aggression and recover China's sovereignty.

Certifier's suggested amendments: This phrase, "Japan's aggression"— it's a matter of usage, but . . . I think that in today's societal circumstances the phrase "aggressive war" has a very strong connotation . . . of criminality; therefore it is a term that in the case of one's own country vis-à-vis another country has a clear value judgment, and I should like to ask you, from an educational point of view, to reconsider its use in your own country's textbook. . . .

Ienaga's response: Aggression against China is objective fact, and not simply judgment, so I will not change it. "Military advance" and the like are the same deception as substituting "change direction" for "retreat" or "the end of the war" for "defeat," and in genuine education such deception should not be allowed. True patriotism expresses itself in recognizing frankly one's own country's mistakes and working so that they will not be repeated

Ministry request in conference to work out differences: Japan's aggression is a phrase that carries the judgment "aggression," so it may be okay for foreign countries to speak of Japan's aggression, but for Japan as subject to speak of aggression? There's no objection if China considers it "aggression." . . . The problem is that you use "advance" to speak of the European countries and "aggression" only of Japan. There would be no objection if you said here that the Chinese "attempted to resist Japan's aggression and recover their own sovereignty. . . ."

Ienaga's second response: . . . To teach "aggression" as "aggression" is correct patriotic education; education that hides "aggression" behind euphemisms and does not exhaust all efforts to prevent the danger that the next generation will again commit mistakes cannot escape the censure that the disastrous wartime education merited.

If Ishihara Shintarō captured the spirit of the 1950s by writing fiction about decadence, and the immorality of 1970s politics by criticizing Prime Minister Tanaka, he encapsulated the 1980s in a more provocative way. He published a book of dialogue between himself and Sony Corporation president Morita Akio—*The Japan That Can Say No*—which sold a million copies in Japan. The book articulates views that Japanese had been espousing privately for a number of years: that Japan had become stronger than America, that America needed Japanese technology for its weapons, that Japan no longer needed to be subservient. It set off a wave of criticism, particularly in the United States, when a pirated translation appeared in English. An official English version of the book, released in 1989 with Morita's sections deleted, is somewhat less inflammatory but still attacks American arrogance and hypocrisy in a blunt way that raised hackles across the Pacific. Ishihara regards even Prime Minister Nakasone as too conciliatory with the United States.

About 1987, the United States began using a new tactic against Japan. Given Gorbachev's popularity in the West and the reduced threat from the "evil empire," Japan-bashing became even more frequent. It was open season on Tokyo as one politician after another made wild, emotional attacks. . . . Instead of carefully weighing all the facts, Congress went off half-cocked. Several members, for example, smashed a Toshiba radio-cassette player to bits with sledgehammers on the steps of the Capitol. This was a disgraceful act.

During my April 1987 visit to Washington, politicians hinted at a detente with the Soviet Union, implying that the two Caucasian races would soon be on much friendlier terms, leaving Japan out in the cold. Our foreign policy makers must not be intimidated by this absurd threat. We control the high technology on which the military power of both countries rests. Unfortunately, Japan has

In addition to regular school, Japanese children typically attend *juku*, or "cram schools," to prepare for high-school or college entrance exams. Historian Harry Wray engaged a child and mother in conversation on a Yokohama bus in the mid-1990s:

Q. How often do you attend *juku* a week and for how many hours?
A. Three times a week, three hours each day.

Mother (with exaggerated pride). But next year you will go four times a week!
A. Yes, that's right. I will attend one four times a week. . . .

Q. Do you have homework from school?
A. Sometimes I do, so I must prepare that before going to bed.

Q. What time to you go to bed?
A. Sometimes 11 o'clock, sometimes later. . . .

Q. Why are you attending one and why will you go more times next year?
A. (The child looked puzzled. . . .) Mama, why am I going to a *juku*?

Mother (With slight embarrassment. . . .). You know, don't you! Remember, you are planning to go to that good private secondary school two years from now.
A. (With pride) Oh yes, I forgot.

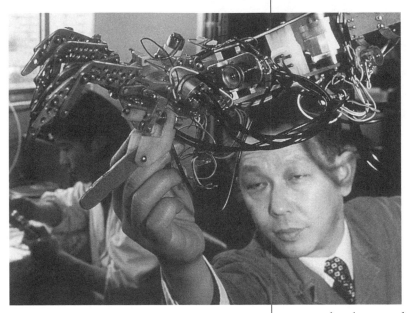

One reason for Japan's dominance of the world economy in the 1980s was its innovative technology and efficient industries. It was a leader in producing and using robotic machines whose "arms" replaced many factory workers.

not used the technology card skillfully. We have the power to say no to the United States, but have not exercised that option. We are like a stud poker player with an ace in the hole who habitually folds his hand. . . .

After the LDP's smashing victory in the 1986 election, Nakasone suddenly and impulsively promised to provide the United States with military technology. Instead of using this asset to bargain for a quid pro quo—no trade sanctions, for example—he gave it away. Nakasone meant it as a great favor to the United States. He was about the only Japanese politician who understood the implications of the commitment, how much the Pentagon needed certain Japanese civilian technology with military applications. There was no outcry from either the LDP or opposition parties. . . . Our politicians still failed to comprehend the importance of Japan's amazing high technology, even though the Americans were beside themselves with fear. This lead in high technology is Japan's greatest strength, but for some reason we have not used it effectively in international politics.

By the time Emperor Hirohito died of cancer on January 7, 1989, the press had been covering his failing health for four months, with the same detail it had given to Emperor Meiji's death watch three-quarters of a century earlier. It gave regular reports on blood pressure and vital signs, always in the most honorific style of language. After his death, however, public discussions turned to philosophical issues about Japan's emperor system: the complexities of Hirohito's reign, the nature of the emperor system, and whether a democratic Japan even should have an emperor. The *Asahi Shimbun* editorialist Kurita Wataru discusses in early 1989 the relationship between the emperor system and Japan's militarist past.

Hirohito's life exemplifies the unresolved contradictions of the tumultuous Shōwa era. He was the last surviving leader of World War II. Because of the U.S. intervention, the International Military Tribunal of the Far East did not indict him as a war criminal, and he escaped the fate of Tōjō Hideki and other top wartime leaders.

After 1945, his royal status confirmed and consolidated by the constitution, Hirohito became the epitome of the law-abiding citizen. His advancing age enhanced that status, and in his twilight years, he projected the image of a kind old man. . . .

With this living link to the past in their midst, most Japanese were reluctant to openly question the imperial institution. . . . The longest reigning monarch in Japanese history, Hirohito's longevity postponed serious discussion of the emperor system for nearly half a century. . . .

Two-thirds of Japan's present population, educated after 1945, are shockingly uninformed about the emperor. Most teachers, themselves products of the post-war school system, are equally ignorant on the subject. Few are equipped to provide their students with a realistic, historically accurate picture of the emperor system. . . .

Shortly after Hirohito's death, the Ministry of Education instructed all elementary school principals to hold a special assembly to honor the late emperor. Some refused to comply with the directive. But even those who obeyed had difficulty explaining Hirohito. Many said simply that the monarch was like an official seal; he stood for the state. Others said he was important because he received foreign dignitaries and represented Japan on state visits abroad. No one could convincingly define the monarch and his official function. . . .

As we bid farewell to Shōwa and enter the Heisei, the era of "achievement of peace," this question must be addressed squarely. If Japan aspires to an equal and honored place in the community of nations, it must come to terms with its militaristic past. That calls for a national reexamination of the emperor system and the role it should play in securing a peaceful, prosperous future.

As the Century Ended

With the dawn of the Heisei era in 1989, Japan entered a stunningly different time. Although social and cultural life remained lively, the political arena became tumultuous, with an endless succession of short-lived cabinets, and the economy plummeted. Land prices fell and eroded the capital base of many companies, revealing the economy's underlying problems. The Nikkei Index, Japan's stock market, dropped nearly 65 percent in just three years; banks were found to have as much as a trillion dollars in bad loans. And by the middle of the 1990s, the region-wide Asian economic crisis

Heisei

Heisei is the reign name of Hirohito's successor, Akihito, as Shōwa was Hirohito's reign name. Japanese refer to an emperor not by his given name but simply as *Heisei tennō*, "the Heisei Emperor," or *tennō heika*, "the emperor." Among other things, the reign name is used for the Japanese calendar, meaning that the year 2000 in Japan was Heisei 12.

Although the Tokyo Stock Market soared in the 1980s, it fell throughout much of the 1990s, hit hard by a loss of confidence fueled by falling real-estate prices and failing financial institutions.

was also hurting Japan. Government officials kept predicting that the worst was past, that solid economic fundamentals such as high savings rates and impressive education levels presaged a coming recovery.

The recovery did not come, however. Although the Japanese economy remained among the most powerful in the world, unemployment reached its highest postwar levels. As the new millennium dawned, major bankruptcies continued to occur, and general national confidence remained shaken. A whimsical, yet serious, piece from the *Asahi Shimbun's* immensely popular column *Tensei jingo* (Voices of God and Man) in March 2002 shows Japan's precarious economic situation. It compares the economies of Japan and Botswana.

Botswana is two-thirds desert and bordered on the south by South Africa. Not too many Japanese are familiar with this African nation at present, but this may change before long.

This has to do with government bonds. The reputation of Japan's long-term government bonds is falling. Late last year, a rating company downgraded their ranking to the Group 4 category. But a further downgrading is reportedly being contemplated now, and if this happens—which is not an entirely unlikely prospect— Japanese government bonds will share their standing with Botswana's.

The ranking is based on the bonds' probable redeemability. The rating company stresses this is different from "ranking the nations" as such. For years, however, Japanese government bonds were consistently ranked in the highest category. The problem is not that the rating company has arbitrarily downgraded the bonds, as some people angrily claim. Japan is becoming like Botswana, say some members of the government's deliberative council on financial affairs.

But Botswana's growth is quite impressive. When it became an independent republic in 1966, Botswana was a poor nation with practically nothing to export except beef. But the economy began to improve with the discovery of a diamond vein some years later. From 1980 to 1992, Botswana grew annually at an average rate of 10 percent.

Unlike other African nations that have yet to end dictatorships and tribal wars, Botswana is politically stable under a multiple-party parliamentary system. The nation's wealth has brought growth. "There are supermarkets, and the streets are quite safe to walk at night," recalls Noboru Tsutsui, who lived in Botswana for two years as a Japan International Cooperation Agency staff member. The government has the support of the entire nation in battling such tough problems as shrinking the gap between rich and poor and dealing with the AIDS epidemic. Botswana exudes the sort of energy that is absent from "mature" Japan.

The century's last decade also marked the fiftieth anniversary of World War II, and the war's memories provoked more questions about Japan's responsibility for the war than celebrations of its recovery from it. When Murayama Tomiichi became the country's first socialist prime minister in fifty years, he pushed for Japan to make an apology to the Asian countries victimized by Japan's wartime aggression. By the time the statement worked its way through the House of Representatives in 1995, however, it had been watered down until it sounded more like an expression of sympathy than an apology. The result was widespread anger among Asian peoples who wanted a full-fledged apology.

On the occasion of the fiftieth anniversary of the end of World War II, this house offers its sincere condolences to those who fell in action and victims of wars and similar actions all over the world.

Solemnly reflecting upon many instances of colonial rule and aggressive acts in the modern history of the world, and recognizing that Japan carried out such acts in the past, inflicting pain and

The bronze Statue of Peace, designed by Kitamura Seibō in 1955, dominates the Nagasaki Peace Park, near the epicenter of the 1945 atomic bomb explosion. Intended to remind visitors of the suffering caused by war, both inside and outside Japan, the man lifts his right hand upward to point toward the bomb and his left hand outward to beckon peace for all people.

Japanese Defense Expenditures

Asian concerns about Japan were partly explained by the size of Japan's military budget. Although Japan kept defense expenditures to one percent of GNP in the 1990s, figures from the *Washington Post* on August 2, 1999, show that the size of its economy made it a massive spender.

	Japan	China	North Korea
Defense budget (1998)	$35.2 billion	$11 billion	$2.4 billion
Defense spending	1% of GNP	5.7% of GNP	27% of GNP
Defense forces	242,600	2,830,000	1,055,000

suffering upon the people of other countries, especially in Asia, the members of this house express a sense of deep remorse.

We must transcend the differences over historical views of the past war and learn humbly the lessons of history so as to build a peaceful international society.

This house expresses its resolve, under the banner of eternal peace enshrined in the Constitution of Japan, to join hands with other nations of the world and to pave the way to a future that allows all human beings to live together.

One reason for the Asian reactions to Japan's war apology was that by the 1990s it had become heavily involved in the international world. In the late 1980s, officials had talked constantly about *kokusaika*, "internationalization." And they put money into the initiative, becoming the world's largest givers of foreign aid, spending millions annually to promote worldwide understanding of Japan and bringing thousands of youths to Japan to study and to assist in teaching English. While critics complained that *kokusaika* was aimed merely at making the world know more about Japan, no one denied that Japan was becoming more influential worldwide. Even private and semi-private foundations joined the effort, working to solve health problems in Asia and improve soil fertility in arid regions of Africa. One symbol of internationalism was the selection of historian Ogata Sadako in 1991 as United Nations High Commissioner of Refugees (UNHCR). Another lay in the new themes that political leaders, including Foreign Minister Kawaguchi Yoriko, brought to international discussions of the world's problems. In a 2003 essay in the public journal *Ronza*, she raises the concept of Japan as a "consolidator of peace."

Conflicts continue to this day around the globe—from the fighting between India and Pakistan over Kashmir and the clashes between Israelis and Palestinians to the separatist movements in places like Sri Lanka and Indonesia. We cannot make sweeping generalizations about the ties between these conflicts and terrorism, but I believe it is possible to see a chain of violence in action. Palestinian suicide bombers and cross-border terrorist strikes over the Kashmir issue can be viewed as outbursts resulting from the hatred and hopelessness that has built up over years of confrontation and conflict. To end terrorism we must cut this chain of violence. . . .

During the last two decades of the 1900s, Japan became the world's largest provider of foreign assistance, sending both money and professional caregivers around the world to help fight poverty, medical problems, and natural disasters.

It goes without saying that diplomatic efforts to resolve conflicts are important. But equally important are efforts to ensure that the temporary ceasefires and spells of stability gained through peace negotiations can be extended and made permanent, preventing the outbreak of further violence. I am positioning the concept of the *consolidation of peace* at the center of Japan's diplomatic efforts—efforts that will include humanitarian and reconstruction aid in regions of conflict, along with cooperation in achieving domestic stability and public safety. This is a relatively new type of initiative for Japan, but we have been gaining experience through our aid efforts in East Timor and Afghanistan. In all these actions aimed at consolidating peace, we begin considering the forms of aid to offer at an early stage—usually when there are signs that reconciliation will be possible. . . .

We must not forget the role that civilians from the private sector have to play in these efforts to bring about lasting peace. The Japanese government needs to lay the groundwork so that the nation's doctors, nurses, election observers, and other private-sector professionals and experts can make full use of their talents and knowledge in overseas operations.

The issue of gender has continued to provoke lively debate among Japanese of all ages and classes in recent years, with a significant number of young women making waves by refusing to marry or have children, so as to avoid the restrictions still placed on housewives by traditional values, even as more and more women enter the workforce. Equal-opportunity employment laws in 1985 and 1997 strengthened women's leverage as workers, and helped to increase women's salaries

Public discussions of the World War II comfort women brought together the issues of gender and war responsibility in the 1990s, when women from Korea, southeast Asia, and even the Netherlands came forward with stories about the way the Japanese military had forced them to serve as prostitutes for Japanese soldiers and sailors. In 2000, a Women's International War Crimes Tribunal, held in Tokyo by activist groups, found Hirohito guilty of war crimes, while nearly all victims sneered at a private fund that the government set up to compensate them. They argued that the use of a "private" fund allowed the government to avoid taking responsibility for its crimes. Money, said many victims, was less important than having the government take responsibility for the comfort women system.

and the numbers of women working outside the home. By the mid-1990s, nearly 40 percent of the workforce was female, with the number of working women having increased by nearly 30 percent in a decade. Nevertheless, women still earned only two-thirds, on average, of what men did. They also made up the majority of part-time workers and were expected in most companies to do "women's work," such as serving tea. A twenty-nine-year-old Okinawa graduate student, activist Tengan Megumi, explains in a 1998 interview that gender equality still has not been achieved. She has created her own female organization, Young Voice, to raise consciousness about women's issues.

What I want people here to understand is that the root of so many of our social problems on Okinawa is inequality between the sexes. Women need to be regarded as equal with men. Too often women are ignored, glossed over, taken for granted. . . .

Also, I don't think we always see the problems people have in their marriages or relationships either; things are hidden well. And because people think women here are so strong, they don't think they could possibly be abused physically or psychologically. If a woman's a victim of physical abuse, she's usually encouraged by those around her not to say anything about it. That's wrong. It's a shame we don't have many support centers here to help out women like that. . . .

I also have aspirations for my daughter. I know as she grows she'll have her own, but there are certain things I want for her in my heart. I honestly hope she'll be her own person and not try to be someone that society tells her she has to be. I want her to develop an independent sense of self, a definition of who she is based on how she feels, not based on how society tells her she has to feel. . . .

What worries me about her starting first grade next spring is that she's already influenced by peers at school. For example, one day I tried to put her in a pair of blue slacks, and she told me "girls don't wear blue; that's a boy's color." I asked her why she thought that. She told me that at school girls wear pink or red, and boys wear blue or green. . . . What scares me is how society can influence us, even a four-year-old, to think a certain way.

The economic doldrums put little damper on the continued development of Japan's popular culture: the cities' throbbing night and entertainment life, the noisy entertainment

game centers, the outpouring of new cartoon books and animation videos, the successful soccer and baseball leagues, the avant-garde urban districts filled with young people with purple hair talking on fashionable cell phones and carrying the latest "cute" bag. Though society remained stable and hard-working, many worried (as the older generations always had) about the materialism of the younger generation. And some worried too that urban Japan had developed its own counterculture and its own problem with juvenile crime—motorcycle gangs, school bullies, computer hackers, and teenage prostitutes—small though that problem was in comparison to other developed nations. As usual, Japan's novelists—writers such as Yoshimoto Banana and Murakami Haruki—described and critiqued this culture at length at century's turn, while politicians and conservative educators decried it. One of the era's most popular poets, Tanikawa Shuntarō, captures the complexity of life in his 1996 poem "A Push of A Button."

Everyone is listening to a song. . . .
   The surgeon who finds an incurable cancer
   And pushes it back into an abdomen;
   A beautiful boy on roller skates
   Coasting down a hill to the stock exchange. . . .

at the push of a button
   a song gushes forth
   at the push of a button
   a salary is settled
   at the push of a button
   the earth is destroyed

Everyone is listening to a song
   The jobless wrapped like mummies in morning papers
   While leaning in dreams on shoulders of fantasy women.
   The astronaut chasing a floating spoon
   While smothering in love for a baby on earth. . . .

at the push of a button
   a song gushes forth
   at the push of a button
   a shirt becomes white
   at the push of a button
   the earth is destroyed

By the early 2000s, dating and public embraces had become as much a part of popular youth culture in Japan as they were in Europe and the United States. This stood in sharp contrast to the early postwar era, when dating was still limited and public displays of affection were sharply discouraged.

One fad that underscored the difference between young people and their parents' generation was the 1999 trend known as yamanba, *"old mountain witch," in which girls lightened their hair to the color of straw, painted their faces dark brown, whitened their lips, and put sparkle round their eyes. This extract shows the reaction of columnist Nakano Midori in the journal Bungei Shunjū to this look in 1999.*

I have lived quite a number of years, but this is probably the first popular fashion that is so beyond my comprehension. Nothing about it is pretty, elegant, or stylish; the main effect, I would say, is to frighten.

Disasters also took their toll on the Japanese psyche in the 1990s. For decades, people had worried about a major earthquake in the Tokyo area, where cyclical quakes had been wreaking major havoc for centuries. They were not prepared, however, for the devastating Hanshin earthquake that toppled freeway overpasses, claimed more than 5,000 lives, and left 400,000 residents of the Kōbe region homeless on January 17, 1995. And the government's initial misjudgment of the disaster only bungled relief efforts. In a time when people's nerves were stretched by economic difficulty and international criticism, the event seemed to symbolize something more serious. A eulogy for Mori Wataru, a Kōbe University student killed in the quake, exemplifies that feeling.

The great earthquake . . . was a vicious sneak attack. . . . In the pitch dark the demon of the earth suddenly lifted houses and slammed them back down. Not satisfied with that, he grabbed them in both hands and ripped them apart. This time he was really out to kill! Despite the dark, I could tell that my rectangular room had been stretched into a diamond shape and that the chest of drawers and TV set were flying around. The whole thing took only twenty seconds or so. . . .

When I think how his family, especially his parents, must feel, words fail me. In my own home, it was sheer luck that the night before the earthquake I had indulged my six-year-old daughter by letting her sleep next to me. I was beside myself with worry, after those lethal twenty seconds, until my older daughter called out from her room across the way. I'm sure every parent felt the same sort of fear. . . .

The 1995 Hanshin earthquake inspired an outpouring of assistance from across Japan. Thousands of volunteers collected money, went to Kōbe to rebuild buildings, and distributed boxes of food to those whose homes had been destroyed.

Why did God have to summon Mori? How absurd it seems! I imagine that Mori, who was a Christian, returned willingly to the Lord when called. Still, he had been about to start a career. He wasn't just looking for a long life but was searching for a life of meaning; he was, I think, the kind of young man who would be prepared to risk his life for a cause. I was looking forward to his company on the uncharted course awaiting us in the post-postwar period. . . .

His life and death will always remain vivid in our hearts. I hope each of us gathered here will be able to carry with us at least a part of his dream and apply it to rebuilding Kōbe and navigating Japan's new course.

Mori, may you rest in peace.

On May 5, 2000, the nation's largest newspaper, *Yomiuri Shimbun*, published its own proposed revision of the 1947 constitution, attempting to ignite a public debate on what constitutional principles Japan should follow in an age of rapid change. The revision includes a rewritten preamble in crisper, more timeless prose and advocates new articles to provide for political parties, assures crime victims of relief aid, and allows citizens to demand disclosure of official information. It attempts to assure both individual rights and public welfare (Article 17). Most important, or at least most controversial, is Article 12, which creates an armed force for "self-defense." It follows immediately after an article that maintains the renunciation of war and adds a prohibition on the manufacture, possession, and use of weapons of mass destruction. Taken as a whole, the proposed constitution shows a desire to move Japan away from many of the tensions and ambiguities of the postwar era. Gone are the direct references to World War II. In their place is a call to balance pacifism and defense. By mid-decade, most observers were convinced that the actual revision of the constitution was only a matter of time.

PREAMBLE

We, the Japanese people, hold sovereign power in Japan and, ultimately, our will shall dictate all State decisions. Government is entrusted to our duly elected representatives, who exercise their power with the trust of the people.

We, the Japanese people, desire peace for all time, respect the spirit of international cooperation and pledge to use our best

As the only country in history to have experienced atomic bombings, I would like to underline Japan's unwavering commitment to its war-renouncing constitution and its three principles: non-possession, non-production, and non-entry of nuclear weapons."

—Prime Minister Koizumi Jun'ichirō, speech at Hiroshima peace ceremony, August 6, 2002

efforts to ensure the peace, prosperity and security of the international community.

We, the Japanese people, aspire to a free and vigorous society, where basic human rights are duly respected, and simultaneously strive for the advancement of the people's welfare.

We, the Japanese people, acknowledge the inheritance of our long history and tradition and the need to preserve our fair landscape and cultural legacy while promoting culture, arts and sciences.

This Constitution is the supreme law of Japan and is to be observed by the Japanese people.

NATIONAL SECURITY
Article 11 (Rejection of war and ban on weapons of mass destruction)

(1) Aspiring sincerely to an international peace based on justice and order, the Japanese people shall never recognize war as a sovereign right of the nation and the threat or use of force as means of settling international disputes.

(2) Seeking to eliminate from the world inhuman and indiscriminate weapons of mass destruction, Japan shall not manufacture, possess or use such weapons.

Article 12 (Armed forces for self-defense, civilian control and denial of forced conscription)

(1) Japan shall form armed forces for self-defense to secure its peace and independence and to maintain its safety.

(2) The Prime Minister shall exercise supreme command authority over the armed forces for self-defense.

(3) The people shall not be forced to participate in the armed forces for self-defense.

RIGHTS AND DUTIES OF THE PEOPLE
Article 17 (The people's responsibility for maintaining freedoms and rights)

The freedoms and rights guaranteed to the people by this Constitution shall be maintained by the constant endeavor of the people, who shall always respect the freedoms and rights of each other, harmonize them with the public good in the form of national security, public order, healthy living environment and other benefits, and who shall refrain from any abuse of them.

Analyses of what Japan needed to regain its economic vitality and self-confidence preoccupied commentators at the beginning of the twenty-first century. One observer, the

Toyota Motor Corporation chose to go its own way after World II, refusing capital alliances with foreign firms. It introduced the popular Toyota Crown in 1955 and the Corona in 1965. Known for aggressive sales and high-quality, fuel-efficient cars, Toyota had become the world's second largest automobile producer by the early 1980s.

renowned architect Andō Tadao, told an interviewer in 2002 that the key lay in emancipating individuals from the conformity produced by Japan's school system. He dates the loss of national energy and creativity to the early 1970s, when affluence brought almost the entire nation into the middle class.

The Japanese as a whole became focused on name-brand goods, and they started making a big deal of labels like Gucci and Hermès. And they turned into a nation of conformists. When bowling became popular, for example, suddenly everyone was bowling. People lost their individuality, and the concept of the responsible individual disappeared. Meanwhile, the middle class spread until it included virtually the entire nation. . . .

In order to create distinctive regions and cities, it's necessary to break free of the concept of democratic uniformity that took root in the postwar period. The eccentric opinions of individuals who differ from the norm should be respected. Any and all ideas should be taken in, and then people should have intense discussions about what to do with the cities where they live. In order for this to happen, someone has to stand up and lead the way. While it may be presumptuous, that's what I've been trying to do in my own part of the country.

What's necessary for the future is the emergence of problem-conscious individuals who will work to build their own society with their own power; Japan must be transformed. In order for this to happen, education needs to be changed from the bottom up. . . . The speedy realization of education that gives birth to independent, problem-conscious individuals is what holds the key to Japan's revitalization.

Timeline

1600
Tokugawa Ieyasu wins control of Japan with battle victory over rival feudal lords at Sekigahara; Edo named capital

1603
Tokugawa Ieyasu takes the title "shogun," establishing his family's formal rule of Japan

1635–41
Government issues decrees to eradicate Christianity and Western traders from Japan; the Dutch are allowed to trade only at Dejima in Nagasaki

1688–1704
Urban culture flourishes, producing Kabuki theater, woodblock prints, popular literature, geisha culture; private schools for commoners, called *terakoya*, are established throughout Japan

1732–33
Massive famine leads to soaring rice prices and urban riots

1774
Sugita Genpaku and Maeno Ryōtaku translate Dutch anatomy book, initiating growth of secret but influential "Dutch learning" in scholarly world

1793–1808
Russian, British, and American ships visit Japan, seeking trade;

Nagasaki magistrate commits suicide when British ship enters his port in 1808

1805
Hanaoka Seishū operates on a breast cancer patient and becomes the world's first doctor to do surgery under general anesthesia

1825
Government issues "no second thought" decree that expels any foreign ships entering Japanese waters

1833–37
Great Tempō era famine results in violent riots in Osaka, demanding increased relief for the poor

1841
Government launches reforms to improve public morals and curb expenses; their ineffectiveness undermines support for Tokugawa government

1853–54
Matthew Perry arrives with an American squadron and demands that Japan open its ports; Kanagawa Treaty of 1854 provides for two open ports and diplomatic relations between the two nations

1858
Japan-U.S. Treaty of Amity and Commerce is signed, opening trade; treaties with other countries follow

1860
Chief minister Ii Naosuke is assassinated for signing the Japan-U.S. Treaty of Amity and Commerce; Japan's first diplomatic mission travels to United States

1864
The domain of Chōshū revolts unsuccessfully against the Tokugawa government

1868
Southwestern samurai overthrow Tokugawa government; Meiji government is launched

1871
Feudal domains are replaced with modern prefectures; Iwakura Mission begins eighteen-month foreign study mission

1872
Government decrees compulsory education and announces military draft

1873
Leading official Saigō Takamori and followers resign from the government in protest over Japan's relations with Korea

1874
Japan defeats China in Taiwan military expedition; demands for a popular assembly initiate freedom and rights movement

1877
Saigō Takamori leads unsuccessful Satsuma Rebellion

1879
Japan seizes Ryūkyū islands and forms Okinawa Prefecture

1881
Scandal over fraudulent sale of government lands in Hokkaidō leads to promise of a constitution; Japan's first political parties are founded

1884–85
Peasants rebel over economic problems, high taxes, and harsh lending practices

1889
Meiji Constitution, Asia's first constitutional monarchy, is promulgated

1890
First national legislature is convened; government issues Imperial Rescript on Education

1894–95
Japan wins Sino-Japanese War, launching its colonial empire; Russia, Germany, and France intervene, requiring Japan to return its holdings in Manchuria to China

1902

Japan signs Anglo-Japanese Alliance, first equal alliance between European and Asian nations

1904–5

Japan wins Russo-Japanese War

1908

Gentlemen's agreement between United States and Japan prohibits immigration of Japanese workers to the United States, triggering wide resentment in Japan

1910

Japan annexes Korea

1912

Emperor Meiji dies and is replaced by Taishō

1915

Japan issues Twenty-One Demands on China

1918

Nationwide riots over rice prices lead to an era when the leading political party chooses prime ministers

1921

Japan signs Washington Conference multinational agreements, which limit Japan's naval spending and replace the Anglo-Japanese Alliance

1923

Tokyo and Yokohama are devastated by Great Kantō Earthquake

1925

Suffrage is granted to all males over twenty-five years of age; Peace Preservation Law prohibits the advocacy of communism, providing impetus for creation of thought police

1926

Emperor Taishō dies and is replaced by Shōwa (Hirohito)

1930

Japan signs London Naval Treaty, which continues Washington naval restrictions, triggering anger among Japanese nationalists

1931

Manchurian Incident launches Japan's takeover of Manchuria as state of Manchukuo

1933

Japan leaves League of Nations after being criticized for its actions in Manchuria

1936

February 26 coup attempt by ultranationalist soldiers fails but propels government to further imperialistic moves in Asia

1937

Second Sino-Japanese War begins and Japan engages in World War II

1941

Japan signs nonaggression pact with Russia, invades Southeast Asia, and bombs U.S. fleet at Pearl Harbor

1942

Battle of Midway turns war tide against Japan, after many early victories

1945

Allies invade Okinawa; United States drops atomic bombs at Hiroshima and Nagasaki; Japan surrenders to the United States, ending World War II; United States-led occupation of Japan begins

1947

Japan's new constitution provides for universal suffrage and makes the emperor a symbol of the state

1948

Tokyo War Crimes Trials end, resulting in seven executions

1950

Beginning of Korean War reinvigorates Japanese economy

1951

Japan signs Mutual Security Treaty, allowing the U.S. to maintain bases in Japan in exchange for providing Japan with military protection

1952

Occupation ends

1954

Self-Defense Force is formed; America's atomic testing at Bikini atoll sparks major protests in Japan

1956

Japan joins the United Nations

1960

Revision of the Mutual Security Treaty improves Japan's position with the United States but causes major anti-American protests

1964

Japan hosts Summer Olympics in Tokyo; bullet train begins operation; economic boom is in full swing

1968–70

Student demonstrations and citizen movements campaign on environmental, educational, and international issues

1972

Diplomatic relations normalized with China; United States returns Okinawa to Japan

1973

Sharp rise in oil prices triggers inflation

1974

Financial scandals lead to Tanaka Kakuei's resignation as prime minister

1982

Nakasone Yasuhiro becomes prime minister and calls for greater Japanese profile on world stage

1989

Emperor Hirohito dies and is replaced by Akihito; economic "bubble" bursts, ending Japan's long period of economic boom

1995

Fiftieth anniversary of World War II surrender sparks discussions of comfort-women issue and Japan's responsibilities toward Asia; Hanshin Earthquake in Kōbe kills more than 5,000; Aum Supreme Truth religion launches fatal gas attack on Tokyo subways

2001

Birth of girl to Crown Princess Masako spurs discussion of law restricting the throne to male heirs

2002

Tensions with North Korea escalate over its nuclear policies and abduction of Japanese citizens in the 1970s

2004

Japan sends more than 1,000 peacekeeping troops to Iraq, its biggest overseas deployment since World War II

Further Reading and Websites

General Works

Aoki, Michiko, and Margaret B. Dardess, eds. *As the Japanese See It: Past and Present*. Honolulu: University of Hawaii Press, 1981.

Bernstein, Gail, ed. *Recreating Japanese Women*. Berkeley: University of California Press, 1991.

Bix, Herbert. *Hirohito and the Making of Modern Japan*. New York: HarperCollins, 2000.

Duus, Peter. *Modern Japan*. 2nd ed. Boston: Houghton Mifflin, 1998.

Gordon, Andrew. *A Modern History of Japan from Tokugawa Times to the Present*. New York: Oxford University Press, 2003.

Hane, Mikiso. *Peasants, Rebels, and Outcastes: The Underside of Modern Japan*. New York: Pantheon, 1983.

Hopper, Helen. *Katō Shidzue: A Japanese Feminist*. New York: Pearson/Longman, 2004.

Huffman, James, ed. *Modern Japan: An Encyclopedia of History, Culture, and Nationalism*. New York: Garland Publishing, 1997.

Imamura, Anne E., ed. *Re-imaging Japanese Women*. Berkeley: University of California Press, 1996.

Irokawa, Daikichi. *The Age of Hirohito: In Search of Modern Japan*. New York: Free Press, 1995.

Keene, Donald. *Dawn to the West: Japanese Literature in the Modern Era: Fiction*. New York: Henry Holt, 1984.

Keene, Donald, ed. *Modern Japanese Literature: An Anthology*. New York: Grove, 1956.

Kodansha Encyclopedia of Japan. 9 vols. Tokyo: Kodansha, 1983.

Lu, David J. *Japan: A Documentary History*. Armonk, N.Y.: M. E. Sharpe, 1997.

McClain, James L. *Japan: A Modern History*. New York: W. W. Norton, 2002.

Pyle, Kenneth B. *The Making of Modern Japan*. 2nd ed. Lexington, Mass.: D. C. Heath, 1996.

Reischauer, Edwin O., and Marius B. Jansen. *The Japanese Today: Change and Continuity*. Cambridge, Mass.: Harvard University Press, 1995.

Saga, Junichi. *Memories of Silk and Straw: A Self-Portrait of Small-Town Japan*. New York: Kodansha, 1987.

Totman, Conrad. *A History of Japan*. Malden, Mass.: Blackwell, 2000.

Tsunoda, Ryusaku, William Theodore De Bary, and Donald Keene, eds. *Sources of Japanese Tradition*, Vol. 2. New York: Columbia University Press, 1958.

Walthall, Anne, ed. *The Human Tradition in Modern Japan*. Wilmington, Del.: SR Books, 2002.

Wray, Harry, and Hilary Conroy, eds. *Japan Examined: Perspectives on Modern Japanese History*. Honolulu: University of Hawaii Press, 1983.

Tokugawa Era

Endo, Shusaku. *Silence*. New York: Taplinger, 1979.

Katsu, Kokichi. *Musui's Story: The Auto-biography of a Tokugawa Samurai*. Tucson: University of Arizona Press, 1988.

Keene, Donald. *The Japanese Discovery of Europe, 1720–1830*. Stanford, Calif.: Stanford University Press, 1969.

Nitobe, Inazo. *Bushido: The Warrior's Code*. Burbank, Calif.: Ohara, 1979.

Perez, Louis G. *Daily Life in Early Modern Japan*. Westport, Conn.: Greenwood, 2002.

Walthall, Anne. *The Weak Body of a Useless Woman: Matsuo Taseko and the Meiji Restoration*. Chicago: University of Chicago Press, 1998.

Yamamoto, Tsunetomo, *Hagakure: The Book of the Samurai*. New York: Kodansha, 1979.

Meiji Era

Chamberlain, Basil Hall. *Japanese Things: Being Notes on Various Subjects Connected with Japan*. Rutland, Vt.: Charles E. Tuttle, 1971.

Duus, Peter. *The Abacus and the Sword: The Japanese Penetration of Korea, 1895–1910*. Berkeley: University of California Press, 1995.

————. *The Japanese Discovery of America: A Brief History with Documents*. Boston: Bedford, 1997.

Fukuzawa, Yukichi. *The Autobiography of Yukichi Fukuzawa*. New York: Schocken, 1966.

Huffman, James L. *A Yankee in Meiji Japan: The Crusading Journalist Edward H. House*. Boulder, Colo.: Rowman and Littlefield, 2003.

Irokawa, Daikichi. *The Culture of the Meiji Period*. Princeton, N.J.: Princeton University Press, 1985.

Ishimitsu, Mahito, ed. *Remembering Aizu: The Testament of Shiba Gorō*. Translated by Teruko Craig. Honolulu: University of Hawaii Press, 1999.

Nagatsuka, Takashi. *The Soil: A Portrait of Rural Life in Meiji Japan*. Berkeley: University of California Press, 1993.

Nakano, Makino. *Makiko's Diary: A Merchant Wife in 1910 Kyoto*. Translated by Kazuko Smith. Stanford, Calif.: Stanford University Press, 1995.

Natsume, Soseki. *Kokoro*. New York: Regnery Gateway, 1957.

Notehelfer, F. G. *American Samurai: Captain L. L. Janes and Japan*. Princeton, N.J.: Princeton University Press, 1985.

Ōsugi, Sakae. *The Autobiography of Ōsugi Sakae*. Berkeley: University of California Press, 1992.

Pyle, Kenneth. *The New Generation in Meiji Japan*. Stanford, Calif.: Stanford University Press, 1969.

Rubin, Jay. *Injurious to Public Morals: Writers and the Meiji State*. Seattle: University of Washington Press, 1984.

Sansom, George. *The Western World and Japan*. New York: Knopf, 1968.

Seidensticker, Edward. *Low City, High City: Tokyo from Edo to the Earthquake*. Rutland, Vt.: Charles E. Tuttle, 1983.

Shibusawa, Eiichi. *The Autobiography of Shibusawa Eiichi*. Translated by Teruko Craig. Tokyo: University of Tokyo Press, 1994.

Sievers, Sharon. *Flowers in Salt: The Beginnings of Feminist Consciousness in Modern Japan*. Stanford, Calif.: Stanford University Press, 1983.

Sugimoto, Etsu Inagaki. *A Daughter of the Samurai.* Rutland, Vt.: Charles E. Tuttle, 1966.

Tsurumi, E. Patricia. *Factory Girls: Women in the Thread Mills of Meiji Japan.* Princeton, N.J.: Princeton University Press, 1990.

Whitney, Clara. *Clara's Diary: An American Girl in Meiji Japan.* New York: Kodansha, 1979.

Taishō Era Through World War II

Butow, Robert. *Tojo and the Coming of War.* Princeton, N.J.: Princeton University Press, 1961.

Cook, Haruko Taya, and Theodore F. Cook. *Japan at War: An Oral History.* New York: New Press, 1992.

Dower, John. *War Without Mercy: Race and Power in the Pacific War.* New York: Pantheon, 1986.

Fogel, Joshua, ed. *The Nanjing Massacre in History and Historiography.* Berkeley: University of California Press, 2000.

Gordon, Andrew. *Labor and Imperial Democracy in Prewar Japan.* Berkeley: University of California Press, 1991.

Hachiya, Michihiko. *Hiroshima Diary.* Chapel Hill: University of North Carolina Press, 1955.

Hane, Mikiso, ed. *Reflections on the Way to the Gallows: Voices of Japanese Rebel Women.* New York: Pantheon, 1988.

Hatano, Isoko, and Ichiro Hatano. *Mother and Son: The Wartime Correspondence of Isoko and Ichiro Hatano.* Boston: Houghton Mifflin, 1962.

Havens, Thomas. *Valley of Darkness: The Japanese People and World War II.* New York: W. W. Norton, 1978.

Hicks, George. *The Comfort Women.* New York: W. W. Norton, 1994.

Ienaga Saburō. *The Pacific War.* New York: Pantheon, 1978.

Iriye, Akira, ed. *Pearl Harbor and the Coming of the Pacific War: A Brief History with Documents and Essays.* Boston: Bedford, 1999.

Ishikawa, Takuboku. *Romaji Diary and Sad Toys.* Rutland, Vt.: Charles E. Tuttle, 1985.

Ishimoto, Shidzue. *Facing Two Ways.* Stanford, Calif.: Stanford University Press, 1963.

Kaneko, Fumiko. *The Prison Memoirs of a Japanese Woman.* Armonk, N.Y.: M. E. Sharpe, 1991.

Mishima, Yukio. *Runaway Horses.* New York: Knopf, 1973.

Nakazawa, Keiji. *Barefoot Gen: A Cartoon Story of Hiroshima.* Philadelphia: New Society, 1987.

Onoda, Hiroo. *No Surrender: My Thirty-year War.* Tokyo: Kodansha, 1974.

Post–World War II Era

Arai, Shinya. *Shoshaman: A Tale of Corporate Japan.* Berkeley: University of California Press, 1991.

Bernstein, Gail. *Haruko's World: A Japanese Farm Woman and Her Community.* Stanford, Calif.: Stanford University Press, 1983.

Bestor, Theodore C. *Neighborhood Tokyo.* Stanford, Calif.: Stanford University Press, 1989.

Dalby, Lisa. *Geisha.* Berkeley: University of California Press, 1983.

Dower, John W. *Embracing Defeat: Japan in the Wake of World War II.* New York: W. W. Norton, 1999.

Field, Norma. *In the Realm of a Dying Emperor: Japan at Century's End.* New York: Pantheon, 1991.

George, Timothy S. *Minamata: Pollution and the Struggle for Democracy in Postwar Japan.* Cambridge, Mass.: Harvard University Asia Center, 2001.

Greenfeld, Karl Taro. *Speed Tribes.* New York: HarperPerennial, 1994.

Ienaga, Saburo. *Japan's Past, Japan's Future: One Historian's Odyssey.* Translated by Richard H. Minear. Boulder, Colo.: Rowman and Littlefield, 2001.

Ishinomori, Shotaro. *Japan Inc.: Introduction to Japanese Economics.* Berkeley: University of California Press, 1988.

Kawabata, Yasunari. *Beauty and Sadness.* New York: Knopf, 1975.

McCargo, Duncan. *Contemporary Japan.* New York: St. Martin's, 2000.

Napier, Susan. *Anime from Akira to Princess Mononoke: Experiencing Contemporary Japanese Animation.* New York: Palgrave, 2001.

Schodt, Frederik. *Manga! Manga! The World of Japanese Comics.* New York: Kodansha, 1983.

Vogel, Ezra F. *Japan as Number One: Lessons for America.* Cambridge, Mass.: Harvard University Press, 1979.

White, Merry. *The Japanese Educational Challenge: A Commitment to Children.* New York: Free Press, 1987.

———. *The Material Child: Coming of Age in Japan and America.* New York: Free Press, 1993.

Websites

Daily Yomiuri Newspaper
http://www.yomiuri.co.jp/index-e.htm
English version of Japan's largest daily newspaper, filled with events, news articles, and information on contemporary life.

Facing East, Facing West
http://www.blackshipsandsamurai.com
Vivid collection of paintings, photographs, and sketches by Japanese and Americans in the mid-1800s, after Japan's opening to the West, prepared by Pulitzer-winning historian John Dower of Massachusetts Institute of Technology.

Hiroshima Archive
http://www.lclark.edu/~history/HIROSHIMA/
Materials on the 1945 dropping of the first atomic bomb; includes photos, art, literature, and historical studies.

Japanese American Relocation Digital Archives
http://jarda.cdlib.org/
Thematic collection of documents in California Digital Library's Online Archive on World War II interment camps for Japanese Americans.

Japanese Surrender Documents of World War II
Modern History of Japan
http://www3.oup-usa.org/sc/0195110609/
Website accompanying Andrew Gordon's 2003 survey history, A Modern History of Japan, including full-text historical documents and study guides.

National Clearinghouse for US-Japan Studies
http://www.indiana.edu/~japan/
Voluminous teaching materials on Japan collected by Indiana University: two-page summaries of Japan-related topics, lesson plans, database of artifact kits, software, published and audiovisual materials.

Text Credits

Note: Japanese titles have been translated except in the cases of newspapers (*shimbun*), where the translation of names produces awkwardness rather than understanding.

Main Text

11. Michael Cooper, ed., *They Came to Japan: An Anthology of European reports on Japan, 1543–1640* (Berkeley: University of California Press, 1965), 60.

12. H. Paul Varley, *Japanese Culture*, Third Edition (Honolulu: University of Hawaii Press, 1984), 21.

13. Basil Hall Chamberlain, *Japanese Things* (Rutland, Vt.: Charles E. Tuttle, 1971), 1.

14. Jay Rubin, *Injurious to Public Morals: Writers and the Meiji State* (Seattle: University of Washington Press, 1984), 18. Reprinted by permission of the University of Washington Press.

15. Irokawa Daikichi, *The Culture of the Meiji Period* (Princeton, N.J.: Princeton University Press, 1985), 151–152.

17. Edward H. House letter to Whitelaw Reid, Sept. 21, 1870, in Reid Papers, Library of Congress.

21. *The Island of Japon : João Rodrigues' Account of 16th Century Japan*, trans. Michael Cooper (Tokyo: Kodansha International Ltd; 1973), 65–66, 69.

22. Cooper, *They Came to Japan*, 55–56.

22–23. Ihara Saikaku, *Tales of Samurai Honor*, trans. Caryl Ann Callahan (Tokyo: Monumenta Nipponica, 1981), 33–34.

23. George Elison, *Deus Destroyed: The Image of Christianity in Early Modern Japan* (Cambridge, Mass.: Council on East Asian Studies, Harvard University, 1973), 335–337.

24–25. Ibid., 193–194. Reprinted by permission of the Harvard University Asia Center. © The President and Fellows of Harvard College, 1973.

26. Engelbert Kaempfer, *Kaempfer's Japan: Tokugawa Culture Observed.* (Honolulu: University of Hawaii Press, 1999), 188–89. Note: Kaempfer used the less-standard spelling "Deshima" instead of "Dejima."

27. Ibid., 364–365.

29–30. Samuel H. Yamashita, *Master Sorai's Responsals: An Annotated Translation of Sorai sensei tomonsho* (Honolulu: University of Hawaii Press, 1994), 40, 64–65, 68–69.

31–32. David J. Lu, *Japan: A Documentary History* (Armonk, N.Y.: M. E. Sharpe, 1997), 206–208. Translation copyright © 1997 by David J. Lu. Reprinted with permission of M. E. Sharpe Inc.

32. Ibid., 208. Translation copyright © 1997 by David J. Lu. Reprinted with permission of M. E. Sharpe Inc.

33–34. Nippon Gakujutsu Shinkōkai, ed. *Man'yōshū* (New York: Columbia University Press, 1965), 29.

34–35. Lady Murasaki Shikibu, *The Tale of Genji*, trans. Edward G. Seidensticker (New York: Vintage Classics, 1990), 3–4. © 1976 by Edward G. Seidensticker. Used by permission of Alfred Λ. Knopf, a division of Random House, Inc.

35. Ryusaku Tsunoda, Wm. Theodore DeBary, and Donald Keene, *Sources of Japanese Tradition*, I (New York: Columbia University Press, 1958), 329–330.

36. Ackroyd, Joyce, trans., *Told Round a Brushwood Fire: The Autobiography of Arai Hakuseki* (Princeton, N.J.: Princeton University Press, 1979), 264–265. © 1979 by UNESCO. Reprinted by permission of Princeton University Press.

37–38. Yamamoto Tsunetomo, *Hagakure: The Book of the Samurai* (Tokyo: Kodansha International, 1979), 17, 22, 31–34, 52, 62.

38–39. Katsu Kokichi, *Musui's Story: The Autobiography of a Tokugawa Samurai*. Trans. by Teruko Craig (Tucson: University of Arizona Press, 1988), 45–46, 156–157. © 1988 The Arizona Board of Regents. Reprinted by permission of the University of Arizona Press.

40. Kaibara Ekiken, *Women and Wisdom of Japan* (London: John Murray, 1905), 33–34, 38–39, 45.

41–42. Ihara Saikaku, "The Eternal Storehouse of Japan," in *Anthology of Japanese Literature from the Earliest Era to the Mid-Nineteenth Century*, ed. Donald Keene (New York: Grove Press, 1955), 357–358, 361–362. © 1955 by Grove Press, Inc. Used by permission of Grove/Atlantic, Inc.

44. Waka Rintarō, *Shiryō Nihon shi* (Documents from Japanese history) (Tokyo: Tokyo Hōrei, 1976), 230.

44–45. Bob Tadaski Wakabayashi, *Anti-Foreignism and Western Learning in Early-Meiji Japan* (Cambridge, Mass.: Council of East Asian Studies, Harvard University Press, 1986), 200–201, 214. Reprinted by permission of the Harvard University Asia Center. © The President and Fellows of Harvard College, 1986.

59. Yukichi Fukuzawa, *The Autobiography of Yukichi Fukuzawa* (New York: Schocken Books, 1972), 314; song, in Stewart Lone, *Army, Empire and Politics in Meiji Japan* (New York: St. Martin's Press, 2000), 8.

60. Text of oath taken from Robert M. Spaulding, Jr., "The Intent of the Charter Oath," in *Studies in Japanese History and Politics* (Ann Arbor: Center for Japanese Studies, 1967), 6–13; preamble adapted from Ryusaku Tsunoda, Wm. Theodore DeBary, and Donald Keene, eds., *Sources of Japanese Tradition*, II (New York: Columbia University Press, 1958), 137.

60–61. S. Lane-Poole and F. V. Dickins, *The Life of Sir Harry Parkes*, II (Wilmington, Del.: Scholarly Resources, 1973), 132–133.

62. Lu, 324.

63–64. Kume Kunitake, *Tokumei zenken taishi Bei-ō kairan jikki*, translated in Peter Duus, *The Japanese Discovery of America: A Brief History with Documents* (Boston: Bedford Books, 1997), 174–178. Copyright © 1997 by Bedford/St. Martin's, from *The Japanese Discovery of America* by Peter Duus. Reprinted with permission of Bedford/St. Martin's.

66–67. Mori Ōgai, "The Incident at Sakai," in *The Historical Fiction of Mori Ōgai*, ed. David Dilworth and J. Thomas Rimer (Honolulu: University of Hawaii Press, 1977), 145–147.

68–69. Ryusaku Tsunoda, et al, 197–198.

70. Essays of students of Margaret Griffis, in the William Elliot Griffis Collection, Rutgers.

70–71. Itagaki Taisuke, "Memorial on the Establishment of a Representative Assembly," in W. W. McLaren, *Japanese Government Documents*, (Tokyo: Asiatic Society of Japan, 1914), 427–432.

71–73. Chiba Takasaburō, "The Way of the King," in Richard Devine, "The Way of the King," first published in *Monumenta Nipponica*, 34, no. 1, 63–72.

73. McLaren, 503.

74. Centre for East Asian Cultural Studies (comp.), *The Meiji Japan Through Contemporary Sources*, II (Tokyo: CEACS, 1969), 93–94.

75–76. Etsu Inagaki Sugimoto, *A Daughter of the Samurai* (Boston; Tokyo; Rutland, Vt.: Charles E. Tuttle, 1966), 25–27.

76. Shibusawa Eiichi, *The Autobiography of Shibusawa Eiichi*, trans. Teruko Craig (Tokyo: University of Tokyo Press, 1994), 139–140.

76–77. Shibusawa Eiichi, *Ginkō o sodatete* (Building banks), in *Gendai Nihon kiroku zenshū* (Comprehensive series on contemporary Japanese documents), 8 (Tokyo: Chikuma Shobō, 1969), 94–95; translation adapted from Lu, 354–356.

78–79. Nagatsuka Takashi, *The Soil*, trans. Ann Waswo (Berkeley: University of California Press, 1993), 47–49. Copyright © 1999 The Regents of the University of California.

79. Donald Keene, ed., *Modern Japanese Literature: An Anthology* (New York: Grove Press, 1956), 56–58.

83. Tokutomi Soho, in Kenneth Pyle, *The New Generation in Meiji Japan: Problems of Cultural Identity, 1885–1895* (Stanford, Calif.: Stanford University Press, 1969).

84. Editorial from *Tokyo Nichi-Nichi Shimbun*, translated in *The Tokio Times*, February 24, 1877, 95.

85–86. Lu, 352–353.

86–87. Ryusaku Tsunoda, et al, II, 139–140.

87–89. Arthur E. Tiedemann, *Modern Japan: A Brief History* (Huntington, N.Y.: Krieger, 1980), 109–112.

89–91. Ubukata Toshirō, "Kenpō happu to Nisshin sensō" (Promulgation of the constitution and the Sino-Japanese War), in Tsurumi Shunsuke, ed., *Jiyānarizumu no shisō* (Journalism thought), vol. 12 of *Gendai Nihon shisō taikei* (Compilation of modern Japanese thought), ed. Tsurumi Shunsuke (Tokyo: Chikuma Shobō, 1965), 87–91.

91–92. Mutsu Munemitsu, *Kenkenroku: A Diplomatic Record of the Sino-Japanese War, 1894–95*, Ed./trans. Gordon Berger (Tokyo: University of Tokyo Press, 1982), 251–252. © 1982 by the Japan Foundation.

93. Katsura Tarō, translated in Lone, 46.

93–94. Ian H. Nish, *The Anglo-Japanese Alliance: The Diplomacy of Two Island Empires, 1894–1907* (London: The Athlone Press, 1966), 216–217. Korea is substituted for Corea, which was used in the original text.

95–96. Irokawa, 305–306.

97–98. Rubin, 56–57. Reprinted by permission of the University of Washington Press.

98–99. *Yorozu Chōhō* editorial, November 1, 1892, in Okano Takeo, *Meiji genron shi* (History of the Japanese press) (Tokyo: Hō Shuppan, 1974), 113.

100–101. Hani Motoko, "Stories of My Life," trans. Chieko Mulhern, in *The Japan Interpreter*, XII, no. 3–4 (Summer 1979), 346–347. Originally published in *Hani Motoko chosakushū* (Collected works of Hani Motoko) (Tokyo: Fujin no Tomosha, 1974).

101. Natsume Soseki, *Kokoro* (Chicago: Regnery Gateway, 1957), 29–30.

102. Futabata Shimei, *Ukigumo*, in *Japan's First Modern Novel: Ukigumo of Futabatei Shimei*, trans. Marleigh Grayer Ryan (New York: Columbia University Press, 1965), 197–198.

103–104. Eiji Yutani, "*Nihon no kaso shakai* of Gennosuke Yoko yama." Ph.D. dissertation, University of California, Berkeley, 1985, 198–200.

104–105. Mikiso Hane, ed., *Reflections on the Way to the Gallows: Voices of Japanese Rebel Women* (New York: University of California Press, 1988), 61, 66, 73. Copyright © by Mikiso Hane.

109–110. Takuboku Ishikawa, *Romaji Diary and Sad Toys* (Boston and Tokyo: Charles E. Tuttle, 1985), 70–71.

110–111. Ibid., 135, 149, 156.

111–112. Hiratsuka Raichō, "Genshi josei wa taiyo de atta" (In the beginning woman was the sun), *Seitō* 1, no. 1 (September 1, 1911), 37–39.

113. Ryusaku Tsunoda, et al, II, 231–233.

114. Frank O. Miller, *Minobe Tatsukichi: Interpreter of Constitutionalism in Japan* (Berkeley: University of California Press, 1965), 64, 65.

115. Junichirō Tanizaki, *Naomi*, trans., Anthony H. Chambers (New York: Knopf, 1985), 35–37.

116. *Heimin Shimbun*, February 5, 1907, translated in John Crump, *The Origins of Socialist Thought in Japan*, (London: Crom Helm, 1983), 341, 350.

116–117. Kaneko Fumiko, *The Prison Memoirs of a Japanese Woman* (Armonk, N.Y.: M. E. Sharpe, 1991), 236–237.

117–118. *Osaka Asahi Shimbun*, August 26, 1918, in *Taishō nyūsu jiten* (Encyclopedia of Taishō news), ed. Uchikawa Yoshima and Matsushima Eiichi, 3 (Tokyo: Mainichi Komiyunikēshiyon Shuppanbu, 1989), 586.

118–119. *Kanpō*, May 5, 1925, in *Taishō nyusu jiten* (Encyclopedia of Taishō News), 7, ed. Uchikawa Yoshimi and Matsushima Eiichi, 293.

120–121. Ryusaku Tsunoda, et al, II, 249–250.

122–123. Shidzue Ishimoto, *Facing Two Ways: The Story of My Life* (Stanford, Calif.: Stanford University Press, 1984), 298–303.

124. Pei-kai Cheng and Michael Lestz, eds., *The Search for Modern China: A Documentary Collection* (New York: W. W. Norton, 1999), 219–220.

125. Yongho Ch'oe, Peter Lee, and Wm. Theodore deBary, eds. *Sources of Korean Tradition*, 2 (New York: Columbia University Press, 2000), 337.

126–127. Based on draft law, *Tokyo Asahi Shimbun*, February 13, 1925, in Uchikawa and Matsushima, eds., *Taishō niyūsu jiten*, 7, 405.

128. Data compiled by Gregory J. Kasza, *The State and the Mass Media in Japan 1918–1945* (Berkeley: University of California Press, 1988), 32.

129. Hane, 198–201. Copyright © by Mikiso Hane.

133–134. Fujii Takashi, *Seisho yori mitaru Japan* (Japan as seen through the Bible) (Tokyo: Kōkōsu, 1947), 185–185. Translation adapted in part from Nobuya Bamba and John F. Howes, *Pacifism in Japan: The Christian and Socialist Tradition* (Kyoto: Minerva Press, 1978), 29–30.

135. Harada Kumao, *Fragile Victory: Saionj-Harada Memoirs*, trans. Thomas Francis Mayer-Oakes (Detroit: Wayne State University Press, 1968), 275–276, 280–282.

136–137. "First Statement of the Japanese Government on the Manchurian Incident— September 24, 1931," *Third Report on Progress in Manchuria: 1907 32* (Dairen: The South Manchuria Railway, 1932), 200.

137–138. Tsunoda, et al., eds, II, 289–290.

139–140. K. K. Kawakami, *The Real Japanese Question* (New York: Macmillan, 1921), 233–234.

140–141. *Kokutai no hongi: Cardinal Principles of the National Entity of Japan*, trans. Robert King Hall (Newton, Mass.: Crofton, 1974), 75–78.

141–142. *Emperor Hirohito and His Chief Aide-de-camp: The Honjō Diary, 1933–36*, trans. Mikiso Hane (Tokyo: University of Tokyo Press, 1982), 208–213.

142–143. Ibid., 215–216.

143–144. Cheng and Lestz, eds., 315–316.

145. *Tazan no ishi* (Stones From a Different Mountain) 2, no. 10 (1935), in Ōta Masao, *Kiryū Yūyū* (Tokyo: Kiinokuniya Company Limited, 1972), 171–172.

145–146. *Tazan no ishi* (Stones From a Different Mountain) 3, no. 5 (1936), in Ōta, 174–175.

146–147. Lu, 441–442.

147. Louise Young, *Japan's Total Empire: Manchuria and the Culture of Wartime Imperialism* (Berkeley: University of California Press, 1998), 390–391. Copyright © by The Regents of the University of California, 1998.

148. *Japan's Decision for War: Records of the 1941 Policy Conferences*, trans. Nobutaka Ike (Stanford, Calif.: Stanford University Press, 1967), 209, 238–239.

148–150. *Communiques Issued by The Imperial General Headquarters (Since the Outbreak of the Greater East Asian War)* (Tokyo: Mainichi Publishing Company, 1943), front matter.

150–151. Haruko Taya Cook and Theodore F. Cook, *Japan at War: An Oral History* (New York: The New Press, 1992), 77–78.

152–153. Lu, ed. 445–447. Translation copyright © 1997 by David J. Lu. Reprinted with permission of M. E. Sharpe Inc.

153–154. Maria Rosa Henson, *Comfort Woman: A Filipina's Story of Prostitution and Slavery Under the Japanese Military* (Boulder, Colo.: Rowman & Littlefield, 1999), 36–38.

154–155. Undated letter, between October 8 and 15, 1944, in Isoko and Ichiro Hatano, *Mother and Son: The Wartime Correspondence of Isoko and Ichiro Hatano* (Boston: Houghton Mifflin, 1962), 61–62.

155–156. Robert J. C. Butow, *Japan's Decision to Surrender* (Stanford, Calif.: Stanford University Press, 1954), 243–244.

156–157. Michihiko Hachiya, *Hiroshima Diary: The Journal of a Japanese Physician, August 6–September 30, 1945*. Trans. Warner Wells (Chapel Hill: University of North Carolina Press, 1955), 1–3. © 1955 by the University of North Carolina Press, renewed 1995. Used with permission of the publisher.

161–163. Kenzaburo Oe, "The Day the Emperor Spoke in a Human voice," *New York Times Magazine*, May 7, 1995, 103–104. Copyright © 1995, Kenzaburo Oe. Reprinted by permission.

163–164. Miyake Setsurei, "Shin-zen-mi nite bunka sōzō" (Creating culture through truth, virtue, and beauty), in Tsurumi, ed., 58–59.

164–165. *Asahi Shimbun* (Osaka), November 7, 1945, in John Dower, *Embracing Defeat: Japan in the Wake of World War II* (New York: W. W. Norton/The New Press, 1999), 97–98.

166–167. Hugh Borton, *Japan's Modern Century* (New York: The Ronald Press, 1955), 490–507.

168–169. Mitsuo Kodama, ed., *CIE (15 February 1946) Education in Japan: Report of the United States Education Mission to Japan* (Tokyo: Meisei University Press, 1983), 12–14.

169–170. *Shiryō: Sengo nijūnen shi* (Documents: A History of the Two Postwar Decades), 6, (Tokyo: Nihon Hyōronsha, 1966), 20–21, translated in John Dower, *Empire and Aftermath: Yoshida Shigeru and the Japanese Experience, 1878–1954* (Cambridge, Mass.: Council on East Asian Studies, Harvard University, 1979), 423.

171–172. Tetsuya Kataoka, *The Price of a Constitution: The Origin of Japan's Postwar Politics* (New York: Crane Russak, 1991), 227–228.

172–173. Shigeru Yoshida, *The Yoshida Memoirs: The Story of Japan in Crisis* (Westport, Conn.: Greenwood Press, 1962), 112–113.

174–175. Shintaro Ishihara, *Season of Violence* (Rutland, Vt.: Charles E. Tuttle, 1966), 26–28.

176–177. Lu, ed., 527–529. Translation copyright © 1997 by David J. Lu. Reprinted with permission of M. E. Sharpe, Inc.

178. "Brundage Praises Role of Japanese," *The Japan Times*, October 25, 1967, 1.

179–180. Tsuneari Fukuda, "Let's Not Make the United States Stand Alone," *Journal of Social and Political Ideas in Japan*, 4, no. 1 (April 1966), 79–83. First published in *Bungei Shunjū*, July 1965, 78–92.

180. Kan'ichi Fukuda, "Japan's Reaction to the Vietnam Crisis," *Journal of Social and Political Ideas in Japan*, 4, no. 2 (August 1966), 25, 30–31.

181. Orihara Hiroshi, "'Test Hell' and Alienation, A Study of Tokyo University Freshmen," *Journal of Social and Political Ideas in Japan*, 5, no. 2–3 (December 1967), 229, 235–237.

182–183. Ishimure Michiko, *Paradise in the Sea of Sorrow: Our Minamata Disease* (Tokyo: Yamaguchi Publishing House, 1990), 135–136.

183. Frank Baldwin, "The Idioms of Contemporary Japan IX: *Junpō-tōsō*," *Japan Interpreter*, 9, no. 2 (Summer-Autumn 1974), 231, 233.

188–189. Mishima Yukio, "An Appeal," *The Japan Interpreter*, 7, no. 1 (Winter 1971), 74, 77. First published in *Sandē Mainichi*, December 13, 1970, 20–21.

190–191. "Joint Statement Following Discussions with Prime Minister Sato of Japan, November 21, 1969," *Public Papers of the Presidents of the United States: Richard Nixon*, I (Washington, D.C.: United States Government Printing Press, 1971), 954–956.

192. Ishihara Shintarō, "Nippon no dōgi" (Japan's moral principles), *Jiyū*, April 1973, in Japan Center for International Exchange, ed., *The Silent Power: Japan's Identity and World Role* (Tokyo: Simul Press, 1976), 87–90.

193–194. Matsushita Kōnosuke, "Double Japan's Land Space," *Japan Interpreter*, 11, no. 3 (Winter 1977), 280–283, 287–288. Originally published in *Bungei Shunjū*, May 1967, 136–142.

195. Onoda Hiroo, *No Surrender: My Thirty-year War* (Tokyo: Kodansha International, 1974), 119–120.

196–197. Shotaro Ishinomori, *Japan Inc.*, trans. Betsey Scheiner (Berkeley: University of California Press, 1988), 304–306. Copyright © by The Regents of the University of California, 1988.

198–199. Ienaga Saburō, *Japan's Past Japan's Future: One Historian's Odyssey*, trans. Richard H. Minear (Boulder, Colo.: Rowman & Littlefield, 2001), 167.

199–200. Shintaro Ishihara, *The Japan That Can Say No: Why Japan will be First Among Equals* (New York: Simon & Schuster, 1991), 42–44. English language edition Copyright © 1991 by Shintaro Ishihara. Reprinted with permission of Simon & Schuster.

200–201. Kurita Wataru, "Making Peace with Hirohito and a Militaristic Past," *Japan Quarterly*, 36, no. 2 (April-June 1989), 191–192.

202–203. "Japanese will be familiar with Botswana soon," *International Herald Tribune/Asahi Shimbun*, March 29, 2002, 176–177.

203–204. Wakamiya Yoshibumi, *The Postwar Conservative View of Asia: How the Political Right Has Delayed Japan's Coming to Terms With its History of Aggression in Asia* (Tokyo: LTCB International Library Foundation, 1995), 9.

204–205. Kawaguchi Yoriko, "A Foreign Policy to Consolidate Peace," *Japan Echo* 30, no. 2 (April 2003), 27–29.

206. Ruth Ann Keyso, *Women of Okinawa: Nine Voices from a Garrison Island* (Ithaca: Cornell University Press, 2000), 123–124.

207. Tanikawa Shuntarō, *Map of Days*, trans. Harold Wright (Honolulu: Katydid Books, University of Hawaii Press, 1996), 103.

208–209. Iokibe Makoto, "Eulogy for a Student," translated from *Yomiuri Shimbun*, January 27, 1995, in *Japan Echo*, 22, no. 2 (Summer 1995), 15.

209–210. Excerpts from the Daily Yomiuri, May 5, 2000. © Daily Yomiuri. Reprinted with permission.

211. Andō Tadao, "Urban Revival Through the Power of the Individual," *Japan Echo*, 29, no. 6 (December 2002), 58–63.

Sidebars

21. Cooper, *They Came to Japan*, 39.

21. Ibid., 191.

22. Ibid., 193.

24. C. R. Boxer, *The Christian Century in Japan* (Berkeley: University of California Press, 1967), 439.

27. Kaempfer, 232.

29. Yamashita, 78.

30. A. L. Sadler, *The Life of Shogun Tokugawa Ieyasu: The Maker of Modern Japan* (Rutland, Vt.: Charles E. Tuttle, 1978), 7.

37. Yamamoto, 85–86.

40. Kaibara, 44.

41. Donald Keene, *Travelers of a Hundred Ages* (New York: Holt, 1989), 293, 297, 304, 308, 310, 316. Copyright © 1989 by Donald Keene. Reprinted by permission of Henry Holt and Company, LLC.

62. Sugimoto, 193.

63. Charles Lanman, ed., *The Japanese In America* (New York: University Publishing Company, 1872), 69–72.

66. Roger Hackett, *Yamagata Aritomo in the Rise of Modern Japan 1838–1922* (Cambridge, Mass.: Harvard University Press, 1971), 81.

70. Nakae Chōmin, *A Discourse by Three Drunkards on Government* (New York: Weatherhill, 1984), 50, 60.

73. *Jiji Shinpō*, December 29, 30, 1887.

74. *Kodansha Encyclopedia of Japan*, V (Tokyo: Kodansha International, 1983), 336.

75. Quoted in Lane R. Earns and Brian Burke-Gaffney, eds., *Crossroads: A Journal of Nagasaki History and Culture*, I (Summer 1993), 76.

76. Sugimoto, 314.

78. Patricia Tsurumi, *Factory Girls: Women in the Thread Mills of Meiji Japan* (Princeton: Princeton University Press, 1990), 98–99, 102. Copyright © Princeton University Press, 1990.

79. Anne Walthall, *The Weak Body of a Useless Woman: Matsuo Taseko and the Meiji Restoration* (Chicago: University of Chicago Press, 1998), 284. Copyright © 1998 by The University of Chicago.

87. Yamagata Aritomo, "Plan to Defend the Sphere of National Interest," in *Modern Japan: An Interpretive Anthology*, ed. Irwin Scheiner (New York: Macmillan, 1974), 179.

88. Pyle, 158.

92. Mutsu, 203.

95. *Nihon shi shiryō shū: zōho kaitei han* (Tokyo: Yamakawa Shuppansha, 2001), 290.

98. Uchimura Kanzō, *The Complete Works of Kanzō Uchimura*, 7 (Tokyo: Kyobunkwan, 1973), 122.

100. Seno Seiichirō and Miyaji Masato, eds., *Shin Nihon shi shiryō shū* (Tokyo: Kirihara Shoten, 1999), 310.

102. Suzuki Jun'ichirō in Shigenobu Okuma, *Fifty Years of New Japan* (London: Smith, Elder and Company, 1910), 547–548. Data are based on *Nihonshi sōgō zuroku (zōhoban)* (Comprehensive statistics of Japanese history: supplement) (Tokyo: Yamakawa Shuppansha, 2001), 99–101.

104. From Kenneth Strong, *Ox Against the Storm: A biography of Tanaka Shozo (1841–1913)* (Vancouver: University of British Columbia Press, 1977), 110. © University of British Columbia Press, 1977.

105. Ono Hideo, "Kuroiwa Shūroku," *Sandai genronjin shū*, 6 (Tokyo: Jiji Tsūshinsha, 1962), 68.

110. Natsume Sōseki, *Sanshiro*, trans. Jay Rubin (New York: Perigree Books, 1977), 15.

111. Laurel Rasplica Rodd, "Yosano Akiko and the Taishō Debate over the 'New Woman,'" in *Recreating Japanese Women, 1600–1945*, ed. Gail Lee Bernstein (Berkeley: University of California Press, 1991), 180. Copyright © by The Regents of the University of California, 1991.

113. Byron K. Marshall, *Academic Freedom and the Japanese Imperial University, 1868–1939* (Berkeley: University of California Press, 1992), 193.

115. Tayama Katai, *Country Teacher*, trans. Kenneth Henshall (Honolulu: University of Hawaii Press, 1984), xix.

115. Table of contents, *Seikō*, 5, no. 1 (February 1, 1914).

116. Data from James L. McClain, *Japan: A Modern History* (New York: Norton, 2002), 372, and Iwao F. Ayusawa, *A History of Labor in Modern Japan* (Honolulu: East-West Center Press, 1966), 154.

117. Vera Mackie, *Creating Socialist Women in Japan: Gender, Labour and Activism, 1900–1937* (Cambridge, UK: Cambridge University Press, 1997), 129.

120. McClain, 387.

122. Rodd, 195.

124. Bamba and Howes, eds., 175.

128. Ōsugi Sakae, *The Autobiography of Ōsugi Sakae*, trans. Byron K. Marshall (Berkeley: University of California Press, 1992), 133.

134. Hashikawa Bunsō, "Antiwar Values The Resistance in Japan," *The Japan Interpreter* 9, no. 1 (Spring 1974), 89.

136. Herbert P. Bix, *Hirohito and the Making of Modern Japan* (New York: HarperCollins, 2000), 262.

140. Mark Peattie, *Ishiwara Kanji and Japan's Confrontatin with the West* (Princeton, N.J.: Princeton University Press, 1975), 57.

148. *Japan's Decision for War*, 284.

148. Thomas A. Bailey and David M. Kennedy, *The American Pageant: A History of the Republic*, II, 6th ed.. (Lexington, Mass.: D. C. Heath, 1979), 810.

151. Roger Daniels, ed., *The Decision to Relocate the Japanese Americans* (Malibar, FL: Robert E. Krieger, 1986), 113–114.

153. Cook and Cook, 185.

154. Ibid., 227.

156. Harry S. Truman, *Memoirs, I: Year of Decisions* (Garden City, N.J.: Doubleday, 1955), 421.

162. Butow, 248.

165. Otis Cary, ed. *War-Wasted Asia: Letters, 1945–46* (Tokyo: Kodansha International, 1975), 53–54.

166. John F. Kennedy, *Profiles in Courage* (New York: Harper and Brothers, 1955), 218.

167. Michael Schaller, *The American Occupation of Japan: The Origins of the Cold War in Asia* (New York: Oxford University Press, 1985), 21.

167. Michiko Y. Aoki and Margaret B. Dardess, eds. *As the Japanese See It: Past and Present* (Honolulu: University Press of Hawaii, 1981), 305–307.

168. Jon Livingston, Joe Moore, and Felicia Oldfather, eds. *The Japan Reader: Postwar Japan, 1945 to the Present* (New York: Pantheon Books, 1973), 118–119.

170. Dower, *Embracing Defeat*, 553.

173. Masataka Kosaka, *A History of Postwar Japan* (Tokyo: Kodansha International, 1972), 141.

175. Figures based on Charles Yuji Horioka, "Consuming and Saving," in *Postwar Japan as History* ed. Andrew Gordon (Berkeley: University of California Press, 1993), 266, 268, 283.175–176. Translation adapated from Katsumi Ueda, "Tabata Shinobu: Defender of the Peace Constitution," in Bamba and Howes, eds., 243–244.

176. George R. Packard III, *Protest in Tokyo: The Security Treaty Crisis of 1960* (Princeton, N.J.: Princeton University Press, 1966), 272.

177. Herman Khan, *The Emerging Japanese Superstate: Challenge and Response* (Englewood Cliffs, N.J.: 1970), 209.

179. "Ei-chan no barādo" (The ballad of Little Ei), *Shūkan Anpō*, 1970, last page (unnumbered).

181. Benjamin C. Duke, *Japan's Militant Teachers: A History of the Left-Wing Teachers' Movement* (Honolulu: University Press of Hawaii, 1973), 228.

188. Kano Tsutomu, "Mishima Yukio 1925–1970," *Japan Interpreter*, 7, no. 1 (Winter 1971), 73.

192. "Citizens Movements," *Japan Quarterly*, 20, no. 4 (October-December 1973), 372–373.

194. Ezra F. Vogel, *Japan As No. One: Lessons for America* (Cambridge: Harvard University Press, 1979), dust jacket.

195. Katō Shūichi, "Beef or Beer," *Japan Interpreter*, 10, no. 3-4 (Winter 1976), 381–384.

195. Yoshio Sugimoto, *An Introduction to Japanese Society* (Cambridge: Cambridge University Press, 1997), 153.

198. Ienaga, 185.

199. Harry Wray, *Japanese and American Education: Attitudes and Practices* (Westport, Conn.: Bergin and Garvey, 1999), 164–165.

204. "Glance at Major Asian Forces," *Washington Post*, August 2, 1999.

207. "Spotlight: Stuff and Nonsense '99: Signs of the Times?" *Japan Echo*, 27, no. 1 (February 2000), 63.

210. "Hiroshima mayor criticizes U.S.," *Springfield (OH) News-Sun*, August 7, 2002, 7.

Acknowledgments

I owe deep thanks for the skillful, gracious editorial team at Oxford University Press, which did so much to turn my feeble words into something more polished: Nancy Toff, Karen Fein, Un Choi, Beth Ammerman, and Martin Coleman (cheers for Tottenham Hotspur!). I also am indebted deeply to several assistants and former students who helped with translations and finding materials, especially to Dukoh Koh and Matt Steele, as well as Yuko Morizono in Kumamoto, Japan. Keiko Higuchi at the International House Library in Tokyo was, as usual, exceptionally helpful—the kind of person who makes you feel that she *wanted* you to ask for assistance! My Wittenberg students in Japanese history also merit special thanks; their talent for encouragement and willingness to put up with my stories is extraordinary. And my children—James, Nao, Kristen, and Dave (as well as their children, Grace and Simon)—deserve more thanks than I'll ever be able to give them, for providing me lodging when I was searching out materials, for giving me advice, for giving me more of everything important than a father and grandfather ever deserved.

Picture Credits

Index

About the Author

James L. Huffman is H. Orth Hirt Professor of History at Wittenberg University in Springfield, Ohio. A newspaper reporter in his early years, he has taught at the University of Nebraska–Lincoln and Indiana Wesleyan University. His other books on Japan include *Creating a Public: People and Press in Meiji Japan* (1997) and *A Yankee in Meiji Japan: The Crusading Journalist Edward H. House* (2003). He also edited *Modern Japan: An Encyclopedia of History, Culture, and Nationalism* (1997).